THE
Canadian Regime

THE
CANADIAN
REGIME

Sixth Edition

AN INTRODUCTION TO PARLIAMENTARY GOVERNMENT IN CANADA

Patrick Malcolmson, Richard Myers, Gerald Baier,
and Thomas M.J. Bateman

UNIVERSITY OF TORONTO PRESS

Library and Archives Canada Cataloguing in Publication

Malcolmson, Patrick N., 1953–, author
    The Canadian regime : an introduction to parliamentary government in Canada / Patrick Malcolmson, Richard Myers, Gerald Baier, and Thomas M.J. Bateman.—Sixth edition.

Includes index.
Issued in print and electronic formats.
ISBN 978-1-4426-3596-8 (paperback).—ISBN 978-1-4426-3597-5 (hardback).—ISBN 978-1-4426-3598-2 (html).—ISBN 978-1-4426-3599-9 (pdf).

    1. Canada—Politics and government—Textbooks. I. Bateman, Thomas Michael Joseph, 1962– author II. Myers, Richard M. (Richard Morley), 1957–, author III. Baier, Gerald, 1971–, author IV. Title.

JL75.M34 2016   320.471   C2016-901201-8

C2016-901202-6

We welcome comments and suggestions regarding any aspect of our publications—please feel free to contact us at news@utphighereducation.com or visit our Internet site at www.utphighereducation.com.

North America
5201 Dufferin Street
North York, Ontario, Canada, M3H 5T8

2250 Military Road
Tonawanda, New York, USA, 14150

ORDERS PHONE: 1-800-565-9523
ORDERS FAX: 1-800-221-9985
ORDERS E-MAIL: utpbooks@utpress.utoronto.ca

UK, Ireland, and continental Europe
NBN International
Estover Road, Plymouth, PL6 7PY, UK
ORDERS PHONE: 44 (0) 1752 202301
ORDERS FAX: 44 (0) 1752 202333
ORDERS E-MAIL: enquiries@nbninternational.com

The University of Toronto Press acknowledges the financial support for its publishing activities of the Government of Canada through the Canada Book Fund.

This book is printed on 100% recycled paper.

Printed in Canada

The authors would like to dedicate this edition of *The Canadian Regime* to Janet Ajzenstat. Her work has made the serious study of the genesis and character of the Canadian regime an essential part of Canadian political science.

CONTENTS

CHAPTER FOUR
FEDERALISM

CHAPTER FIVE
THE CANADIAN CHARTER OF RIGHTS AND FREEDOMS

PART THREE
INSTITUTIONS

CHAPTER SIX
THE CROWN AND ITS SERVANTS

PREFACE

Of all regimes, the democratic regime is in greatest need of a politically educated populace. The democratic principle requires the rule of the people. Such rule demands that the people have an education in politics that makes "government by the people" both possible and prudent. If the great body of voting citizens lacks such an education, two consequences follow. First, people become passive and unwitting followers of the opinion leaders of the day. Demagoguery becomes indistinguishable from principled political rhetoric, and the tyranny of the majority—the Achilles' heel of democracy—grows more probable. Second, people come to have entirely unrealistic expectations of politics. Lacking any clear understanding of what is possible, they let their hopes, desires, and dreams govern their political demands.

There is ample evidence to suggest that both of these characteristics are easily observable in Canadian politics today. We believe that this is due, in large part, to the poor condition of civic education in contemporary Canada. This book has been written in the hope of strengthening Canadian civic education.

Our book is an attempt to explain and describe the most important political institutions of Canada's national government. Its premise is that Canadians—citizens, university students, and even many of our politicians—need a straightforward, explanatory introduction to these institutions. Our aim is to educate Canadians to a sober and realistic set of expectations about politics by explaining the institutional limitations that structure all political action. The connection between institutions and issues is very clear. How can one intelligently discuss problems concerning the tax structure without some understanding of federalism? Or laws governing assisted suicide without some understanding of the Charter of Rights and Freedoms and the Supreme Court? Or the role of a Member of Parliament (MP) without understanding the nature of parliamentary or responsible government? Yet all too often one finds that people want to discuss current political problems without giving any consideration to how these issues are tied to the structures and institutions of government. Thus, the local MP is criticized for always voting the party line, with little consideration of how the Canadian form of parliamentary democracy makes it exceedingly difficult for MPs to vote against their party on any crucial political issue. One might liken such discussions to criticizing a chess move without understanding the rules of chess.

Our basic objective is to present the reader with a short and clear account of Canadian government. We have tried to focus on the logic of how our institutions work and how they fit together. For that reason, this book, unlike similar texts, concentrates more on explaining basic principles and less on describing the arcane details of our institutions. We have tried to ensure that our account is written in straightforward language and that all technical terms are clearly explained. We have also tried to write the book so that it presupposes little prior knowledge of the subject matter. It is gratifying to hear from readers of previous editions that its clarity has been appreciated.

While our primary objective has been to provide the reader with a clear account of Canadian government, we have also been guided by a second objective. There is a thread that runs through the entire book, an underlying theme that endows it with unity and purpose. We have used the term "regime" to suggest that a country's political institutions form an organic whole, a kind of complex ecosystem with an inner logic and coherence that holds it together.[1] The Canadian regime is a political ecosystem whose inner logic derives from its unique combination of responsible government and federalism, a combination that explains why our institutions are what they are and why we do things the way we do. By extension, it also explains why we do so many things differently from our neighbours to the south: the American regime is built on a different

---

1   James W. Ceaser, *Liberal Democracy and Political Science* (Baltimore: Johns Hopkins University Press, 1990), 41: "The regime or form of government is the most inclusive concept of traditional political science: it refers to the form or shape of a society, as fixed by who or what rules, and by the principles of justice and the sentiments that dominate society."

combination of core principles, namely, separation of powers and federalism. Throughout the book, we try to explain Canadian institutions and practices in terms of the underlying regime principles that govern them. Frequently, one of the best ways to make our point is to contrast Canadian practices with those of the United States, showing how our approach is the logical consequence of responsible government while theirs is the logical consequence of the separation of powers. This direct comparison of regime principles makes it easier for readers on both sides of the border to understand the regime logic of both countries. That, in turn, makes our book particularly useful for political science instructors in the United States who want their students to learn about the parliamentary alternative to separation of powers and find it more appropriate to use their northern neighbours as the test case rather than European countries such as Britain, Italy, or Germany.

Our primary concern, however, is to provide Canadian students with a greater appreciation of, and respect for, their own country's regime. For whatever reasons, it has become fashionable in Canada to advocate the adoption of American political practices in place of our own. In 1982, our Constitution was expanded to include an American-style charter of rights. We continue to hear calls for an American-style Senate, an American-style procedure for screening Supreme Court nominees, American-style primaries for leadership selection, and American-style representation (so that MPs pay less attention to the "party line" and vote more in accordance with the wishes of their constituents). After the much-hyped debate between Senator Biden and Governor Palin in the 2008 American presidential race, some commentators went so far as to suggest that Canada also needs an American-style vice-presidential debate! Such innovations strike many Canadians as being more "democratic" or more "progressive" than what we have here now, but it is doubtful whether many appreciate the complexities involved in grafting features from one regime onto a very different one.

Years ago, Canadians adopted the American practice of choosing their party leaders at leadership conventions. It was thought that this innovation would further democratize our regime by taking leadership selection out of the hands of a small minority (the caucus) and sharing it with a wider number of Canadians. In practice, however, the introduction of leadership conventions has probably made our institutions *less* democratic. When the leader was chosen by the caucus, the caucus maintained a certain influence over the leader. Because today's party leaders are chosen by several thousand party delegates, they have a "mandate" that allows them to dominate their caucus to an unprecedented degree. It is in this innovation as much as in anything else that we find the roots of "prime ministerial government." Thus an American-inspired innovation that was designed to democratize our party leadership has in the long run made it even more elitist. The point here is not to say that leadership conventions (or primaries or reviewing nominations to the Supreme Court) are bad in some general way. Nor do we argue that it is impossible to adopt practices from the United States. Our point is that features that work well as part of one system of government are likely to cause unanticipated complications when indiscriminately plugged into a very different one. To return to our analogy of the ecosystem, it is certainly possible to introduce American bullfrogs into our lakes and ponds, as was done recently in British Columbia, but biologists in that province are now reporting a host of ecological complications as this new species either displaces or disrupts the lives of the native species.

Canadian political scientists have not always been helpful in terms of defending the integrity of our regime; indeed, they sometimes contribute to the problem. It is surprising to us how many Canadian textbooks discuss our institutions in terms of the legislative and executive "branches" of government. Such a framework makes perfect sense for a book on the government of the United States given that the American Constitution is built around the theory of "separation of powers" into distinct "branches." But the Canadian Constitution is not built on such principles. Our Constitution provides for a "fusion of powers" rather than a "separation of powers." The work done by cabinet ministers is of both a legislative and executive nature. It is therefore misleading and confusing to frame one's discussion of Canadian government in terms of chapters on the legislative and executive "branches." We have no such thing, and pretending we do leads to significant deficiencies in the way Canadian government is described. For instance, because they are composed in light of assumptions about a "separation of powers," many texts are inadequate in their accounts of the principles of responsible government, the principles that create our "fusion of powers." Canadians' general ignorance of those principles became starkly evident during the parliamentary crisis of late 2008 when a number of grossly incorrect claims were in circulation as to how governments are formed. In this book, by contrast, we describe the institutions of Canadian government on their own terms. Instead of fitting Canadian institutions into some foreign framework, we present them in terms of responsible government, the framework that is appropriate to them.

The underlying objective of our book, then, is to provide Canadians with an account of their regime that permits them to grasp and appreciate its inner logic so as to minimize the appeal of seductive but facile calls for further Americanization. By approaching Canadian institutions on their own terms, we hope to articulate the inner logic and coherence of the regime as a whole. This should make the reader more aware of the problems inherent in borrowing practices from other regimes. More important, it should give the reader a deeper appreciation of, and respect for, our own.

We would like to think Michael Harrison of the University of Toronto Press for his ongoing support for this textbook. We are especially grateful for his foresight in asking us to prepare a new edition by December of 2015. That timeline has allowed us to cover a number of significant developments emerging from the election held that October. We would also like to acknowledge the helpful suggestions made by Dr. Denis Pilon of York University for improving this edition of the book, as well those made by anonymous reviewers and by our students over the years.

Dr. Patrick Malcolmson,
Department of Political Science,
St. Thomas University

Dr. Richard Myers,
Principal,
St. Paul's University College

Dr. Gerald Baier,
Department of Political Science,
University of British Columbia

Dr. Thomas M.J. Bateman,
Department of Political Science,
St. Thomas University

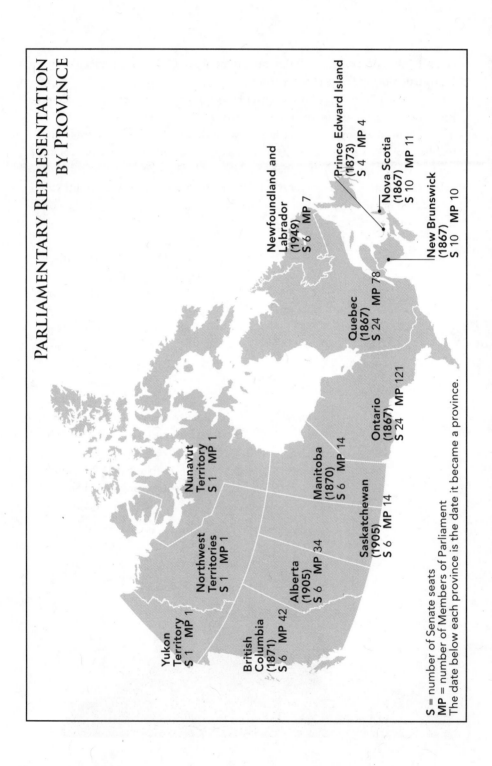

PARLIAMENTARY REPRESENTATION BY PROVINCE

Yukon Territory
S 1   MP 1

Northwest Territories
S 1   MP 1

Nunavut Territory
S 1   MP 1

British Columbia (1871)
S 6   MP 42

Alberta (1905)
S 6   MP 34

Saskatchewan (1905)
S 6   MP 14

Manitoba (1870)
S 6   MP 14

Ontario (1867)
S 24   MP 121

Quebec (1867)
S 24   MP 78

Newfoundland and Labrador (1949)
S 6   MP 7

Prince Edward Island (1873)
S 4   MP 4

Nova Scotia (1867)
S 10   MP 11

New Brunswick (1867)
S 10   MP 10

S = number of Senate seats
MP = number of Members of Parliament
The date below each province is the date it became a province.

PART ONE
INTRODUCTION

Chapter One

Canada's Regime Principles

1.1 Political Regimes

To the casual observer, it may seem that Canada's political institutions are an arbitrary, perhaps even whimsical, hodgepodge of archaic ideas and quaintly named offices. To the political scientist, however, the political institutions of this, or any other country, have an inner logic that ties them all together into a coherent whole. The term traditionally used by political scientists to describe that whole is **regime**.

The English word "regime" is derived from the Latin word *regere*, which means to rule. From this Latin root come related words like "regent" (the person who rules on behalf of a monarch who is not yet of age) and "regulate." In common speech, the word "regime" is sometimes used to refer to a particular group of rulers (we might talk, for example, of "the Castro regime" in Cuba). In political science, however, the term "regime" has a more precise meaning. It refers to the form of government *and* the underlying political principles that provide the legitimate basis for that form of government. It thus provides the answer to the question: who rules and why? The question of what sort of political institutions a state ought to have will logically follow from the question of what sort of regime it has. The principles of the regime must support the political institutions and vice versa. And questions of the efficacy of particular institutions will be settled by assessing how well they fit with the principles of the regime. A democracy, for example, will necessarily have political institutions based upon democratic elections. As we shall see, the question of whether an institution like our current Senate fits with the liberal democratic principles of our regime is one Canadians continue to debate.

The classic discussion of regime types is to be found in Aristotle's *Politics*. His account is not comprehensive enough to provide a complete analysis of contemporary regimes, but it provides an excellent starting point for understanding the differences between them. According to Aristotle, the first question one must ask about any particular political order is how those who rule understand the purpose of political rule. This is the question that each of us would likely ask first if we were being ruled: are the rulers just or unjust? Do they rule in their own interest, or do they look to the common good of the political community? The second question that Aristotle asks is who rules: one person, the few, or the many?

Applying these two considerations, Aristotle generated a typology that included six regimes, three of them just and three of them unjust:

Figure 1.1: To What Purpose Do the Rulers Rule?

Who Rules?	Common Good	Own Interest
One	Kingship	Tyranny
Few	Aristocracy	Oligarchy
Many	Polity	Democracy

When we look back on history, we commonly and quite correctly distinguish between good and bad monarchs. Some kings and queens ruled with the interests of their country and subjects uppermost in mind. Others were concerned primarily with their own benefit. Aristotle calls a monarchy of the first type **kingship** and one of the second type **tyranny**.

The distinction between the common good and self-interest forms the basis of the other regime types. Aristotle calls an elite few ruling for the sake of the common good an **aristocracy**. However, political history does not provide many examples of small elites ruling for the common good. In most cases where political power is in the hands of the few, they use it for their private economic advantage. Aristotle calls this unjust regime **oligarchy**. Today we find oligarchies in many developing countries where rich elites use political power to maintain and increase their wealth.

Aristotle's analysis of rule by the many will come as something of a surprise to the reader. He says that a regime in which the many rule for the sake of the common good could be called **polity**, but he argues that such a regime is non-existent. The reason for this is that in his time political communities were divided into two classes: the many poor—the *demos*—and the few rich. Aristotle had never seen a community in which rule by the demos was anything but an attempt by the poor majority to use its superior force to despoil the rich minority. In other words, ancient Greek democracies had a tendency to degenerate into mob rule. This explains why Aristotle puts **democracy**—rule by the demos—on his list of bad or selfish regimes.

Aristotle's unflattering portrait of majority rule may offend our democratic sensibilities, but his point merits serious consideration. It is undeniable that majority rule can, and too often does, involve unjust treatment of those in the minority. For instance, a majority of voters could elect a government that would forbid members of a non-white minority to own property. Such legislation would be democratic in that it expresses the will of the majority, but it would also be unjust. The fact that something is democratic does not necessarily mean that it is right. In contemporary terms, we would distinguish between a decent democratic regime and **tyranny of the majority**. For us, democracy has come to mean rule by the majority that respects the rights of all individuals, including those who may be in the minority. We use constitutions to provide protection against unrestrained majoritarianism.

It is important to appreciate the danger posed by tyranny of the majority if one is to understand the foundations of the Canadian regime. Canada's regime, as we all know, is a democratic regime. But it has been carefully crafted so as to minimize the dangers of tyranny of the majority. This will become apparent as we examine our most fundamental principles. We call these "regime principles," and there are two of them: **equality** and **liberty**.

1.2 Equality and Democracy: Direct versus Indirect Government

The fundamental principle of democracy is the principle of equality. In its pure form, democracy grants political power to all citizens equally (excluding children) because democrats believe that no one has any special title to rule. In a democratic regime, there is no formal political privilege granted to those who come from particular families or to people who own particular lands or businesses.

It should be noted that the democratic principle of equality is a political principle, not a social or economic one. Strictly speaking, democracy means that people share equally in political rule; it does not mean that they share equally (or even equitably) in wealth or social status. Still, there are some respects in which political equality is interconnected with questions of social and economic equality. Genuine political equality may be undermined by massive social or economic inequalities. For instance, if those with great wealth are able to use their money to influence the political process in a significant way, that gives them unequal political power. This is why democracies usually enact legislation to regulate donations to political campaigns.

The basic democratic principle of political equality can take different forms. In the democracies observed by Aristotle, the principle was given its fullest expression. The democrats of ancient Greece understood equality to mean that all citizens were equally capable of exercising political power. These were **direct democracies**—regimes in which all of the citizens were directly involved in political decision making. Moreover, to the extent that special officers were needed, they were to be chosen by lottery on the assumption that all citizens are equally capable of exercising political power. The Fathers of Confederation were democrats, but they did not support such a fully egalitarian form of democracy. Their preference was for **parliamentary democracy**, a regime they thought superior to direct democracy precisely because it was a more limited form of democracy.

Parliamentary democracy is best understood in the first instance as a variety of **representative democracy**. The direct form of democracy practised by the ancient Greeks has been replaced by an indirect form. Instead of managing political matters themselves, the equal citizens of modern democracies delegate the responsibility for public matters to a small group of elected representatives. There are two chief reasons for the emergence of representative democracy. The most obvious is that modern democracies are simply too large to be governed by the people directly: while the direct democracies of ancient Greece may have had only a few thousand citizens, the democracies of the modern world typically have millions. The second justification for representative democracy, though somewhat less obvious, is no less important. We are used to thinking of elections as a democratic exercise, and in one sense they obviously are: all voters get an equal say in the choice of the winner. But elections are also an aristocratic exercise: to attain office, the candidate has to convince the voters that he or she is the *best* person for the job. The founders of modern democracies believed that the introduction of representation would minimize the tendency to mob rule observed in the direct democracies of ancient Greece. The fact that the representatives would be accountable to the people through elections would keep the regime democratic. But at the same time, the exercise of power would be given to a small elite of the best people, an elite that would be less likely than the people as a whole to behave like a mob.

Parliamentary democracy is a regime in which political decisions are made by a representative body called parliament. It is, therefore, like all representative democracies, an indirect and, hence, limited form of democracy. Indeed, it is important to understand that the Fathers of Confederation valued the institutions of parliamentary democracy precisely because it was a more limited form of representative democracy than the alternative.

As we shall see in subsequent chapters, when the Fathers of Confederation created our regime, they borrowed heavily from the United States in some respects. When it came to representative government, however, they emphatically rejected the American congressional/presidential model in favour of the British model of parliamentary government. Their concern was that American-style democracy, though indirect, was nonetheless still too directly linked to the people and thus subject to the dangers of mob rule. One of the problems they noted was that the chief officers of the American regime—the president, the governors, and some of the judges—were chosen directly by the people. The Fathers of Confederation preferred the model of parliamentary government in which (as we shall see in Chapter Three) the chief officers of the government are chosen only indirectly: the voters do not directly elect either the prime minister or the ministers of the cabinet; through a complex process called "responsible government," those officers are selected by our elected representatives. Parliamentary democracy is thus in some sense the most indirect of indirect democracies.[1]

The other feature of parliamentary democracy that was important to the Fathers of Confederation was the fact that it gave the Crown a role (albeit a weak one) as a last-chance safety valve. The Constitution of the United States established a **republican** regime, that is, a regime in which full and final authority is placed in the hands of the people's elected representatives and officers. The Fathers of Confederation believed that it would be important to have the monarchy present as a stabilizing influence, one that would prevent democratic politicians from rash action. Today, of course, it would be unthinkable for the Crown to interfere in the normal political process. Still, the anti-republican attitudes of the Fathers

---

1   Contemporary thinking on this point has changed somewhat. Canadians now believe that our indirect democracy should provide clear and direct lines of accountability to the electorate. See Chapter Nine, section 9.1.

of Confederation are worth noting, for it was precisely their desire to avoid the "evils of republicanism" that led them to reject annexation to the United States and to work so hard to create an independent Canada.

While there has been some evolution in our political ideas since the time of the Fathers of Confederation, it is still important to appreciate that the Canadian regime is a relatively limited form of democracy. We do not believe that people are so equal that all of us should share equally in the making of political decisions. Nor do we believe that all citizens ought to share equally in the election of all political officers. What makes our regime a fundamentally democratic one is the notion that *the regime belongs to us all equally*: Canadian political equality is an equality of citizenship. This implies two things. The first is that we all have an equal right to run for public office. Second (and more important), whoever is elected or appointed to political office must in some way be accountable (i.e., answerable) to the people as a whole for his or her actions and decisions.

1.3 Liberty

Though Canadians view democracy as a key political principle, we do not see it as the only fundamental principle of our regime. Indeed, Canadians believe that democracy can go wrong if it is not tempered by another fundamental principle— the principle of liberty. This explains why our regime is commonly referred to as a **liberal democracy**: it combines the political principles of liberty and democracy.

Liberty is the idea that there is a sphere of human thought and action that is private and that, within that **private sphere**, all individuals have the right to make choices for themselves. According to the political theory of **liberalism**, then, we are free to do whatever we wish provided there is no law prohibiting us from doing so. We have rights, which means that we are free to decide for ourselves whether we will or will not do something. This freedom to decide for ourselves about such matters as which ideas we shall believe and what religion we shall practise is an essential element of the liberal understanding of politics. And from these initial freedoms flow a number of others, notably freedom of expression, freedom of the press, and freedom of association.

But what provides the philosophical foundation for the principle of liberty? In contemporary liberal democracies, there are two schools of thought that predominate: **natural rights** and **utilitarianism**. The natural rights school argues that all individuals possess certain rights—for example, the right to life, liberty, property, or privacy—simply because they are human beings. These rights, now often called human rights, are rights that each human being possesses everywhere and always, whether they are legally recognized or not. They are "inalienable" rights in that they cannot be given up or taken away. According to the natural rights school, these inalienable or natural rights establish both the purpose and the limits of political power. The purpose of government is to secure these universal and permanent rights, and no government should ever act in a manner that violates them.

The utilitarian justification for liberty is fundamentally different. For a utilitarian, the importance of liberty derives from its usefulness ("utility") as a means of promoting human happiness. Utilitarians do not believe that there are universal and permanently valid "natural" rights. They believe, rather, that rights are created within each regime in response to circumstances. For example, if it is conducive to the general well-being of the citizens to establish a right to separate schools for Roman Catholics, then such a right could be established by law. But utilitarians would deny that such a right exists by nature; they deny, in other words, that the establishment of separate schools is a universal moral imperative binding all governments in all times and places.

It is important to appreciate, however, that utilitarians believe the articulation of rights to be guided by certain fundamental rules. The most important of these rules would be the famous **harm principle** elaborated by John Stuart Mill.[2] According to the harm principle, governments cannot interfere with the actions of individuals so long as those individuals are not harming others. Mill argued that happiness was most likely to be achieved if all individuals were allowed to develop their own individuality as fully as possible. The full development of our individuality requires that we each be left as free as possible to explore our own ideas and to act on the basis of those ideas. Provided we do not harm others, even harming ourselves is, according to Mill, properly within the sphere of individual liberty.

The harm principle means two things for politics. The first point is that the onus of proof is always on the government to show why any law that limits our individual liberty is necessary. The second point is that such a law will be valid only if it is necessary to prevent some direct harm to other human beings. We cannot, for example, pass laws forbidding people to smoke or drink when they are acting in ways that harm only themselves. But when their actions harm others, such as driving while drunk, we are allowed to curtail their liberty for the protection of others' rights.

The best examples of liberal democratic regimes that take their bearings from the natural rights school of liberalism are the United States and France. The leading example of the utilitarian approach to liberty is Britain. Here in Canada, our liberalism was historically of the utilitarian type. The doctrine of

---

2   This argument is elaborated in Mill's famous essay *On Liberty*, 1859.

natural rights was for many years seen as an abstraction foreign to our traditions. In recent years, however, especially since the adoption of the Charter of Rights and Freedoms, Canadian thinking about rights has shifted dramatically. Although our traditional utilitarian approach to rights remains, it is now common for Canadians to think of many of their rights as human rights, just as our American neighbours do. Given that the utilitarian and the natural rights schools are incompatible in important respects, it seems likely that our thinking about rights will be in flux for some time to come.

The list of specific rights enjoyed by citizens of liberal democracies is a long one. It is also a list that varies from one liberal democracy to another. Still, it is possible to summarize the essence of those rights in three general principles:

1. *Protection of the private sphere.* Liberals draw a deep (though not necessarily sharp) distinction between the private sphere and the public sphere. The public sphere includes those areas of human activity where governmental regulation of our conduct is necessary to protect the rights of everyone. The private sphere includes everything else, and liberals insist that governments may not interfere in these areas of our lives. For a liberal, then, government may legitimately tell us how fast we may drive a car or what kind of guns we may own, but it has no right to tell us what religion to believe in or whether we should refrain from engaging in extramarital sex. Former Prime Minister Pierre Trudeau once articulated this principle of liberalism in his famous remark that "there's no place for the state in the bedrooms of the nation."[3]

2. *Respect for minority rights.* A liberal regime will proscribe all discrimination on the basis of race, religion, and other politically irrelevant characteristics. This injunction against discrimination is part of a wider principle, the principle that those in power must assure equal treatment for those in the minority. According to liberals, the fact that 51 per cent of the population can win any vote does not entitle that majority to do anything it pleases. For instance, would it not be unjust for a majority of the population to compel an ethnic, religious, or regional minority to pay all of the taxes?

3. *The rule of law.* Liberals believe that the effective protection of the various rights of citizens depends on the principle of the **rule of law**. At a minimum, this

---

3   *CBC Digital Archives*, December 21, 1967, http://www.cbc.ca/archives/entry/omnibus-bill-theres-no-place-for-the-state-in-the-bedrooms-of-the-nation.

principle states that citizens must be able to count on what we often call "law and order," for without the protection of an effective legal order, the rights of everyone would be in jeopardy. But the principle of the rule of law goes far beyond simple law and order. It dictates, first of all, that the government is not itself above the law. Second, it stipulates that the law must be applied equally and impartially. Finally, every action taken by the government must be grounded in some legal authority. The reason for this principle is simple: if those in control of public power were able to treat citizens arbitrarily—that is, however they liked—we would all be at the mercy of the powerful.

Insisting that government act on the basis of established legal authority is a crucial mechanism for guaranteeing our rights. One especially important aspect of the rule of law is the idea of **constitutionalism**, the idea that the regime itself must be ordered in accordance with agreed-upon rules that will be supreme. A dictatorship may be defined as a regime in which those in power rule by force and recognize no limitations on their capacity to act. In a liberal regime, however, we insist on fixing clear limitations on the power of those who rule, and these limitations are to be found in a set of fundamental rules called the constitution.

1.4 The Canadian Regime

Equality and liberty constitute the regime principles of all of the world's liberal democracies. Sweden, Australia, Japan, Germany, Mexico, Israel—all are liberal democracies. They are founded on the regime principles sketched above. It is important to note, however, that every liberal democracy will apply those principles in its own way. What the student of politics must first understand is the kind of regime a state has. On that basis, one can then turn to an examination of its political institutions and to a fuller study of its political culture.

In Part II of this book (Chapters Three–Five), "The Pillars of the Canadian Constitution," we will explain the way in which the Canadian Constitution adapts and applies the regime principles of liberal democracy to create a uniquely Canadian regime. Chapter Three discusses the principle of responsible government. We will see in that chapter that the rules of responsible government are the mechanism we use in Canada to apply the principles of democracy in general and parliamentary democracy in particular. In Chapter Four, we examine federalism, the division of political authority between a national government in Ottawa and the ten provincial and three territorial governments. As we will see, Canadians adopted a federal regime as the best means of ensuring respect for the rights of regional and linguistic minorities. In Chapter Five, we turn to the Charter of

Rights and Freedoms, the constitutional document that serves to protect our liberal rights and freedoms from violation by the governments.

Before turning to Part II, however, we must first complete our introduction to the Canadian regime by describing and explaining Canada's Constitution. We have seen in section 1.3 that liberal democracies are based on constitutionalism, the idea that the rules of the regime must be set down in a constitution. The constitution is thus the skeleton or framework of the regime, and any study of the regime will therefore entail frequent reference to it. For this reason, it is important to begin by familiarizing the reader with Canada's Constitution.

Key Terms

regime	parliamentary democracy
kingship	representative democracy
tyranny	republican
aristocracy	liberal democracy
oligarchy	private sphere
polity	liberalism
democracy	natural rights
tyranny of the majority	utilitarianism
equality	harm principle
liberty	rule of law
direct democracy	constitutionalism

Discussion Questions

1. Developments in information technology have made direct democracy more possible. What are the pros and cons of having a more direct democracy?

2. Can you think of any examples from the past decade or two when the Canadian government has acted as a tyranny of the majority?

CHAPTER TWO

THE CONSTITUTION

2.1 Constitutions and Their Functions

A constitution may be defined as *a set of rules that authoritatively establishes both the structure and the fundamental principles of the political regime.* We call this set of rules a "constitution" because it is these rules that "constitute" (i.e., create or establish) the regime. A constitution will normally do so by performing four major functions.

The *first major function of a constitution* is to establish what person or persons will exercise the various forms of political authority. In modern times, political power is understood to consist of three distinct types. **Legislative power** is the power to make law or policy. For instance, a political community might use its legislative power to pass a law stipulating that no one whose blood has an alcohol content above .05 per cent may drive an automobile. **Executive power** is the power to "execute" or administer that law or policy. This would include the power to establish and maintain a police force to catch impaired drivers. **Judicial power** is the power to settle questions about specific violations of law (is there adequate evidence to prove the driver's blood-alcohol level exceeded .05 per cent?) and to choose a suitable punishment from among those permitted in the relevant legislation for those found guilty.

Every constitution will, at some point, assign legislative, executive, and judicial powers to some specific persons or bodies of persons. Almost any organization or governing body, from the national government to the local chapter of the SPCA, will have a constitution that performs this function. The constitution of a student council, for example, might stipulate that legislative power, the power to set policy, will be exercised by a council consisting of some fixed number of persons who represent specific constituencies of the student population: the senior class, the off-campus students, and so on. It will probably also establish certain fundamental rules to govern the manner in which the council will proceed in its work (for instance, how many members must be present to make a meeting official). The student council's constitution will also specify who is to exercise the executive power. It may, for example, confer this power on a group called "the executive" and stipulate that this executive will have a number of specific members (president, secretary, treasurer), each of whom will have certain specific responsibilities.

The constitution of a political regime will set down these types of rules. It will stipulate that legislative power is to be exercised by a "parliament," a "congress," an "assembly," or some other body. It will then dictate the composition of that body (one chamber or two, how many members, how they are to be selected) and probably establish some basic ground rules for its functioning. The constitution will also determine whether executive power will be in the hands of a president, prime minister, cabinet, or perhaps even a monarch. Finally, it must establish the broad outlines of a judicial system by stipulating what kind of courts the country will have and by setting down rules for the selection of their judges.

The *second major function of a constitution* is to provide an authoritative division of powers between national and regional governments in federal countries. Countries such as Britain or France are said to have "unitary" regimes in the sense that they have only one government for the entire country. Yet, in very large countries (e.g., the United States) or in countries divided into distinct ethnic or cultural regions (Russia or Germany), it is common to establish two independent levels of government. In these "federal" regimes, a "national" or "federal" government will handle those matters on which it is thought there should be common policy across the country (national defence, for instance). At the same time, however, "state" or "provincial" governments take responsibility for matters on which different parts of the country want distinct policies (education, for example) or which might be more effectively managed by local authorities (the construction and maintenance of roads).

A workable federal system requires a clear division of powers between the two levels of government. If it were left up to each level to decide for itself what its powers were, the result would be political instability, if not chaos. Citizens might find themselves torn between a federal law requiring them to drive on the right-hand side of the road and a state or provincial law requiring them to drive on the left! In order to avoid such conflicts, federal constitutions provide a clear division of powers and areas of responsibility for each of the two levels of government. In theory, such a division can be neatly accomplished by drawing up two lists, each of which spells out the specific jurisdictions of each level of government. The practical problem, however, is that it is difficult, if not impossible, to make the two lists sufficiently comprehensive; moreover, there will also be overlapping areas of jurisdiction. Governments legislate in a wide variety of areas, and new areas emerge on a regular basis (regulating the use of the Internet, for example). It is therefore typical for a constitution in a federal regime to furnish a list of specific jurisdictions reserved for the exclusive attention of one level of government and then to stipulate that everything else (the "**residual power**") be reserved for the other. In addition, such a constitution will probably set down a process by which disagreements over jurisdiction can be settled.

The *third major function of a constitution* is to delineate the limits of governmental power. The very existence of a constitution is in some sense a limitation on the power of government. The idea of constitutionalism implies that the constitution is supreme and that government is subordinate to it. Beyond this general limitation, it is not uncommon for constitutions to establish a list of fundamental rights and liberties in some sort of charter or "bill" of rights. Such a charter might specify, for example, that the citizens of a country have a right to freedom of religion. What this means is that no government, national or provincial, has the power to take measures that would violate its citizens' right to religious freedom. Thus, even though a provincial government might, under the division of powers, have jurisdiction over education, it could not use that jurisdiction to pass legislation requiring schools to indoctrinate their students in some specific religious tradition.

Finally, the *fourth function of a constitution* is to provide for an orderly way to make changes to it. Political regimes do not remain static, so constitutions must accommodate and structure change. Most constitutions contain clear provisions for amendment. As we shall see, the Constitution of Canada contains a number of provisions for its amendment.

2.2 Constitutional Forms: Conventions and Laws

In saying that a constitution consists of the regime's most fundamental rules, we need to first look at what types of rules these are. A rule is a principle or condition that customarily governs behaviour. Such rules might be written down or unwritten; they might be legally enforced or enforced by public opinion and political custom. Hence, some of these rules are likely to be legal rules while others may be rules that everyone generally understands and follows without any threat of legal sanction. As we shall see, both types of rules can be of fundamental importance.

When it comes to examining the political nature of constitutions, we find that the fundamental rules that make up a regime's constitution are of two basic types: conventions and laws. Conventions are political rules; laws are judicially enforceable rules. A political rule is typically followed because one fears the political consequences of breaking the rule. A judicially enforceable rule is typically followed because one fears the consequences of punishment.[1]

A constitution will thus be a set of fundamental rules, consisting of conventions and laws. *The distinction between conventions and laws is not that the former are unwritten and the latter are written*; the distinction is in how the rule is enforced. Consider the following: statutory law is written down, common law is not.[2] Both are rules enforced by courts. What makes conventions different from laws is that conventions are rules enforced by politics, whereas constitutional laws are rules enforced by courts.

Constitutional laws may in turn be divided into two types: organic statutes and entrenched constitutional laws. Canada's Constitution consists, then, of a combination of constitutional conventions, entrenched constitutional laws, and organic statutes. It is a complex constitution, and one whose clear understanding often seems to elude many good minds. It poses a challenge to effective democratic citizenship, for a democracy needs to have citizens who are well informed in its most fundamental rules. Let us look at these different forms of constitutional rules.

---

1   This discussion relies on the work of A.V. Dicey, whose *Introduction to the Study of Law of the Constitution*, 8th ed. (1915; repr., Indianapolis: Liberty Fund, 1982) remains essential reading for anyone who wishes to understand the British and Canadian constitutions.

2   We discuss common law in more detail in Chapter Eight. In all provinces of Canada except Quebec, common law is used to govern most commercial relations and transactions such as contracts. It is a body of law made over time by the resolution of disputes by judges and the binding character of those rulings as a precedent for future disputes. It is law, but not law written by a legislature.

1. Constitutional Conventions. When it comes to understanding the constitution, it is important to grasp that, in referring to a **constitutional convention**, we are not referring to a big meeting where people get together to talk about the constitution. (Such meetings do take place from time to time, but they are unusual events and are sometimes, but not exclusively, referred to as conventions.) In constitutional terms, the word "convention" refers to a constitutional rule based on implicit political agreement and enforced in the political arena rather than by the courts. Courts have been occasionally called upon to give better definition to conventions, but they are unable to enforce them. A convention is thus similar to a custom. Think, for example, of the custom of shaking hands when you meet someone. There is no law that says people must shake right hands, but everyone accepts that it is the right hand one offers to another person (except, perhaps, in extraordinary circumstances). Constitutional rules in the form of conventions can operate in much the same way. For instance, traditionally in the British Constitution, a long-established political rule stipulates that the monarch will not refuse to provide royal assent to legislation that has been passed by both the House of Lords and the House of Commons. This rule takes the form of an unwritten agreement, accepted as binding by everyone and sanctioned by the force of tradition. But it is not mere tradition that makes a particular practice a convention. The essential point in any convention is its rationale. Today, we shake right hands because that just happens to be the custom. Originally, however, people greeted others by extending their right hand for a specific reason: that was the hand in which one would normally hold one's weapon. Extending an empty right hand was thus a way of demonstrating that one's intentions were not hostile. The British convention requiring royal assent is also based on an obvious rationale: as Britain evolved from a monarchy to a democracy, the House of Commons became the primary political power, and withholding royal assent would thus not be viewed as politically legitimate. This convention is now well established, but its legitimacy rests on the perception that there are good reasons for such a rule, not on how constitutionally ingrained it is.

The question, of course, is what happens if someone violates a convention. If politicians break a law, they can be brought before a court, tried, and punished if found guilty. But precisely because the court is a "court of law" and not a "court of conventions," its judges cannot, and will not, enforce constitutional conventions. So who does enforce them? The answer is the voting public. In a constitutional system based on conventions, the voters, it is assumed, will know what those conventions are and will guard them jealously. Therefore, those holding political office will respect these conventions out of fear of invoking the wrath of the voters. But this is not to say that constitutional conventions are always respected. The great advantage of having constitutional rules in the form of conventions rather than laws is that they can be applied with a certain amount of flexibility. We normally greet other people by offering our right hand to shake, but if one's right hand is in a cast, it is acceptable to offer the left. This same flexibility is evident in the realm of constitutional convention. The British electorate would never permit a monarch to violate the convention on royal assent, unless there was some obvious necessity for doing so. What might constitute such a necessity is hard to imagine, but the possibility is still there. The public would have to decide whether that specific departure from the rule was justified. Similarly, in Canada there is no constitutional law stating that the Senate cannot vote against a bill that has been passed by the House of Commons. But there is a constitutional convention that the Senate will ultimately defer to the will of the House of Commons. Occasionally, however, it has refused to do so. In 1988, the Senate refused to pass legislation that would implement a free trade agreement with the United States. This refusal triggered a national election on the issue. Prime Minister Mulroney's government was returned with a majority, and the legislation was ultimately passed. But Canadians did not react negatively to the fact that the Senate had triggered the election, thus proving that a convention can be ignored, but only for the right reason. In both the previous examples, if the convention had been ignored for light and transient reasons, the likely consequence would have been immediate: political pressure for the reform of the institutions of the monarchy and the Senate.

2. Constitutional Law. The second form in which a country may embody its constitutional rules is in constitutional laws: rules of a constitutional nature that are enforced by courts. **Constitutional laws** may, in turn, be divided into two distinct categories: organic statutes and entrenched constitutional acts.

The term "statute" refers to an act of the authoritative legislative body, which, in Canada, is Parliament or a provincial legislature. Statutes establishing constitutional rules are called "**organic statutes**" to distinguish them from statutes dealing with non-constitutional matters—statutes regulating health care, automobile traffic, or unemployment insurance, for example. The classic parliamentary model using these constitutional rules is found, once again, in Britain. Because of that country's extensive use of constitutional convention, textbooks will often describe the British Constitution as an "unwritten" one. This description is somewhat misleading. A good deal of the British Constitution is actually written out in the form of organic statutes, laws passed by the British Parliament to spell out certain constitutional rules in black and white. The Bill of Rights of 1689, which placed important new restrictions on the powers of the Crown, is a classic example of such a statute. So too are the Reform Act of 1832 and the Parliament Act of 1911, both of which dramatically altered the nature and functioning of Britain's legislative institutions. An illustrative category of examples in Canada would be human rights codes; these are simply provincial statutes, but they deal with fundamental rights such as equality and protection against discrimination (e.g., in housing and employment).

There are two basic reasons for adopting some constitutional rules as organic statutes rather than conventions. The first is that some rules, especially those that establish and describe institutions, are probably too complex and too detailed to be left to the realm of unwritten agreement. The second is that organic statutes provide a more effective means of introducing substantial innovation to the existing constitutional order. Each of the three statutes cited as examples in the previous paragraph represented a dramatic change in the nature of the British regime. Putting those measures in statute form improved their chances of taking hold because statutes, unlike conventions, can be enforced by the courts. For instance, if in 1690 the king had tried to impose new taxes without Parliament's consent (an act prohibited by the Bill of Rights of 1689), his subjects could have used the courts to resist the new taxes on the grounds that they were in violation of British law.

Constitutional law may also take the form of an **entrenched constitutional act**. Like organic statutes, entrenched constitutional acts are written and enforceable by courts, but they differ from organic statutes in two important respects. The first difference is that entrenched constitutional acts tend to be more comprehensive than organic statutes: while organic statutes usually deal with one particular institution or situation, entrenched constitutional acts tend to be comprehensive codifications of a wide variety of major constitutional rules. The second and more important difference is one of status or authority. The authority of an organic statute derives from the fact that it represents the will of the body that exercises legislative power. This means its authority is always somewhat precarious because any body that has a right to adopt a statute must, of necessity, have the right to repeal or amend it. The British Parliament that adopted the Reform Act of 1832 could have repealed that same bill the day after it was passed. The authority of an entrenched constitutional act is more absolute because entrenched acts are not as easily changed as statutes. In the United States, for example, the Constitution itself proclaims that changes (or "amendments") may be made to that country's entrenched act only if they are supported by two-thirds of the members of each chamber of Congress and by the legislatures of three-quarters of the states.

The logic of this concept is best explained in the writings of the great British political philosopher John Locke.[3] Locke's theory of government begins with the argument that, because no one has any natural title to rule over anyone else, government can be legitimate only if it is based on the consent of all those who are governed. In saying this, Locke does not mean that all political decisions have to be made democratically. He means only that the regime has to meet with the approval of its citizens. Locke suggests that this approval comes in a two-stage process, which he calls the "social contract." In the first stage of the contract, human beings who are naturally free and equal decide to come together in "civil society" and establish a political regime to govern themselves. In the second stage, they establish the ground rules of the regime by majority vote. They can vote to set up a democratic regime, but they also have the right to institute an aristocracy or even a monarchy. It is not the institutions that have to be democratic for government to be legitimate but the underlying contract that establishes them.

According to Locke, once the people have put the social contract in place, they turn the process of governing over to those who fill the offices established by the contract. But this government is not free to act in any way it pleases. It is always limited by any conditions stipulated in the social contract because the legitimacy of the government's very existence depends on that contract. If the social contract says that the government may not tax citizens without obtaining the consent of their representatives, then a new tax that has not been approved by the representatives of the people would be in violation of the social contract and hence illegitimate.

In conceptual terms, what we mean by an "entrenched constitutional act" is very close to what Locke meant by a "social contract." An entrenched constitutional act is a kind of fundamental pact emanating from the will of the people, which provides the foundation for the entire regime. It is therefore of higher status than ordinary laws—statutes adopted by legislative bodies—because those bodies owe their very existence to it. An entrenched act is thus a kind of "super-law," the supreme law of the regime, and this means that any action or statute inconsistent with it can have no validity.

The special authority or status of an entrenched constitutional act is embodied in the descriptor "entrenched." There are many political principles so

---

3   See Locke's *Two Treatises of Government* (1690; repr. Cambridge: Cambridge University Press, 1967). See also Janet Ajzenstat, *The Canadian Founding: John Locke and Parliament* (Montreal: McGill-Queen's University Press, 2007), and Guy Laforest, *Trudeau and the End of a Canadian Dream* (Montreal: McGill-Queen's University Press, 1995).

fundamental that citizens will want to ensure that their government will never be able to violate them legally. Freedom of religion might be an example of such a principle or the right to use either French or English in the courts. The best way to ensure the inviolability of such principles is to "entrench" them by writing them into the text of the constitution. The foundational status of that law will then serve to put those principles safely out of the reach of any institution of government that might seek to violate them. Section 52 of Canada's 1982 Constitution Act affirms that document, as well as previous Canadian constitutional acts, as the "supreme law" of the country—amendable only by extraordinary means and superior to all other laws in the regime.

The prototype of an entrenched constitutional act is the Constitution of the United States. Prior to declaring their independence, the American colonists were, of course, British subjects. As such, their constitutional traditions might have led them to opt for a constitution similar in form to the British one, a constitution based on conventions and organic statutes. But for a number of reasons, the Americans opted instead to embody many of their constitutional rules in a more permanent and inviolable form. One reason was the fact that the leading figures in colonial America—people such as Jefferson, Franklin, and Madison— were profoundly influenced by the works of John Locke. The so-called Founding Fathers insisted that the Constitution of the United States take the form of a fundamental law emanating from the will of the people (rather than from a set of conventions and organic statutes devised by those politicians who held the legislative power) because this was the approach most consistent with Lockean theory.

But the Americans also had two practical reasons for using an entrenched constitutional act instead of conventions and organic statutes. One was that they had decided to establish a federal regime in which responsibilities were to be divided between a "federal" government and a number of "state" governments. It would have been impractical to establish a federal division of powers in the form of a constitutional convention because a federal division of powers has to be formulated in more precise, detailed, and rigid terms than can be managed in unwritten agreements. It would have been equally impractical to try to embody the division of powers in an organic statute because that statute would have to be adopted by some particular legislative body. But which one? The state governments would never agree to concede the task to the legislative body of the federal government, for then that body, by virtue of its right to amend its own statutes, would be able at any time to rewrite the division of powers so as to transfer jurisdictions from the state governments to itself. By the same token, leaving the adoption of a division of powers to the state legislatures would put the federal government at the mercy of the state governments. The federal division of powers had to be put in a constitutional form that would be beyond the unilateral reach of either the state or federal governments. This meant it had to take the form of a more entrenched set of constitutional rules.

The other reason for preferring an entrenched act to convention or organic statutes was the belief that the **entrenchment** of a constitution provides the most effective means of guaranteeing citizens' rights and liberties. It should not be forgotten that the 13 colonies broke away from Britain precisely because they believed that the British government was not respecting the American colonists' constitutional rights (e.g., the right to "no taxation without representation"). These rights had been guaranteed to all British subjects, including the American colonists, by various conventions and organic statutes. But guarantees offered by conventions and statutes are not iron clad. A government could ignore conventions or repeal statutes if it had strong public support for such actions. And in the 1770s, the American colonists believed that their constitutional rights were being systematically violated by a government more concerned with the interests of the British majority than with the rights of the American minority.

Here, then, was another reason to place the constitutional rules of the new American regime in an entrenched form. Entrenched constitutional acts are the preferred constitutional form for rights and liberties because these acts have a higher status than any particular political institution. In a constitutional system based on convention and statute, politicians can adopt the most oppressive of measures as long as they have the support of a majority of voters. But no matter how much public support they have, politicians cannot legally adopt measures that violate an entrenched guarantee.

2.3 The Canadian Constitution

In subsequent chapters, we will see that the Canadian regime is, to a large extent, a mixture of the British and American regimes. This intermingling is evident in the form of the Canadian Constitution. Like the Americans, we have embodied many, if not most, of our constitutional rules in entrenched constitutional acts: the Constitution Act, 1867 (CA 1867)[4] and the Constitution Act, 1982 (CA 1982). Like the British, however, we also rely on constitutional conventions and organic statutes for a substantial number of our constitutional rules. Our entire system of responsible government, for example, is embedded in constitutional convention

---

4   Canada's first constitutional law was originally called the British North America Act (BNA Act). Its name was changed to Constitution Act, 1867 in 1982.

rather than in constitutional law.[5] Specific examples of Canadian constitutional conventions and organic statutes will be discussed later. In this section, we will focus our attention on Canada's two constitutional acts.

It is essential that students of the Canadian regime learn to work with CA 1867 and CA 1982, and, for that reason, we have included a copy of each of these acts in the appendix. It will be useful to examine them briefly in order to familiarize the reader with their structure and contents.

Figure 2.1: Main Elements of Canada's Constitutional Acts

CA 1867	CA 1982
Executive power	Charter of Rights and Freedoms
Legislative power	Aboriginal rights
Provincial constitutions	Equalization and regional disparities
Federal division of power	Amending formulas
Judicial power	Definition of the Canadian Constitution

1. CA 1867. This act served to create a union of three British colonies into a new political entity called the "Dominion of Canada." The term "dominion" was new, invented to describe a regime that was too self-governing to be considered a colony but not entirely independent of the mother country either. Under the terms of Confederation, Canadians were to remain subjects of the British Crown; their foreign policy was to be directed by the British government; the Judicial Committee of the Privy Council, Britain's highest court, would be the final court of appeal for Canadian legal disputes; and Britain would maintain control of Canada's Constitution.

It is this last point that is of particular interest to us here. Entrenched acts normally derive their supreme status from the fact that they emanate from the will of the people, usually as expressed in some kind of popular referendum. Because those creating the new confederation were already subjects of the British Crown, however, their new constitution was not adopted as some kind of Lockean social contract; instead, it was legislated for them, at the request of

---

5   It is important to note that, though constitutions may use entrenched constitutional law to a greater or lesser degree, there will almost always be some role played by constitutional convention. Although it is common to point to the United States as an example of a constitutional order based on constitutional law, the American constitutional order also depends on certain conventions. A good example would be the way the Electoral College functions in that country.

their colonial legislatures, by the British Parliament. Thus, the status of CA 1867 as Canada's supreme law depended on the fact that it was an act of our colonial mother country and on the fact that we Canadians, being less than fully independent of her, had no right to disobey her laws.

CA 1867 consists of a **preamble** (an introduction stating the reasons for the act that follows) and 11 "parts." The most noteworthy feature in the preamble is the suggestion that Canada is to have "a Constitution similar in Principle to that of the United Kingdom." This clause is of the greatest importance for understanding the Canadian Constitution. As we have seen, the British Constitution is to a large extent based on conventions. In declaring that Canada's Constitution is to be "similar in Principle to that of the United Kingdom," the preamble serves notice that many of those conventions are to be incorporated into it. Certain to be included were those conventions governing the operation of "responsible government," a subject we shall discuss in detail in Chapter Three.

Part I of CA 1867 deals with relatively unimportant preliminary matters. Part II establishes some basic points about the union of the provinces. Parts III and IV are much more important, for it is here that CA 1867 sketches the fundamental outlines of executive and legislative power in the federal government. We shall examine the particular sections of Parts III and IV in some detail in Chapter Six ("The Crown and Its Servants") and Chapter Seven ("Parliament"). Part V deals with "provincial constitutions" and describes some of their distinctive features. For the most part, the constitutions of the provinces are governed by the same principles as those governing the federal government.

In Part VI, we find the division of powers between the two levels of government. Of particular importance are the description of the legislative authority of the federal government in section 91 and the list of provincial jurisdictions in section 92. Part VII lays down some of the fundamental rules governing judicial power in Canada. Note, however, that nothing is said about the Supreme Court of Canada. Section 101 gives the federal Parliament the right to establish a "General Court of Appeal for Canada," and, in 1875, Ottawa used this power to create a supreme court in the Supreme Court of Canada Act. Because the Supreme Court of Canada is this country's highest institution of judicial power, the act that establishes it must certainly be considered a constitutional law, even though it is not an entrenched constitutional act. Here, then, is a good example of a Canadian "organic statute." Part VIII establishes various provisions governing the financial details of Confederation. Part IX lays down a number of miscellaneous provisions, including section 133 on the use of the French and English languages.

Part X, which committed the federal government to the immediate construction of the Intercolonial Railway between Quebec and Halifax, became obsolete upon the termination of that project and was repealed in 1893. It is a good example of the way in which a constitutional act is sometimes used in Canada to entrench guarantees that have nothing to do with constitutional matters. Part XI establishes two procedures for the admission of new provinces. Existing colonies, such as British Columbia or Prince Edward Island, may be admitted to Canada by an act of the British Parliament if it receives a request to that effect by both the colony and the federal government of Canada. The federal government may pass acts of its own to create new provinces out of "Rupert's Land" and did so when it founded the provinces of Manitoba, Saskatchewan, and Alberta. In either case, the act creating a new province is a constitutional measure and may thus be classified as an "organic statute."

2. CA 1982. For well over 100 years, CA 1867 and its attendant statutes and conventions formed the core of Canada's constitutional order. Through much of that period, however, there was a sense that this constitutional order was significantly incomplete. From the 1920s right up to the beginning of the 1980s, Canadian politicians struggled to add another element to our constitution: a constitutional amending formula.

Constitutions need to be amended from time to time when certain of their provisions either become outdated (e.g., the section of CA 1867 dealing with the Intercolonial Railway) or are found to be problematic. Entrenched constitutional acts will therefore always (or almost always) contain an amending formula, a rule explaining how the law can be changed. The Constitution of the United States, for example, specifies that it may be amended if the text of a proposed amendment is supported by a two-thirds vote in each of the two houses of Congress and then a majority vote in three-quarters of the state legislatures.

CA 1867 is perhaps the only entrenched constitutional act in the history of the world that contained no comprehensive amending formula. Until 1982, section 92.1 gave each province the right to amend its own internal constitution. From 1949 to 1982, section 91.1 gave the federal Parliament the right to make changes to most aspects of its own internal structure. But nowhere in the act is there a formula for the amendment of such crucial matters as the federal-provincial division of powers, the judiciary, or language rights. This, of course, did not mean that the constitutional provisions governing such matters could not be amended. Because CA 1867 was a statute of the British Parliament, that body retained the right to amend any of its sections. Until 1982, then, Canada could initiate changes to those parts of CA 1867 not governed by section 91.1 or 92.1 by sending a formal request for amendment to the British Parliament at Westminster. The request took the form of a resolution of the federal Parliament, but a practice emerged according to which Ottawa would not request any amendments that would alter the powers of the provincial governments without first obtaining their consent.

Over time, this arrangement came to be seen as unsatisfactory. As a result of our nation's substantial contributions and sacrifices during World War I, Britain and Canada agreed that the time had come for the Canadian regime to become fully independent. This meant, among other things, that it was time for Canada to take full control of its own constitution. As early as the 1920s, Britain had invited Canada to **patriate** (literally, to "bring to the fatherland") its constitution, but Canada was unable to do so. The problem was that before the British government could hand CA 1867 over to us, it had to put a comprehensive amending formula into the act. Unfortunately, Canadian politicians were unable to agree upon what that formula should be. Numerous constitutional conferences were held over the years, but agreement remained elusive.

The problem in these negotiations was not patriation itself: everyone agreed that patriation was a good idea. The catch was that various parties insisted on using the patriation negotiations to pursue other agendas. From the early 1960s on, the government of Quebec took the position that it would agree to patriation only if it were accompanied by the transfer of specific legislative jurisdictions from Ottawa to Quebec City. In the 1970s, many other provincial governments made similar demands. On the other side of the table, Pierre Trudeau, then prime minister, opposed any such transfer and sought to link patriation of the Constitution to a project of his own: the adoption of an entrenched bill of rights that would, among other things, provide constitutional protection for the bilingual regime of language rights he favoured. His proposal was fiercely resisted by the government of Quebec.

In the early 1980s, Trudeau brought the matter to a head by announcing that if Ottawa and the provinces did not soon come to an agreement on patriating the Constitution, his government was ready to proceed with a patriation request unilaterally. Two provincial governments supported Trudeau, but the other eight (the "Gang of Eight") opposed him and went to court to challenge the constitutionality of a unilateral initiative.[6] The case was eventually heard by the Supreme Court of Canada, which handed down a complicated split decision: in terms of constitutional law, there was nothing to prevent the federal government from making a unilateral request for patriation, but the court also declared that Trudeau's proposed amendment would diminish the powers of the provincial governments and that it was now a convention that amendments having an impact on the powers

---

6   Ontario and New Brunswick sided with the federal government, and the remaining eight provinces were opposed.

of the provinces required the support of a substantial number of the provinces. The effect of this decision was to compel both sides to go back to the negotiating table and show more flexibility. The "Gang of Eight" could not be intransigent knowing that Ottawa had the legal right to proceed unilaterally if no agreement was reached, and Ottawa had a powerful incentive to compromise because it wanted to avoid the stigma that comes from violating constitutional convention.

These negotiations resulted in a compromise agreement that obtained the support of every provincial government except Quebec. On the basis of that agreement, the British Parliament passed the Canada Act, 1982, which created a second major constitutional law for Canada, the Constitution Act, 1982 (CA 1982).

CA 1982 is divided into seven parts. Part I is the Canadian Charter of Rights and Freedoms, a document we shall examine in Chapter Five. Part II is a constitutional declaration of the rights of Canada's Aboriginal peoples. Part III entrenches the principle of the federal government making equalization payments to provinces whose revenues are below the national average. This practice will be explained in Chapter Four. The fourth part committed the governments of Canada, the provinces, and the territories to hold a conference on Aboriginal people's constitutional concerns. The conference was held soon after the adoption of CA 1982 and resulted in certain amendments to its section 35. Part V outlines the new procedure for amending the Constitution of Canada, and we shall examine its contents in detail in the next section of this chapter. Part VI makes an amendment to section 92 of CA 1867 strengthening the powers of provincial governments in the areas of energy, forestry, and non-renewable resources. This was one of the demands of the "Gang of Eight." Part VII contains a number of miscellaneous provisions. For our purposes, the most noteworthy is section 52, which gives a legal definition of the Constitution of Canada and proclaims in no uncertain terms its status as Canada's "supreme law."

It should not be forgotten, however, that section 52 is a clause in an act that is itself a creation of Britain's Canada Act, 1982. The supremacy of Canada's constitutional acts is thus still grounded in the fact that they are statutes of our mother-parliament in Westminster. Some suggested that the federal Parliament and the ten provincial legislatures should each pass a resolution adopting the Constitution Act of 1982, so as to give our constitutional order a more independent foundation and make it more like a Lockean social contract. The problem with this strategy, however, is that the government of Quebec, which has always opposed the agreement now embodied in CA 1982, refused—and continues to refuse—to pass such a resolution. Nevertheless, the Constitution Act of 1982 is valid in Quebec, as well as in the rest of Canada, because the British Parliament has declared it so by the Canada Act, 1982.

Figure 2.2: The Five Amending Formulas

Sections of CA 1982	Subject of Amendment	Amending Formula
General Procedure (ss. 38–40; 42)	All sections of the Constitution not exempted by ss. 41, 43, 44, 45	Parliament + seven provinces with 50% of the population
	Prov. representation in the Senate	
	Supreme Court reform	
	Principle of proportionate rep. in the House of Commons	
	The establishment of new provinces	
	Extension of provincial boundaries into the territories	
Unanimous Agreement (Queen, Gov. Gen., Lt. Gov.) (s. 41)	Changes to the Crown	Parliament + all provinces
	Right of province to have no fewer MPs than Senators	
	Use of French and English languages	
	Composition of the Supreme Court	
	Amendments to the amending formulas	
Some Provinces (s. 43)	Alteration of boundaries between provinces	Parliament + relevant provinces
	Provisions relating to the use of French and English languages within the province(s)	
Parliament (s. 44)	Amendments to the executive government of Canada, and to the Senate and House of Commons, aside from those matters falling under ss. 41–42	
One Province (s. 45)	Amendments to the Constitution of a provincial govt. alone (not falling under s. 41)	province

2.4 Amending Canada's Constitution

Part V of CA 1982 establishes an amending formula for the Constitution, or, to speak more precisely, five distinct formulas for five distinct situations. A brief summary is sketched in Figure 2.2.

Section 44 stipulates that amendments to constitutional provisions regarding the executive or legislative offices of the federal government may be made by Parliament[7] on its own. This is essentially the same provision that formerly existed as section 91.1 of CA 1867. In like fashion, section 45 reproduces the former section 92.1 of CA 1867, stipulating that amendments to the constitution of a province may be made by the legislature of that province. Section 43 contains a third amending formula. It stipulates that amendments that concern some but not all provinces (e.g., the alteration of a provincial boundary) or that deal with constitutionally entrenched language rights in a particular province may be made only with the consent of Parliament and the province concerned. The reason for including the second category of amendments is to ensure that a temporary majority in a single province cannot unilaterally diminish or abolish the constitutional language rights of a minority.

The other two formulas are somewhat more complex. Section 41 provides that for five specific matters—the Crown, the right of provinces to a number of MPs not less than the number of its senators, the use of French and English, the composition of the Supreme Court, and the amending procedures themselves—a constitutional amendment must have the support of the federal Parliament and the legislatures of every province. This is an extremely rigid amending formula, but it is argued that the matters in question are so fundamental that they should not be altered without the unanimous consent of Canada's federal and provincial governments.

Any provision of the Constitution not covered by one of these four formulas is to be amended with the "general" formula established in section 38, which requires the consent of the federal Parliament and the legislatures of two-thirds of the provinces that, taken together, contain at least half of Canada's population. This formula ensures that no single province can **veto** (i.e., block) a proposed amendment, but at the same time it ensures that no amendment can be adopted without widespread support, including the support of one of the two largest provinces, Ontario and Quebec. Section 38 also establishes that a province

---

7   In constitutional language, the term "Parliament" refers to the Parliament of Canada. Provincial governments do not have parliaments; the provincial equivalent of Parliament is a "legislature."

may choose to exempt itself from an amendment made under this formula. If, for example, nine provinces were willing to transfer jurisdiction over prisons (a provincial responsibility under CA 1867, 92.6) to Ottawa but Quebec was not, the amendment could be made, and prisons would thereafter be a federal responsibility in the other nine provinces and a provincial responsibility in Quebec. Section 40 adds an interesting twist to this arrangement. This section stipulates that if an amendment involves a transfer of some part of provincial jurisdiction over education or culture, the federal government, which will now take up those responsibilities in all the other provinces, must offer financial compensation to the province that is retaining them. This compensation is granted because it would be unfair for the taxpayers of a particular province to have to pay a share of the cost of those responsibilities in the other nine provinces through their federal taxes as well as the total cost of those responsibilities in their own province.

2.5 Judicial Review of the Constitution

Our overview of the Constitution would be incomplete if we did not say a word about judicial review.

By their very nature, constitutions have to regulate every single aspect and activity of a political regime. This means that constitutional rules must be applicable to an almost infinite number of possible situations. But the number of constitutional rules cannot itself be infinite. For this reason, constitutional laws are of necessity written in language that is highly general and even vague. A constitutional division of powers cannot list every possible object of legislative activity: the regulation of automobile engine emissions, the regulation of industrial effluents, the regulation of garbage disposal, and so on. It will therefore collect all of these matters under a general heading such as "protection of the environment." By the same token, the Charter of Rights and Freedoms cannot specify all the types of police searches that are acceptable and all those that are not. It therefore defines our rights in general terms: the right to be secure against "unreasonable" searches.

The problem, however, is that it is often difficult to know how to apply general rules in specific cases. Let us take as a hypothetical example a constitution that stipulates that "protection of the environment" is a jurisdiction of the federal government and that "management of natural resources" is a provincial jurisdiction. Which level of government has the authority to regulate the clear-cutting of forests? The answer is not self-evident, and it is likely that each of them would insist that it had exclusive jurisdiction over the matter. Obviously, then, someone has to be in a position to offer an authoritative interpretation of what the Constitution means in these circumstances.

This interpretive task often falls to the judiciary. Judicial review of the Constitution refers to the judiciary's task of defining constitutional terms and determining whether laws or actions taken by government are consistent with them. The courts will decide, for example, whether the Constitution says that a particular legislative matter is of federal or provincial jurisdiction. To do so, they will determine the concrete meaning of abstract phrases such as "the Peace, Order, and good Government of Canada," "subject only to such reasonable limits prescribed by law as can be demonstrably justified in a free and democratic society," or "the right to be secure against unreasonable search or seizure." It is therefore essential that students of Canadian politics pay close attention to judicial review, for to understand our regime one has to understand the Constitution, and to understand the Constitution, one must understand how the courts have interpreted and applied it.

2.6 Constitutional Politics Since 1982

Canada's constitutional struggles did not end with the adoption of CA 1982. The government of the province of Quebec was resolutely opposed to the agreement made by Ottawa and the other nine provinces in 1982. This led Prime Minister Mulroney to initiate negotiations between Ottawa and the ten provincial premiers aimed at producing a new package of constitutional amendments designed to meet Quebec's concerns. The result of those negotiations was the Meech Lake Accord. Among other things, this accord would have declared Quebec to be a "distinct society" and would have given Quebec and all the other provinces a veto over constitutional amendments affecting the matters listed in section 42, matters that in CA 1982 are governed by the two-thirds/50-per-cent formula in section 38.

Because the accord proposed a change to the amending formula—one of the subjects mentioned in section 41 of CA 1982—its adoption required the consent of all the provincial legislatures. This proved to be a problem. Although all the premiers who participated in the Meech Lake negotiations personally endorsed the final package, a number of them were defeated in provincial elections before they were able to get the necessary resolution of approval passed in their legislatures. In the face of mounting public opposition to the Meech Lake Accord, the new governments that replaced them were reluctant to proceed. A series of complex federal-provincial negotiations ensued in a last-ditch effort to save it. Finally, in 1990, with the three-year window for approval fast closing, Elijah Harper, an Aboriginal member of the Manitoba Legislature, effectively killed the accord by opposing a crucial procedural motion that required unanimous consent.

Two years later, Prime Minister Mulroney initiated a new round of negotiations. One of the reasons for the defeat of the Meech Lake Accord was that it focused almost exclusively on the constitutional concerns of the government of Quebec. Aboriginal Canadians, women's groups, and Western Canadians, among others, were unwilling to endorse a constitutional package that did not address their constitutional concerns. The 1992 negotiations produced a new proposal, the Charlottetown Accord, which was designed to address the concerns of not only Quebec but other constituencies as well. The Charlottetown Accord retained the essential elements of Meech Lake: a "distinct society" clause, the Meech Lake amending formula, and limitations on new federal spending in provincial jurisdictions. It added to that formula a constitutional commitment to Aboriginal self-government, a new Senate designed to meet the demands of Westerners (as well as, perhaps, of women) for better representation in Ottawa, and a "Canada Clause" that was meant to encapsulate the fundamental political principles of the regime.

Once the Charlottetown Accord was drafted, the federal government announced that it would not be willing to support a parliamentary resolution adopting it unless a majority of voters in each province gave it their approval in a national referendum, because there had been many complaints that the process that produced the Meech Lake Accord had been "undemocratic." Although CA 1982 places the responsibility for amending the Constitution in the hands of Parliament and the ten legislatures, many Canadians thought they should have been directly consulted on the matter. Confident that the "something-for-everyone" approach of Charlottetown would prove popular, Prime Minister Mulroney gave in to those who advocated putting the accord to a referendum. To the surprise of many, however, a majority of voters in six provinces voted against it. The "something-for-everyone" approach turned out also to be a "something-to-offend-everyone" approach.

Ottawa's recourse to a referendum leaves us with an interesting constitutional question: do proposed amendments to the Constitution now have to be submitted to the people for a popular vote of approval? If we look at the relevant constitutional law, Part V of CA 1982, in which there is no mention of the term "referendum," the answer appears to be no. Nevertheless, it is difficult to believe that Canadian voters would not insist on the right to have a direct voice in future decisions about the Constitution now that they have had that opportunity in the Charlottetown process. If this is so, then perhaps we are witnessing the emergence of a new constitutional convention.

The most significant constitutional development since the rejection of the Charlottetown Accord was the Supreme Court of Canada's decision in the 1998 case *Reference re Secession of Québec*. After separatist forces had come within a whisker of winning a referendum on Quebec sovereignty in 1995, the Chrétien government asked the Supreme Court of Canada to clarify whether unilateral secession was permitted under the Canadian Constitution. The court held unanimously that the Constitution does not permit unilateral declarations of independence but went on to say that if a "clear majority" of Quebeckers voted in favour of a clear proposal for secession, that would confer on the rest of Canada an obligation to enter into negotiations for separation. The court also stipulated that it would be up to political leaders to determine what constitutes "a clear majority on a clear question." Acting upon the judges' invitation, Parliament adopted in 2000 the **Clarity Act**, under which the right to determine whether a "question" and a "majority" are "clear" is reserved to Parliament itself. Predictably, the adoption of the Clarity Act was denounced by a wide range of Quebeckers as an intrusion on what they took to be their province's right to decide its future on its own. Yet if Ottawa's strategy was to deflate the separatist cause by making separation appear even more complicated and risky, it seems to have been quite successful. In the years since the adoption of the Clarity Act, support in Quebec for separation has declined significantly. Moreover, studies tabled by the separatist Parti Québécois government in March of 2002 conceded that there would be major obstacles to any attempt to negotiate independence.

Canada has been through 30 years of what can be called "constitutional politics"—the major political issues being of a constitutional nature. In recent years, the fires of constitutional politics no longer burn as hot, and the country has returned to a more normal politics focusing primarily on issues of public and foreign policy. The fall from power of the Parti Québécois and the seven years of national minority governments that ended in 2011 probably effected this change.

In the past 10 years, the Harper government did not make constitutional reform a high priority. Constitutional discussions have focused on the perennial issue of Senate reform. Attempts to reform the Senate by way of unilateral legislative change by Parliament have proven unsuccessful, and it remains to be seen whether the various recent scandals involving a number of senators will provide the necessary political impetus for change.

Key Terms

legislative power

executive power

judicial power

residual power

constitutional convention

constitutional law

organic statutes

entrenched constitutional act

entrenchment

preamble

patriate

veto

judicial review

Clarity Act

Discussion Questions

1. As Canada is a democracy based on majority rule, why should a minority of provinces be able to block constitutional amendments?

2. Would the Canadian Constitution be improved if it were revised so that key conventions were made into laws?

THE PILLARS OF THE CANADIAN CONSTITUTION: RESPONSIBLE GOVERNMENT, FEDERALISM, AND THE CHARTER

CHAPTER THREE
RESPONSIBLE GOVERNMENT

We have seen that one of the chief functions of a constitution is to determine who will exercise legislative, executive, and judicial power. It is therefore not surprising that this should be one of the very first topics addressed in CA 1867. In the preamble to that act, it is stipulated that Canada is to have "a Constitution similar in Principle to that of the United Kingdom." Above all else, this phrase means that legislative and executive power are to be organized in accordance with a set of principles that may be summarized by the term "responsible government." The purpose of this chapter is to explain the meaning, the application, and the rationale of those principles.

3.1 The Emergence of Responsible Government

The British regime is a monarchy that has evolved through a number of different forms. In the earliest stage of that regime, the Crown wielded both legislative and executive power. In other words, the king or queen both made the laws and administered them. But the possession of so much power by unelected (and hence unaccountable) monarchs inevitably led to abuses of that power. In reaction to such abuses, the English nobles and commoners were gradually able to compel the Crown to turn legislative power over to their assembly, which they called Parliament.

By the mid-eighteenth century, the political philosopher Montesquieu could cite the British regime as an example of the principle of the **separation of powers**. Following an argument first made by John Locke, Montesquieu claimed that the best way to protect freedom and to prevent the abuse of political power is to ensure that legislative and executive powers are assigned to separate people or bodies. As any tyrannical act would ultimately require the application of both legislative and executive power, placing those powers in different hands would minimize the chances that such acts could be taken. Because it assigned executive power to the Crown and legislative power to Parliament, the British Constitution of his day was held by Montesquieu to be the very model of a free political order.

The principle of the separation of powers also became one of the cornerstones of the American regime. The American Founding Fathers were well versed in the ideas of Montesquieu and Locke, and their experience with what they regarded as "tyrannical" British colonial rule made them keenly concerned about the control of political power. They therefore opted for a constitution that placed legislative power in the hands of a bicameral legislature known as Congress and executive power in the hands of a president. Indeed, the Americans extended Montesquieu's principle. Not only did they place legislative and executive power in separate hands but also, because both the president and the Congress were elected democratically, each would to some extent be in competition with the other for public favour. It was thought that this competition or rivalry would reduce further still the chances of tyrannical collusion between the two branches of government.

In the early years of British rule, the colonies of what would later become Canada were ruled by imperial governors appointed by the British Crown. As early as 1758, the subjects of Nova Scotia gained the right to elect legislative assemblies with authority to legislate on most internal matters. The subjects of Upper Canada (Ontario) and Lower Canada (Quebec) received the same right late in the eighteenth century. Yet, because executive power remained in the hands of the governors and their advisers, our colonial constitutions were based on a kind of separation of powers, such as that set out in the American Constitution. The difference, of course, was that we had a separation of powers for imperial reasons (i.e., to ensure British control) rather than for the liberal reasons advanced by Montesquieu and Locke. These colonial constitutions were unworkable precisely because of the separation between legislative and executive powers. When those powers are placed in different hands, friction between the two branches of government is inevitable. Such friction is tolerable when each of the branches is elected, as is the case in the United States. But when only the legislative branch is elected, as was the case in our colonial constitutions, conflict between the two branches comes to be seen in terms of democratic rights.

The experience of Upper Canada provides a good illustration of the problem. In the early nineteenth century, political life in Upper Canada centred on the attempts of "reformers" to break the power of the so-called Family Compact, a small clique of wealthy citizens who controlled much of the colony's political and economic life. Even when the reformers won control of the legislative assembly, they found the governors unwilling to cooperate in the implementation of the reform program because they had appointed as their advisers an executive council composed almost exclusively of members of the Family Compact. For Upper Canada's reformers, the separation of legislative and executive powers amounted to a constitutional subversion of democratic self-rule. Discontent with this constitutional order led to armed rebellions in both Upper and Lower Canada in 1837. These were easily crushed by British troops, but they showed the British government that some kind of reform was necessary. The government therefore dispatched to the Canadas one of the leading political figures of the day, Lord Durham, asking him to investigate the situation and to recommend appropriate measures. The central recommendation of Durham's famous *Report on the Affairs of British North America* was that the colonial constitutions be amended so as to replace the principle of separation of powers by the principle of **responsible government**. The fundamental feature of responsible government is that it makes the executive responsible for its actions to a democratically elected legislative body. Instead of choosing as his advisers anyone he liked, the governor would have to choose them from among those who had been democratically elected to a legislative assembly. This principle had recently been incorporated into the ever-evolving British regime, and the Canadian rebels of 1837 had demanded that the same step be taken in the colonies. The British government hesitated at first, but agreed in 1848 to introduce responsible government first in Nova Scotia and then in the other colonies. By the time of Confederation, then, responsible government was well established as a fundamental principle of Canadian political life.

3.2 The Conventions of Responsible Government

In the British and Canadian regimes, responsible government makes the executive accountable to the House of Commons. This accountability implies first that the executive is required to defend its actions in the House. But accountability is meaningless if the House before which the executive defends its actions is unable to do anything about executive actions it finds unacceptable. The principle of responsible government, therefore, demands of those exercising executive power that they obtain the approval of the House for their use of that power. In this way, responsible government allows for meaningful democratic control of executive power.

The achievement of responsible government requires the adoption of a number of rules, which take the form of constitutional conventions. The **five conventions of responsible government** may be summarized as follows.

1. The *first convention* is that the Crown, which still has formal title to executive power, will use that power only "on the advice of" its ministers. In other words, it is the ministers themselves who exercise executive power; their "advice" to the Crown is really a command, and the Crown is thus a mere figurehead when it comes to the use of executive power.[1]

2. The *second convention* is that the Crown normally appoints as ministers or advisers only persons who are Members of Parliament (MPs). This rule is intended to facilitate executive accountability: putting the Crown's ministers in the House itself makes them more accessible to other MPs who wish to question or criticize them. A certain amount of flexibility is always shown in the application of this rule. It is generally acceptable to appoint one or two senators as ministers. It is also possible to appoint people who are neither senators nor MPs, as happened in 1996 when Université de Montréal political scientist Stéphane Dion was named Minister of Intergovernmental Affairs. In such cases, however, the persons appointed must take the first possible opportunity to run for a seat in the House of Commons; if they lose that election, they must immediately resign their position as minister.

3. The *third convention* is that the ministers will act together as a team or "ministry," led by a prime minister (or "first" minister), with each minister sharing in

---

1   There are some respects in which the Crown is not merely a figurehead, but they relate to the Crown's role in the management of responsible government not to its use of executive power. See especially 6.3 below.

the responsibility for all policy decisions made by any member of the ministry. This third rule is known as the convention of **collective responsibility**.

4. The *fourth convention* is that the Crown will appoint and maintain as ministers only people who "have the **confidence** of" the House of Commons (i.e., the support of a majority of the members of the House). Without this rule, responsible government would not necessarily be democratic, for the Crown could appoint a ministry consisting only of MPs from some minor party whose views were representative of only a small minority of the electorate.

5. If the House of Commons expresses a lack of confidence in a ministry (either by adopting an explicit motion of non-confidence or by voting down a proposal that the ministry deems a matter of confidence), the democratic linkage provided through responsible government has, in a sense, broken down because the executive is no longer acting in a manner that reflects the wishes of a majority of the people's representatives. In order to keep responsible government going, then, either the ministry or the House must be replaced. Therefore the *fifth convention* of responsible government is that when the ministry loses the confidence of the House, the prime minister must either resign (which entails the resignation of the entire ministry) or request new elections. The first of these options clears the way for the formation of a new ministry, one in which the House, in the governor general's estimate, will have confidence. The second option (elections) will resolve the problem by producing one of two possible results. One is that the voters will take the side of the ministry and return a new contingent of MPs who will be more favourably disposed toward it. (This is what happened in the 2011 election. The Harper ministry had lost a vote of confidence in the House, but in the subsequent election, the voters elected a majority of MPs who supported that ministry. Mr. Harper therefore remained in office.) The other possibility is that the voters will take the side of the House and elect a majority of MPs who do not support the existing ministry. (This happened in the election of 2015, when voters elected a House with a strong majority of members who would not support the Conservative ministry headed by Prime Minister Harper. Mr. Harper, seeing that he would not have the confidence of the House, promptly resigned.)

Taken together, these five conventions create a political order that makes those who exercise executive power fully accountable to the elected representatives of the people and, thus, indirectly accountable to the people themselves. (This relationship is expressed schematically in Figure 3.1.) By law, executive power is vested in the Crown. But the conventions described above modify the law of the Constitution dramatically. Under the principle of responsible government, the Crown in effect delegates its executive power to a ministry composed of MPs. This ministry (or "cabinet" as it is usually called) must have the confidence of the House of Commons and must resign or face an election if it loses that confidence. In sum, these arrangements provide the kind of democratic accountability sought by the reformers of 1837.

Figure 3.1: Responsible Government

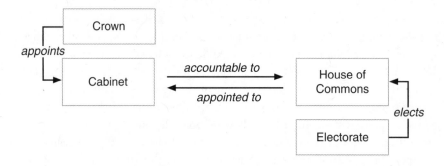

3.3. Responsible Government as "Cabinet Government"

From the description of the principle of responsible government given above, one would likely conclude that the introduction of that principle substantially weakened the cabinet by subordinating it to the control of the House of Commons. This is why responsible government is often referred to as **parliamentary government**. In theory, responsible government makes the House of Commons (the dominant chamber of Parliament) the ultimate authority for both legislative and executive action.

In reality, however, the introduction of responsible government actually strengthened the power of the cabinet. It is therefore more accurate to think of responsible government as **cabinet government**. To understand why, we must grasp how the rise of strong political parties facilitated the transfer of effective legislative power from the House to the cabinet. We have noted that the cabinet must be composed of MPs who have the confidence of a majority of the members of the House. If that majority consists of MPs from the same party as the cabinet, and these MPs will loyally support the measures proposed by the cabinet in order to keep their party in office, then the cabinet has de facto control of the legislative activity of the House.

In a regime based on responsible government, with strong, disciplined parties, the cabinet becomes the dominant political institution. Under the law of the constitution, it possesses no power of its own, but the conventions of responsible government give it control of both executive and legislative power. Although constitutional law places legislative and executive powers in separate hands, responsible government leads in practice to a **fusion of powers** in the hands of the cabinet. Indeed, one may say that responsible government is best defined as *a regime in which legislative and executive power are fused together in a cabinet that is accountable to an assembly of the people's elected representatives.*

3.4 Forming a Government

To say that Canada is governed by a cabinet is to imply something very surprising about our regime: we do not elect our government—at least, not directly. People often talk about having "elected" the "Harper government" or the "Trudeau government," but in this they are mistaken. The truth is that citizens elect only their local Member of Parliament. In a regime based on the principle of responsible government, then, the people's role in the selection of their government is merely an indirect one.

This is no accident. The principle of responsible government is inconsistent with the notion of a directly elected executive. We have seen that at the core of responsible government is the idea that the government must be accountable to the House of Commons. Having the people elect the government directly would necessarily make the government accountable to the people as well. As the old proverb teaches, however, no one can serve two masters because the two masters may demand contradictory things. What if the voters were to elect a Conservative government pledged to free trade and a House of Commons dominated by Liberal and New Democratic Party (NDP) members who were opposed to it? The government would either have to drop its free trade policy (thereby repudiating its accountability to the voters) or it would have to introduce free trade by executive decree (thereby repudiating responsible government).

In responsible government, then, we do not elect our government directly. It is more accurate to speak of the "formation" of a government. This is a complex process in which the Crown, the prime minister, and the House of Commons work together to provide Canadians with a government that has the confidence of the elected representatives of the people. One may summarize this process in **four conventions for the formation of a government**, some of which overlap with those described in 3.2 above.

1. The *first convention* is that the ultimate responsibility for choosing the government must rest with the Crown. In practice, this means that the Crown will select a prime minister, who will, in turn, nominate the other members of the government. There are good reasons for this rule. First, the Crown is uniquely

suited for choosing the government. For obvious reasons, the government cannot choose itself: in that case, every Member of Parliament might proclaim himself or herself the head of a new government. It would be workable (though perhaps cumbersome) to leave the choice of government in the hands of the House of Commons, but this would be inconsistent with certain aspects of our regime. It will be recalled that, formally speaking, the ministers who compose the government are merely advising the Crown on the use of the Crown's powers. The Crown must, therefore, have a formal role in the appointment of its own advisers.

2. The *second convention* for forming a government is that, in appointing a prime minister, the Crown must choose the person whose government is most likely to have the confidence of the House of Commons. This rule is obviously necessary for the functioning of responsible government, the regime in which the executive is accountable to the legislature. It also brings a democratic element into the process by ensuring that the person who heads the government and chooses its other members has the support of a majority of the elected representatives of the people.

3. The *third convention* for forming a government is that the government remains in power until the prime minister resigns on its behalf.

4. The *fourth convention* is that the prime minister must resign if his or her government has lost the confidence of the House of Commons and has no prospect of winning the confidence of a newly elected House.

These rules may seem complicated, but working through a couple of historical examples will make them easier to understand.

At the beginning of 1993, Brian Mulroney was Canada's prime minister. He was the leader of the Progressive Conservative Party (the PCs), which held a substantial majority of the seats in the House of Commons. Mr. Mulroney announced his intention to retire from politics. The PCs called a leadership convention at which Kim Campbell, a Progressive Conservative MP and a member of Mr. Mulroney's cabinet, was chosen to succeed him as party leader. Governor General Ramon Hnatyshyn, then, had no difficulty deciding whom to appoint as the new prime minister when Mr. Mulroney formally resigned. The PCs still controlled a majority of the seats in the House of Commons, Ms. Campbell was their leader, and therefore Ms. Campbell would obviously be able to form a government that would command the confidence of the House.

In October 1993, a parliamentary election was held. In that election, Ms. Campbell was defeated in her own constituency, and her party lost all its seats but two. Technically, she was still the prime minister because governments remain in office until the prime minister resigns. Yet it was obvious to Ms. Campbell that when the new House convened, it would not have confidence in her government. It was equally obvious that a government headed by Liberal leader Jean Chrétien would be able to command the confidence of the House of Commons. Consequently, within a few days of the election, Ms. Campbell resigned and the Governor General invited Mr. Chrétien to form a government.

It is important to appreciate that it is actually the prime minister, and not the voters, who decides the future of his or her government. As a result of the 1957 election, Louis St. Laurent's Liberals no longer had a majority of seats in the House of Commons and actually had seven fewer seats than the PCs. Mr. St. Laurent might have tried to govern by cultivating the support of one or more of the other parties, but he interpreted the results of the election to mean that the voters were not happy with his government and suspected that he would not have the confidence of the House. He therefore resigned. The Governor General then invited John Diefenbaker, the PC leader, to form a new government. From 1968 to 1972, Pierre Trudeau's Liberal Party held well over half of the seats in the House of Commons. In the election of 1972, the Liberals won fewer than half the seats, and only two more than their main rivals, the PCs. Mr. Trudeau suspected that the not insignificant block of members elected for the NDP would prefer his government to the PC alternative, and he knew that this would give him enough votes to command the confidence of the House. He therefore chose not to resign. It is important to note that Mr. Trudeau could have made exactly the same decision in 1972 had he won two fewer seats than the Conservatives instead of two more. In a regime based on responsible government, the crucial question is not which party leader has the most seats but which party leader has the confidence of the House of Commons.[2]

---

2   It is interesting to note that in the run-up to the 2015 election, both Prime Minister Harper and the Liberal leader Justin Trudeau opined that whichever party won the most seats in the election should form the government. As we shall see in Chapter Nine, this kind of "first-past-the-post" approach is indeed the principle by which we determine winners in the election of individual members to the House of Commons, but it is certainly not the principle that governs the operation of responsible government. The legitimacy of parliamentary democracy is grounded in the requirement that those who exercise power must have the support of a majority of the people's representatives. In a multi-party parliament, the largest single party may not always speak for the majority of the people's representatives; if it does not, it has no title to rule, even if it did win more seats than any other party.

What these examples demonstrate is that the process of forming a government is more complex than it appears. Canadians like to think that they elected a Trudeau government or a Harper government; in fact, however, they elect members of the House of Commons. Because no ministry may govern without the confidence of the House, the choices made by the voters have an important, and usually decisive, influence on the formation of government. Yet that influence is not always decisive. After the 1993 election, it was obvious that Kim Campbell would have to step down, and it was equally obvious that the new prime minister would have to be Jean Chrétien. As the elections of 1957 and 1972 demonstrate, however, when the voters give no party a clear majority in the House, the prime minister may have the decisive first move in determining who will form the government. Alternatively, if several opposition parties with a majority of seats between them publicly agree to a **coalition**—a formal sharing of the cabinet—the governor general would have to appoint as prime minister the person they had designated as the leader of the coalition. In this case—which is essentially what happened in the Ontario election of 1985[3]—the decisive role was played by the opposition parties, not by the prime minister. Finally, should Canadians ever elect a House in which no party has a majority, and there are multiple parties of roughly equal strength, the choice of the new prime minister (should the incumbent resign) might well require the exercise of some discretion by the governor general. Such a situation is unlikely and has never yet occurred, but would be somewhat more probable if we accepted proposals to change our electoral system to one based on proportional representation.[4]

Canadians' understanding of how governments are formed was put to the test in late 2008. Six weeks after the 2008 election, the minority Conservative government delivered a "fiscal update" to Parliament that was unacceptable to the three opposition parties. Liberal leader Stéphane Dion, NDP leader Jack Layton, and Bloc leader Gilles Duceppe announced that they intended to defeat the government in the House by passing a motion of non-confidence. They also announced that the Liberals and the NDP had agreed to then replace the Conservatives with a coalition government. In this case, the Liberals and the NDP had agreed that Mr. Dion would serve as the prime minister of the proposed coalition and that the Liberals and the NDP would share the seats in cabinet based on the number of seats each of them had in the House. The Bloc would

---

3. In that election, the ruling PC party won the most seats but not a majority. The NDP formally supported the Liberal Party, and the Liberals subsequently formed the new government.

4 See Chapter 9.7.

not participate in the government, but Mr. Duceppe pledged to support it for at least 18 months provided that his party was consulted on all matters affecting the interests of Quebec. (The Bloc's support was critical because the Liberals and NDP did not have enough seats between them to command a majority of votes in the House.) Mr. Harper denounced the proposed coalition as a "coup d'état," insisting that he had won the election because he had the most seats and that the coalition could not legitimately take power until it had won a mandate from the people in an election. Though a large majority of Canadians were opposed to the proposed coalition (largely because it relied on support from the separatist Bloc), Mr. Harper was surely wrong to claim that Canadians had elected him prime minister and that the coalition had no right to take office. Strictly speaking, the only Canadians who voted for Mr. Harper were the people in Calgary Southwest, who elected him as their MP. Moreover, winning the most seats in the House does not give a party a mandate to form the government and does not make its leader prime minister. The only legitimate prime minister in our regime is the person who commands the confidence of the House of Commons.

3.5 Majority and Minority Government

In a political order based on the principle of responsible government, the ministry that takes office is said to have either a **majority government** or a **minority government**. The term "majority government" refers to a situation in which the party that forms the government controls over half the seats in the House of Commons. Because party organizations are able to exercise a high degree of control over the way their members vote, a cabinet backed by a parliamentary majority is almost guaranteed the automatic confidence of the House. This does not mean that such a ministry can do whatever it likes: the cabinet will back away from any measure that is resolutely opposed by its parliamentary **caucus** (the group of MPs who are members of that party), whose votes are essential for sustaining the House's confidence in the government. But a majority government that has the support of its caucus can govern as it sees fit.

The term "minority government" refers to a situation in which no single party controls a majority of the seats in the House of Commons. In such a situation, the government must be formed by some party that controls less than half the seats. In the 1963 election, for example, 265 members were elected: 129 of these were members of the Liberal Party, 95 were PCs, 17 were members of the NDP, and 24 were members of the Social Credit Party. Obviously, no party had a majority of seats. Prime Minister John Diefenbaker did not expect that his government would maintain the confidence of the House, and he therefore resigned. The governor general called on the leader of the Liberals, Lester Pearson, to form a government. Mr. Pearson's party did not have enough seats to control the House of Commons. Under the rules of responsible government, however, it is sufficient if a government is able to command the confidence of the House. Mr. Pearson knew that he would be able to win and maintain that confidence as long as he adopted policies that would either find favour with or not be opposed by the members of one of the two smaller parties. In this, he was quite successful: his Liberal government remained in office for two terms totalling five years, despite the fact that it never had a majority of seats in the House. More recently, Prime Minister Harper duplicated this feat for five years before winning a majority in 2011.

In Canada, it has been more common to have majority rather than minority governments, but minority governments are not rare: since 1867, there have been 12 of them. Not all of these governments have been as stable as Mr. Pearson's or Mr. Harper's. Arthur Meighen's minority government lasted a mere three months in 1926 before the House declared a lack of confidence in it. In 1979, Joe Clark formed a minority government for the PCs yet announced that he would govern as if he had a majority. By this he meant that, unlike Pearson, he would not attempt to tailor his policies to maintain the confidence of the House. This rather bold stance cost Clark dearly: his government lost the confidence of the House after eight months in office, and a new election was held. In that election the Liberals won a majority of seats in the House, and Clark was therefore compelled to resign.

It is worth noting, however, that Mr. Clark's government fell only because both the PCs and the Liberals believed that a new election would be in their interest. The PCs thought they had momentum on their side. The Liberals, on the other hand, thought that the electorate had merely wanted to give them a spanking in 1979 and would now prefer to have them back. As both parties hoped to improve their fortunes through a new general election, Mr. Clark's government was unlikely to last very long.

Often, however, the situation is just the reverse. A minority government can draw a certain amount of strength from the fact that it is rarely in the interests of everyone to fight another election campaign. For one thing, campaigns are quite expensive. Moreover, individual MPs who have just been elected are, in many cases, nervous about going back to the polls: why risk the seats they have just worked so hard to win? Most important, though, the defeat of a minority government requires the collaboration of at least two opposition parties who can combine for a majority of votes in the House. Are there likely to be two opposition parties with good reason to believe that they will come out of fresh elections with more seats than they currently have? Not often. After the election of 2006, Stephen Harper led a Conservative minority government that, for a time, operated with the self-confidence of a majority government. Mr. Harper realized that the Liberals were afraid of an election at that time due to a lack of money and an unpopular leader. He was therefore certain that the Liberals would not join the other opposition parties in voting against the government and forcing new elections. Consequently, Mr. Harper brought forward a number of pieces of legislation that the Liberals did not like but could not afford to oppose, and their failure to vote against those measures simply added to the general perception that they were weak and indecisive.

In reality, minority government creates a fascinating game of political cat-and-mouse. A government that wishes to stay in power has to try to keep the opposition divided. It typically does so by introducing measures that it hopes at least one of the major opposition parties cannot possibly disagree with. For instance, after the Liberals, the NDP, and the Bloc made it clear that they were ready to vote the Conservative government out and replace it with a coalition in the late fall of 2008, Mr. Harper suddenly reversed his aggressive tactics; the budget introduced in January 2009 was designed to look as much as possible like a Liberal budget so as to ensure that the Liberal Party would support it and leave Mr. Harper in office. On the other hand, when a minority government feels that public support is swinging behind it, it may try to introduce legislation that the opposition parties cannot possibly agree with. Why? This way, the government not only gets the election it would like, but it can blame the opposition for "forcing" the country to go through an election the government will surely present as wasteful, bothersome, and unnecessary!

There is a general (though far from universal) opinion in Canada that majority government is better than minority government. The superiority of majority government is said to rest on its greater stability, longevity, and vigour. But this opinion is open to debate; certainly, many Canadians welcomed a return to minority government in 2004 after 24 years of majority government. Moreover, as the examples cited above suggest, minority government is not necessarily unstable and short-lived. In the right circumstances, and with appropriate leadership, minority governments can last as long as majority governments. Concerning the relative vigour of minority and majority governments, one should consider the arguments made by the distinguished constitutional specialist Eugene Forsey. Forsey notes that sometimes a government backed by an absolute majority of seats may vigorously ride off in the wrong direction. Conversely, minority governments are often compelled by their need for support from outside their own party to govern in a more moderate and less arrogant fashion.[5] In sum, it is probably wrong-headed to ask which form is superior, minority or majority. It is more sensible to recognize that each has potential advantages and disadvantages, and that circumstances and personalities will do much to determine which form is more desirable in a given situation.

3.6 Institutional Implications of Responsible Government

As was mentioned in the first chapter of this book, we have chosen the term "regime" to emphasize the extent to which political rules and institutions form a complex web with an internal logic of its own. Nowhere is this more evident than when one considers the principle of responsible government. For the most part, our arrangements with respect to legislative and executive power are highly complex—certainly much more complex than the relatively straightforward arrangements to be found in the Constitution of the United States. Canadians often wonder why we don't jettison some of our quaint practices and institutions and adopt American alternatives instead. The difficulty, of course, is that the logic of responsible government will not easily permit it.

It is essential to appreciate that each of these two quite different constitutional principles—responsible government and separation of powers—has its own internal logic, a logic that will then determine many of the regime's institutional features. The decision to adopt responsible government as a fundamental principle will, by the internal logic of the principle, necessitate certain institutional arrangements and rule out others. The same would be true if one opted for the principle of the separation of powers. To demonstrate this point, let us explore a few of the key institutional differences between Canada's regime and that of the United States: elections, cabinet appointments, head of state, and party discipline.

1. The timing of elections. In the United States, the principle of separation of powers implies that each "branch" of government is elected separately. Congress is chosen by the people in one set of elections; the president is chosen by the people in a separate election. Each branch thus has its own mandate, and neither depends on the confidence of the other for its legitimacy; even if the Congress believes the president is doing a terrible job, the president will remain in office for four full years because the presidential election gives him or her a four-year mandate. Because the term of office is fixed by the Constitution

---

5   Eugene Forsey, "The Problem of 'Minority' Government in Canada," *The Canadian Journal of Economics and Political Science* 30, 1 (February 1964): 1–11.

(two years for the House of Representatives, four years for the presidency, and six years for the Senate), elections in the United States are held at fixed, predictable intervals. President Barack Obama was elected on the first Tuesday of November in 2008. We know that the next American presidential elections will be held on the Tuesday after the first Monday of November in 2016, 2020, 2024, and so on.

In a regime based on the principle of responsible government, the fundamental logic of the regime makes such an orderly and predictable schedule difficult, to say the least. In Canada, the timing of parliamentary elections has traditionally been decided by the prime minister. Strictly speaking, it is the Crown (i.e., the governor general) that dissolves Parliament and calls elections, but the decision to do so is made on the basis of "advice" tendered by the prime minister, advice that is almost always followed. There is one fixed rule governing the prime minister's choice of election date: section 4(1) of CA 1982 specifies that the interval between elections may not exceed five years. In the Canadian tradition of responsible government, the prime minister traditionally looks to call new elections after four years.

Of course, leaving the timing of the elections to the prime minister gives him or her a significant partisan advantage over the opposition. The prime minister will typically call elections when the polls are most favourable for his or her own party, or perhaps when the main opposition party is in disarray. Jean Chrétien twice called elections (1997 and 2000) after less than three and a half years in office, primarily because opinion polls indicated that early elections would work to his advantage. Each time, Chrétien's decision led to (somewhat predictable) calls to change Canada's electoral practice in this respect and to adopt the American practice of holding elections at fixed intervals.

In the past decade, both Ottawa and the majority of provinces have passed legislation that creates fixed election dates. There is little doubt that the adoption of fixed election dates makes the timing of elections more equitable. The problem, however, is that the practice of fixed election dates is not compatible with the principle of responsible government. Under responsible government, the prime minister and cabinet are not directly elected by the people (as is the American president) and therefore have no direct mandate of their own. Their democratic legitimacy thus depends entirely on their capacity to maintain the confidence of the House of Commons. Because a ministry can, in principle, lose that confidence at any time (especially if no party commands a majority in the House), it is essential to be able to hold elections at any time; as we have seen, holding new elections is sometimes the only way to resolve the impasse that results when the House and the ministry are in disagreement. The existence of a floating or non-fixed election date is thus an inescapable consequence of the logic of responsible government. Accordingly, when Mr. Harper's government passed legislation stipulating that elections were to be held in the third week of October of every fourth year, that legislation had to make allowance for the need to call elections at other times should a government lose the confidence of the House.

2. Cabinet appointments. A second important institutional difference between Canada and the United States is the selection of cabinet ministers (or cabinet secretaries, as they are called in the United States). Here the practice in one country is almost the exact opposite of what is done across the border. An American president may choose for the cabinet virtually any citizen of the United States; the only restriction is that, if the president selects a member of Congress, that person must resign his or her congressional seat. This flexibility allows presidents to seek out the most talented people in the nation to run the government. John F. Kennedy, for instance, plucked Robert McNamara from the presidency of the Ford Motor Company to be his Secretary of Defence. Richard Nixon reached out to Harvard University to bring to Washington the famous international relations expert Dr. Henry Kissinger as his Secretary of State. More recently, George W. Bush, during his first term, chose retired General Colin Powell to be his Secretary of State, and Barack Obama chose Timothy Geithner, president of the Federal Reserve Bank of New York, as his Secretary of the Treasury. In Canada, on the other hand, a prime minister looking for cabinet material is essentially restricted to the membership of the House of Commons; other Canadians might be appointed to cabinet temporarily but may not stay unless they are able to get themselves elected quickly to a vacant seat in the House. A Canadian prime minister's choice of cabinet ministers is thus restricted to a very small group of people, few of whom have meaningful technical expertise in the area for which they will be responsible.

Here, too, the difference between the two regimes is a direct consequence of the difference between the principles of separation of powers and those of responsible government. The Constitution of the United States bars members of Congress from holding cabinet posts precisely because its underlying objective is to have the two branches of government "check and balance" each other as a means of protecting liberty. In Canada, on the other hand, the logic of responsible government requires us to restrict a prime minister's choice of cabinet ministers to members of the House of Commons. Because the prime minister and cabinet are not directly elected to their positions by the people, their democratic legitimacy depends on their capacity to maintain the confidence of the House of Commons. If the prime minister and cabinet were not themselves members of the House, it is hard to imagine how the House would be in a position to hold them accountable for their actions and to determine whether they deserve its continued confidence.

3. Head of government and head of state. Another noteworthy difference between the two regimes is that the Canadian regime draws a distinction between the "**head of government**" (the prime minister) and the "formal **head of state**" (the Queen). No such distinction exists in the United States, where the president fulfills both roles. Why this difference? Once again, the crucial point is the difference between the logic of responsible government and the logic of the separation of powers. In a regime based on the principle of responsible government, democratic legitimacy depends on the capacity to maintain agreement between the House and the government to ensure that the government commands the confidence of the House of Commons. Yet such agreement does not arise on its own; someone must intervene actively to ensure that a ministry that has lost the confidence of the House steps down and that a new ministry more likely to have the confidence of the House will take its place. In the Canadian version of responsible government, that official is the governor general (who represents the Queen). As the official whose job it is to keep the system of responsible government running, the governor general is, in effect, responsible for the regime; and that is why, logically, the prime minister cannot serve as Canada's formal head of state. In the United States, on the other hand, there is no office corresponding to that of our governor general because, in a regime based on separation of powers, democratic legitimacy is maintained automatically by the system itself. Each branch of government is elected by the people for a fixed period of time and thus has its own democratic mandate. No one is required to oversee the system or to intervene to ensure that one branch has confidence in the other.

4. Party discipline. One final illustration of our general point is the matter of **party discipline**. Party discipline in Canada is quite strong—so strong that it is common for Canadians to complain that their MPs, who almost always vote the party line in the House of Commons, are "little better than trained seals." In the United States, by contrast, members of both the Senate and the House of Representatives are freer to vote as they wish, and it is not unusual for them to vote against the position favoured by their own party. This is a practice many Canadians would like to see adopted in this country.

The difficulty, however, is that here, too, the different approach of the two countries is to a large extent determined by a basic difference in fundamental principles. The United States can afford to have weaker party discipline because, under separation of powers, the president's mandate does not depend on the support of Congress. The president has a direct mandate from the people and can legitimately remain in office even if Congress consistently votes against his program. There is thus no pressing reason for members of Congress to follow their party line. In Canada, on the other hand, the internal logic of responsible government makes necessary a relatively strict form of party discipline. Because the prime minister and cabinet are not directly elected by the people, their democratic legitimacy depends entirely on the continued confidence of the House of Commons. If members of the party in power do not stick together in support of the ministry, that ministry will not have the confidence of the House and will thereby lose its only title to rule. Unless they are willing to see their governments change on a semi-annual basis, Canadians have to accept that responsible government will, of necessity, require a high level of party discipline.

As these examples illustrate, when contemplating reforms to our political institutions and practices, we must consider very carefully whether specific proposals for change are consistent with the internal logic of responsible government. The fact that certain practices work well in the United States does not mean that they will work here. A political regime is somewhat like an ecosystem. Species from one ecosystem may not be able to adapt to another. Or they may be able to adapt, provided certain adjustments are made. Of course, the introduction of a new plant or animal species to a particular ecosystem may have unintended (and undesirable) side effects as well. Our point, then, is not that change is undesirable or impossible; rather, it is that advocates of reform need to reflect very carefully on whether—and to what extent—practices imported from other regimes are consistent with the internal logic of responsible government.

3.7 Responsible Government and Separation of Powers Compared

The principle of responsible government is of British origin, but it now forms the cornerstone of many, if not most, liberal democratic regimes. In one way or another, all the nations of Western Europe, as well as most members of the British Commonwealth, subscribe to the principle that the executive must be responsible for its actions to a legislative body consisting of the elected representatives of the people. In almost all of the world's other liberal democratic regimes, the most influential constitutional model has been the United States rather than Britain. (This is especially true in Latin America.) One may thus think of responsible government and separation of powers as the two great alternative principles for the formation of a liberal democratic regime.

As we have noted, the political objective that inspires the principle of the separation of powers is liberty. Montesquieu and Locke argued for a separation of powers on the grounds that placing legislative and executive power in different hands would minimize the chances of the government becoming tyrannical. What they argued for in theory seems to be validated by the experience of the

United States. In that country, even when the legislative and executive branches of government are held by members of the same political party, the relationship between them is often one of rivalry rather than collusion. It is thus very difficult to imagine the two branches cooperating for anti-democratic purposes. Indeed, the rivalry between the two is so strong that it typically becomes a problem. In 1995, for example, the government of the United States came to a standstill when the president and the Congress could not agree on a budget. A series of similar crises occurred in 2011. One may thus say that the price of liberty in regimes based on the separation of powers is a substantial inefficiency in government.

In contrast, regimes based on the principle of responsible government are remarkable for their efficiency, particularly during majority governments. Because of the fusion of powers, the same small group exercises both legislative and executive power. In such regimes, standstills of the sort seen in the United States simply do not take place. Once a cabinet backed by a parliamentary majority decides what it wants to do, there is almost nothing to stand in its way. When the Pearson cabinet decided to introduce universal medical insurance in Canada, the adoption and implementation of the policy followed quickly and smoothly. This political efficiency is in striking contrast to the inefficiency experienced in the United States. Though most Americans agree that action is needed to extend coverage of medical insurance, former President Clinton's initiatives on that issue were stalled and then blocked by Congress, which favoured different policies. President Obama eventually succeeded, but only after new congressional elections gave his party a majority in both the Senate and the House of Representatives; and even then, the adoption of his program was not without challenges.

Yet some people would argue that the efficiency of responsible government is purchased at the price of a certain loss of political liberty. Because it is difficult to stop a cabinet that has a solid majority supporting it in the House of Commons, it is sometimes said that responsible government amounts to a four-year elected dictatorship. Critics of our regime will point to the introduction of the highly unpopular Goods and Services Tax (GST) as an example of the way in which Canadian governments can introduce and impose policies that lack public support. It is probably safe to speculate that the separation of powers in the Constitution of the United States would make it far more difficult for politicians to introduce a similar tax in that country.

Nevertheless, it would be an exaggeration to suggest that responsible government equals an elected dictatorship. In the first place, it should not be forgotten that all governments seek re-election. Because no government will be re-elected if it consistently or conspicuously ignores public opinion, those in power will have great incentives to behave democratically. Second, one must keep in mind that the activity of the government is subject to the authority of the Constitution, especially the Charter of Rights and Freedoms. Finally, in responsible government, there is an important political check on the power of the cabinet: the presence of an institutionalized parliamentary opposition. As we shall see in Chapter Seven, the House of Commons, to which the cabinet is responsible, affords those who oppose government policy a wide range of opportunities to question and attack the government, opportunities that do not exist in a regime like that of the United States. One can thus plausibly argue that the cabinet's accountability to the House of Commons makes responsible government as favourable to liberty as does a regime based on the separation of powers.

There is, of course, a more general issue of accountability to be considered: accountability to the voters. In certain respects, democratic accountability appears to be stronger under separation of powers. The leading executive and legislative officers are directly elected by the people under separation of powers, but only the legislative officers are directly elected in responsible government. Moreover, under separation of powers, legislative officers can respond more directly to the wishes of their constituents because they are not restricted by party discipline. In responsible government, when MPs have to choose between voting in support of their party and voting in response to the wishes of their constituents, they will almost always take the side of their party.

On the other hand, responsible government offers substantially greater accountability in that it is much easier for the voters to judge the performance of their elected servants. Under separation of powers, it is often difficult to know who is responsible for the state of the nation's affairs. When the economy is doing well, for example, both the president and the Congress will take credit for it. On the other hand, when the economy is doing poorly (or when there is a crisis over the budget, Medicare, or some other issue), the president and the Congress will each insist that everything is the fault of the other branch. The voter has a difficult time evaluating office-holders because it is frequently difficult to know who was responsible for what. In responsible government, one always knows exactly who deserves praise or blame for the state of things. Because responsible government fuses legislative and executive power in the hands of the prime minister and cabinet, there is no debate over whom to praise or blame for specific situations. American President Harry Truman was famous for having a sign on his desk that said "The Buck Stops Here." Such a sign would be far more appropriate on the desk of a prime minister, as a president has relatively little control over the nation's legislative activity while a prime minister backed by a majority in the House controls it quite firmly. Accountability to the voters is in this sense much greater in regimes based on responsible government than in regimes based on the separation of powers.

In a simple, abstract comparison, then, a strong case can be made that responsible government is a superior choice to the separation of powers. This case is especially compelling in the twenty-first century, when people are generally less inclined to worry about government tyranny than were the American Founding Fathers and more inclined to expect government to intervene effectively in economic and social life. This probably explains why one regularly sees influential figures in the United States advocating reforms that would move the American regime in the direction of responsible government. Yet politics does not take place in a vacuum, and abstractions that do not take proper account of context can be very dangerous. The attractions of responsible government may not be equally compelling in all situations. One variable that has a considerable impact on the debate over the relative merits of responsible government and separation of powers is federalism. As we shall see in the next chapter, responsible government is substantially inferior to separation of powers with respect to the capacity to manage the tensions that arise in countries that decided to embrace the principle of federalism.

Key Terms

separation of powers

responsible government

five conventions of responsible
  government

collective responsibility

confidence

parliamentary government

cabinet government

fusion of powers

four conventions for the formation
  of a government

coalition

majority government

minority government

head of government

head of state

party discipline

caucus

Discussion Questions

1. Between 1993 and October 2015, Canada had four majority governments and three minority governments. Which type do you think has provided better government?

2. The American form of government allows the people to elect both their executive (the president) and their legislators (Congress) directly. It is in this respect more democratic than the Canadian regime, in which citizens merely elect a local Member of Parliament. In this case, does "more democratic" mean "better"?

CHAPTER FOUR

FEDERALISM

The preamble to CA 1867 indicates that the Dominion of Canada is to have "a Constitution similar in Principle to that of the United Kingdom." We have seen, in Chapter Three, that this phrase is primarily a reference to Canada's adoption of the British tradition of responsible government. Yet the British Constitution was not the only model for the Fathers of Confederation. Their new dominion was to be a *federal* union, although the principle of federalism was not one to be found in the British Constitution. In developing the federal aspects of the Canadian regime, then, the Fathers of Confederation looked south of the border to see what could be learned from the Constitution of the United States, the blueprint of the first great modern federal regime.

4.1 What Is Federalism?

In order to understand what federalism is, we must first understand the distinction between **unitary** and **federal** systems of government. As the name suggests, a unitary system of government is a system in which all sovereign authority of that nation-state resides in one governing body—the national government. That national government may delegate some of its authority to lower levels of government, such as the governments of counties, towns, cities, or administrative districts. But the national government decides how much power it will delegate—it gives the power, and it can always take that power away. In a unitary system, there may be other governments besides the national government, but these will always be simply the servants of the national government. The country has one sovereign government.

Though many ancient regimes resembled federations, modern federalism is a relatively recent phenomenon, invented by the American founders in 1787 when they designed the Constitution of the United States. Canada, Australia, India, Switzerland, and Germany are examples of countries that have used some version of the federal principle to organize their governments. They stand in contrast to countries such as the United Kingdom, France, the Republic of Ireland, Sweden, and Japan—all of which have unitary systems of government.

In a federal system of government, authority is constitutionally divided between two levels of government. This means that neither level of government can be understood to have sovereign authority. Each receives its authority from the nation's constitution and is thus subordinate to it. The constitution gives legal jurisdiction over matters of national concern to the national legislature and legal jurisdiction over matters of local or regional concern to the provincial or state legislatures. In some instances, the two levels of government may share jurisdiction. The point of fundamental importance is that, in a federal system, the provincial or state governments are not beholden to the national government in the way that local governments are beholden in a unitary system. In a unitary system, authority flows from the centre out; in a federal system, authority is constitutionally divided.

In Canada, we commonly refer to the national government as the federal government because it is the government of the whole federal union. It is important to understand that the relationship between the federal and provincial governments is not the same as that between the provincial and municipal governments. Municipal governments fall within the jurisdiction of the provincial governments, which can alter, reorganize, or abolish them.[1] They are subordinate to their respective provincial governments. But the provincial governments are not subordinates of the federal government any more than the federal government is subordinate to the provinces. Both are equally subordinate to Canada's Constitution.

This equal subordination is made clear in the Constitution itself. CA 1982 contains complex amending formulae, which work on the basic principle that the provinces and the federal government must agree on changes to the federal division of powers. In this respect, federalism can be understood as a contract between two levels of government. Neither party can change the terms of the contract on its own.

4.2 Why a Federal Union?

In order to understand why the Fathers of Confederation opted for a federal union, we must consider the political situation that confronted the founders of the country in the 1860s. British North America consisted of six colonies—British Columbia, New Brunswick, Nova Scotia, Prince Edward Island, Newfoundland, and the Province of Canada (formerly Upper and Lower Canada, united at the time, and now Ontario and Quebec). It also included a vast expanse of territory, largely inhabited by First Nations people, but under the control of the Hudson's Bay Company. Each of the six colonies had its own colonial government and legislature. The government of the Province of Canada was a massive failure, as the divisions that existed between the French and English colonists made it unworkable. Politicians from the Province of Canada were thus eager, if not desperate, to reform the system of government.

The scheme that seemed most logical was to unite the British colonies within North America under one government. This idea ultimately proved appealing to three of the colonies that would go on to make up the first four provinces of Canada. First, the new arrangements would break the deadlock that existed between the French and English in the largest colony (the United Canadas) by tilting the balance of power in the new, bigger union in favour of the English-speaking colonists. Second, the new government of the Dominion of

---

1   A parallel relationship exists between the federal government and the three "territorial" governments in Canada's North. In those parts of Canada not under control of a province, the federal government has a free hand to establish territorial boundaries and territorial governments as it wishes. Territorial and municipal government will be discussed below in 4.6.

Canada could provide a coordinated plan of economic development of railways, canals, and roads. Third, it could provide greater security for both the small colonies, which were concerned about American imperial designs on them, and the uncolonized parts of North America. Fourth, it would help to relieve the burden on Britain of providing troops and personnel to administer the colonies; furthermore, the British believed that the time had come for Canada to begin to stand on its own. Finally, it would make Canadian expansion into the western part of North America easier. The intention to include British Columbia and other existing British holdings in Confederation was there from the start. Linking this western colony with the rest of Canada would help ensure that the United States would not be able to expand northward.

Those seeking union faced immense political obstacles. The English-speaking colonists in central Canada were enthusiastically in favour of a "legislative union" (a unitary system) rather than a federal union. But a legislative union was not a realistic political option. The French-speaking colonists in Lower Canada would never have agreed to a unitary system in which they would be a minority. They had to have their own provincial government, which would have jurisdiction over those matters relating to their preservation as a people. And the Maritime colonies were similarly ill disposed toward a legislative union. They were among the oldest British colonies, and their governments were long established. They were not inclined to see their interests submerged as they became a regional minority in a large dominion dominated by central Canada. Thus, from the very beginning, Canada was confronted with two serious political divisions: the split between the French and the English and a division between the centre and the periphery.

The obvious solution to the objections of the French Canadians and the Maritimers was the creation of a federal union. Yet, for a number of good reasons, Canadians were reluctant to organize the government on the federal principle. First, federalism was perceived to have failed in the United States. That country had just emerged from one of the worst civil wars in human history, a war fought to preserve the United States as one country without slavery. The Southern states had argued that every state had the right to decide for itself whether it should be a slave state or a free state. Federalism and the assertion of states' rights were thus associated with war and slavery. Moreover, it was often argued that federalism had created a divided system of government and that the weakness of the national government in Washington was one of the main causes of the war. Given the obvious problems that plagued our federal neighbour to the south, it is easy to see why the framers of the new dominion would have been less than enthusiastic about federalism.

The second objection to federalism was that it would create two levels of government and hence be more costly than unitary government. The colonies in British North America could not easily afford one level of government, let alone two. Moreover, it was suggested that federalism would be a weaker regime. Who would speak for Canadians? Under a unitary system, the people of the country could speak with one voice. But federalism would mean that each Canadian would be part of a provincial as well as federal community, and it was easy to foresee that this would create divided loyalties. The challenge for the Fathers of Confederation, then, was to find a form of federalism that would minimize the perceived defects of federal unions and yet meet the objections of those colonists who opposed a unitary system.

4.3 The Original Design of the Federal Union

The Fathers of Confederation believed that the federal arrangements agreed to at the Quebec Conference of 1864 constituted a workable solution to their problem. The key was the creation of a federal system in which the federal government would have a clear preponderance of power. A brief examination of some of the essential sections of CA 1867 will make that preponderance obvious.

The first point to notice is evident in those sections of the Constitution that outline the division of powers between the two levels of government. Sir John A. Macdonald argued that the Fathers of Confederation had given "all the great subjects of legislation" to the federal Parliament. A comparison of **section 91** (which establishes the exclusive legislative jurisdictions of the federal government) and **section 92** (which establishes those of the provinces) shows that Macdonald was indeed correct. That, at least, was how it looked in 1867.

Unlike the Constitution of the United States, which restricted Washington to the regulation of international and interstate commerce, section 91.2 grants to the federal Parliament exclusive jurisdiction over trade and commerce. This was intended to provide a constitutional basis for putting the general management of the economy in Ottawa's hands. Section 91.27 gives the federal government exclusive control over the important matter of criminal law, a jurisdiction that had been reserved for the individual states in the American Constitution. Section 91.3 makes Ottawa the financial powerhouse of Confederation, granting it the right to any form of taxation. Finally, section 91 appears to place the **residual power** in the hands of the federal government; anything not specifically reserved for the provinces is to be part of a general federal power to legislate for the "peace, order, and good government of Canada."

In comparison, the powers of the provincial governments appear paltry. The legislatures of the provinces are to have jurisdiction over "all matters of a strictly local or private nature in the province" (92.16). This includes such mundane items as hospitals and charities (92.7), local works (92.10), property and civil rights (92.13), and municipal institutions (92.8). Significantly, the provinces' powers to raise revenue are limited to two modest sources: "direct taxation" (92.3), which was relatively unimportant in 1867, and "shop, saloon, tavern, auctioneer and other licenses" (92.9).

The pre-eminence of the federal government was evident in a number of other provisions of CA 1867. Section 58 provides that the representative of the Crown for each of the provincial governments—the lieutenant governor—is to be appointed by Ottawa. The lieutenant governors are given the right to reserve provincial legislation, that is, to withhold royal assent, so as to give the federal government a chance to examine it. Under section 90, Ottawa is granted the power of **disallowance**, by which means the federal government can annul provincial legislation of which it disapproves. These powers of **reservation** and disallowance actually make the provincial level subordinate to the federal in a certain sense. Since true federalism rests on the principle that the two levels of government are equally sovereign in their own jurisdictions, it has been said that CA 1867 establishes not a federal system but a quasi-federal system, in which the federal government is the dominant partner.[2]

4.4 The Historical Development of Federalism in Canada

Although the Fathers of Confederation intended to create a highly **centralized** federal union—one in which the federal government would dominate—Canada now has one of the most **decentralized** federal unions in the world. This may sound confusing, but one must remember that federal systems, like the constitutions that describe them, are not rigid; they evolve over time in response to a number of factors.

We saw in Chapter Two that the meaning of a constitution will depend on judicial review—how the courts interpret it. Constitutional provisions that appear to establish a highly centralized form of federalism may be given a decentralized interpretation, thus changing the nature of the federal system. Moreover, jurisdictions that were unimportant in the nineteenth century have become extremely important in the twenty-first. Because medical science was relatively crude in

---

2   The powers of reservation and disallowance have not been used for decades, and there is widespread agreement that they should not be used. It would be fair to argue that it has become a constitutional convention that the federal government not exercise these powers.

1867, it seemed to the Fathers of Confederation that jurisdiction over hospitals (and, by extension, health) was not a major item. Today, however, health care is one of the largest areas of public expenditure. The fact that it is a provincial jurisdiction makes provincial governments more important than they were in 1867. The same is true of provincial taxing powers. CA 1867 restricts provincial governments to "direct taxation." Before the invention of personal and corporate income taxes, direct taxation was not very lucrative. Today, the use of such taxes by provincial governments has given those governments revenue sources that would have made the premiers of 1867 green with envy.

Perhaps the most influential factor shaping the relative strength of the two levels of government is public favour. There are a number of decentralizing forces that sometimes lead the public to favour a greater role for provincial governments, including the regional pattern of economic development in Canada, the lack of a strong Canadian identity and the corresponding strength of local attachments, and the demands of Québécois nationalists for a strong *état du Québec*. On the other hand, a number of forces can push the public to favour a strong central government, including the desire for national standards in both social services and human rights, the desire to protect our economy and our culture from American domination, and the need to address global issues such as climate change. The balance between these forces at a given point in time will determine whether the public favours greater centralization, greater decentralization, or the status quo.

Over the years, the interplay of these various factors has left us with remarkably different balances between federal and provincial power at different points in our history. Without undue simplification, one can divide the historical development of Canadian federalism into five basic periods.

1. Quasi-federalism (1867–1896). The era of John A. Macdonald's long tenure as prime minister and the ascendancy of the Conservative Party was one in which the national government, true to the founders' hopes, proved much stronger than the provincial governments. For most of this era, the relationship between the national and provincial governments was analogous to the colonial relationship between Britain and Canada. Provincial legislation was occasionally reserved or disallowed, and most of the great initiatives were undertaken by Ottawa, not the provinces.

2. Classical federalism (1896–1914). Beginning with the election of Wilfrid Laurier and the rise of the Liberal Party to national pre-eminence, the balance of power clearly shifted to a more equal relationship between the provinces and Ottawa. The Liberal Party had championed provincial rights in Ontario, and a French-Canadian prime minister was naturally more sensitive to such rights for Quebec. During this period, the courts handed down a series of important constitutional decisions, each of which contributed to a steady erosion of important federal powers (notably the "peace, order, and good government" clause and the trade and commerce powers granted in section 91.2). At the same time the scope of provincial jurisdictions expanded in areas such as property and civil rights (section 92.13). Of particular note was the *Maritime Bank* case of 1892, in which the Judicial Committee of the Privy Council (then Canada's highest court) explicitly repudiated the notion that provincial governments are subordinates of the federal government. The Judicial Committee declared that the Constitution would henceforth be interpreted in light of the principles of classical federalism, according to which each level of government is sovereign in the jurisdictions assigned to it.

3. Emergency federalism (1914–1960). In this era, the balance of power swung back toward the federal government. The two world wars required strong and decisive leadership and command of the economy and society that could be provided only by a national government. Moreover, the period between the wars was marked by the economic collapse of the Western democracies and the massive depression that ensued. The Great Depression fostered increased centralization because it led to the idea that the purpose of government should be expanded to include ensuring the welfare of the people; as the Depression had virtually bankrupted most of the provincial governments, it was evident that only Ottawa would be able to afford the costs involved in this new responsibility.

4. "Cooperative" federalism (1960–1995). In the postwar era, the economies of the Western democracies grew steadily. Canada's provincial governments now have a much greater ability to raise revenues and exercise power over their respective jurisdictions. Moreover, as public expectations continue to rise and people demand ever more services from government, the jurisdictions of the provincial government continue to grow in importance. The federal government sought relevance in this period by spending in tandem with the provinces. Thus, federalism became a system of federal-provincial "cooperation," meaning that the two levels of government constantly bargained and coordinated their actions. Increasingly, this process of federal-provincial negotiations involved regular meetings of first ministers and of cabinet ministers with common responsibilities. Because of the proliferation of such meetings between federal and provincial executive officers, this era is sometimes referred to as the age of **executive federalism**.

5. **"Collaborative" and "Open" Federalism (1995–present)**. In 1995, the federal budget made massive changes to the long-standing fiscal arrangements between the provinces and Ottawa. Transfers were simplified and effectively shrunk. At the same time, the conditions related to that spending were also loosened, leaving the provinces more leeway to spend money as they saw fit and reducing the need for cooperation between the two levels of government. That said, the federal government has still occasionally been interested in working with the provinces to realize collective goals. Much of that work has been more about setting mutual expectations and standards collaboratively rather than imposing federal norms upon the provinces with the lure of increased transfer funds. Hence, Canadians have seen a number of different sectoral agreements that commit provincial and federal governments to mutually agreed (and often flexible) standards in areas such as environmental assessment, early learning and child care, and other discrete policy foci.

This period has been marked by differing approaches to federal-provincial relations by individual prime ministers. Prime Minister Chrétien generally avoided much formal engagement with the premiers, preferring bilateral relations with individual premiers and modest federal-provincial programming. Prime Minister Martin was much more engaged with the premiers, meeting with them collectively on many occasions and attempting to resolve many outstanding issues through formal agreements and accords with the provinces. Prime Minister Harper returned to the pattern of less frequent meetings with the premiers and engaged in much less collaboration, leaving the provinces to their own devices and providing relatively stable federal transfers. His practice of "open federalism" was more classical in orientation, leaving governments to do their own thing in their own jurisdictions, despite the reality that effective policymaking at either level requires some interaction between the two governments. This led to some bitter disputes between the federal government and the provinces. Prime Minister Trudeau has signalled an intention to re-engage with the provinces, promising to involve premiers more in federal policymaking in matters such as the environment and addressing climate change.

4.5 Financing Government and Federal-Provincial Relations

One of the major problems associated with federalism is the need to balance a government's responsibilities with its ability to finance its role. A federal system will not work well if this balance is not attained, for it does little good to give a level of government the responsibility for providing a service if it cannot afford to provide it. The jurisdictional rights and responsibilities of government are mere legal niceties if the government lacks the will or the means to act.

This problem of balancing revenues with jurisdiction has plagued the Canadian federal system from the outset. In one sense, our federal system was designed to create an imbalance so that the provinces would always be subordinated to the federal government. But as the provinces grew more powerful, their inability to finance their programs and services also grew, which in turn has put enormous stress on the federal system. In response to that stress, federal and provincial politicians have developed an elaborate web of financial relations that usually goes by the name of **fiscal federalism**. This fiscal federalism may be divided into three distinct branches: taxation, federal spending power, and equalization payments.

1. Taxation. If we examine CA 1867, we find that the federal government was given both a much greater ability than the provinces to raise revenues and the power to spend money within areas of provincial jurisdiction. It was clear from the outset that the provincial governments were to be the poor cousins of the federal government and that the federal government would be able to play a major role in areas of provincial jurisdiction because it would have the superior financial resources.

In the area of jurisdiction over taxation, the federal government can raise money "by any mode or system of taxation" (section 91.3), whereas the provincial government has only the more specific jurisdiction over "direct taxation within the province" (section 92.2). At the time CA 1867 was written, government financing was done largely through systems of indirect, as opposed to direct, taxation. A **direct tax** is one in which the taxpayer is taxed directly by the government. A good example is the income tax. An **indirect tax** is one in which the tax is not collected directly from the taxpayer. Examples of such taxes are custom duties and the excise taxes that are built into the retail price of goods. The merchant or manufacturer pays the tax but then passes it on in the price charged to the consumer.

Jurisdiction over taxation was thus divided between the federal and provincial governments so as to favour the former. As the field of government responsibilities expanded, governments sought new sources of revenue. In the early part of the twentieth century, both the federal and the provincial governments introduced income taxes. Both levels of government have resorted to sales taxes.[3]

---

3   It was thought, in 1867, that a sales tax was a form of indirect tax and hence not within the jurisdiction of the provinces. In the 1943 case of *Atlantic Smoke Shops Ltd. v. Conlon*, however, the courts declared that a sales tax could be seen as a direct tax if one considered the merchant as a government tax collector. This decision opened the door to provincial sales taxes.

What is important to note is that the federal government has historically been ahead of the provincial governments in occupying and thus dominating these fields. It is politically difficult for the provincial governments to raise provincial income taxes when the federal tax is already widely perceived as burdensome enough. Taxation is thus one of the major areas of conflict between federal and provincial governments. Joint occupancy of what are now the major fields of taxation requires constant negotiation between the two levels of government over "**tax room**." Rather than simply transfer its own revenues to the provinces in support of provincial programs, Ottawa can relinquish some of its tax room and allow the provinces to take over the vacated "tax points."

2. Federal spending power. The federal division of powers divides the areas of jurisdiction in a fairly precise fashion. Nonetheless, today we find the federal government involved in many important areas of provincial jurisdiction. One reason is that the federal government has the financial resources, which it uses to aid the provinces in areas such as education and health care. Although health care is a matter of provincial jurisdiction, that need not prevent the federal government from establishing and financing programs in that area. The **federal spending power** (Ottawa's power to spend its money as it pleases) has been a major factor in determining how the federal system operates.

The most important aspect of this spending power is the way it has allowed the federal government to wield policy influence in areas that constitutionally belong to the provinces. The federal government will supply monies for programs in health care, education, or transportation, for example, but will also attach conditions as to how that money can be spent. Thus, while the federal government is not exercising direct legal control over an area of provincial jurisdiction, it can nonetheless establish substantial influence over the shape and outcome of programs. Perhaps the best-known example is in the area of health care. The federal government transfers billions of dollars to the provinces so that they may run their provincial health-care programs. In exchange for this money, however, the federal government demands that provinces respect certain principles (such as the prohibition of user fees). Although it is constitutionally within a province's power to allow for medical user fees, it is difficult for a province to do so if that means losing millions of dollars in federal monies.

This type of federal spending was traditionally known as a **conditional grant**. In response to political pressure from the provinces, particularly Quebec, the federal government has in recent decades moved more in the direction of **unconditional grants**. These involve the transfer of a large block of funds to each province, which allows for greater provincial discretion in how the monies are spent. Programs must still meet some broad national standards set by the federal government. Most federal funding to the provinces is used to finance health care, post-secondary education, welfare, and social services. This funding is now accomplished mainly through the Canada Health Transfer (CHT) and the Canada Social Transfer (CST). For 2014–2015, the total transfer to the provinces and territories through these grants was approximately $45 billion.

3. Equalization payments. The federal government is also responsible for providing monies to provinces whose tax revenues fall below the national average economically. The precedent for such responsibility was established by CA 1867, which required the federal government to provide subsidies to the provinces for the expense of their governments. This commitment has developed into a responsibility to ensure that social and economic conditions across the country remain roughly equal and that regional disparities do not become too great.

Attempts by the federal government to ameliorate regional disparities were once made mainly by means of shared-cost programs and federal grants. But today the more well-known means for doing this are the unconditional **equalization payments**. This type of financing was established in the 1950s and was entrenched in the Constitution in section 36 of CA 1982. Equalization payments are a redistribution of federal tax revenue to provinces whose tax revenues fall below a national average standard in order to ensure that Canadian citizens have roughly the same level of government services and taxation. Though the principle of equalization is entrenched in CA 1982, the implementation of it is governed by federal regulations. In essence, a formula is used to determine the average fiscal capacity of provincial governments, assuming average tax rates. (Fiscal capacity is the amount of revenue a government can raise through taxation.) Provinces with a fiscal capacity below the national average receive a transfer of funds from Ottawa sufficient to bring them closer to the national average. These transfers are unconditional, meaning the provincial government that receives them may spend the money on any area within its jurisdiction. Currently, the total amount of equalization payments is approximately $17 billion per year. In 2015, six provinces received equalization payments. Ontario has historically not been a recipient of equalization, but it has now received these payments for more than five years (since fiscal year 2009–10). For many provinces, equalization payments are extremely important. In New Brunswick and Prince Edward Island, for instance, equalization payments alone account for at least 20 per cent of the provincial governments' revenues and are larger than the health and social transfers combined.

4.6   Other Orders of Government: Territorial, Municipal, and First Nations

Up to this point, we have spoken only of the federal government and of provincial governments. That is because, strictly speaking, the Constitution divides all authority between those two levels[4] of government. Yet even a casual observer of Canadian politics understands that there are other sorts of governments in this country as well: territorial governments, municipal governments, and First Nations. Where do they fit into our federal regime?

Territorial Governments. At the time of Confederation, Canada consisted only of New Brunswick, Nova Scotia, what is now Southern Ontario, and those parts of Quebec that bordered the St. Lawrence River. Newfoundland, Prince Edward Island, and British Columbia were separate British colonies. The rest of what now constitutes Canada was known as Rupert's Land—property of the British Crown that had been assigned by charter to the Hudson's Bay Company. The federal government acquired Rupert's Land in 1869–70, and a small part of it became the Province of Manitoba in 1870. The rest was administered directly by the federal government as a dependent "territory." Over time, large tracts of this land were either assigned to existing provinces such as Ontario or Quebec or used to create new provinces such as Saskatchewan and Alberta. The remainder—all of which is north of the 60th parallel—is currently divided into three territories: Yukon, Northwest Territories, and Nunavut. Each of these territories has a premier and cabinet who are responsible to an elected territorial legislature. (A federally appointed "commissioner" is the territorial equivalent of the provincial lieutenant governors.) The territorial governments take responsibility for many of the same matters that are handled by provincial governments elsewhere in the country. The key difference, however, is that, while the provinces are sovereign, the territories exercise only those powers that are delegated to them by the federal government. The federal government is the main source of their revenues and, theoretically, has the authority to change their powers, change their boundaries, or even abolish them altogether. In many respects, however, territorial governments are treated like small provinces. For instance, their premiers and ministers will attend relevant federal-provincial meetings, and their governments will share in many of the arrangements governing fiscal federalism.

---

4   Legally and constitutionally, the provinces and the federal government are coordinate levels of government, each having its own independent areas of jurisdiction. In speaking of "levels" of government, we are in no way implying that the provincial governments are subordinate to the federal government.

Municipal Governments. The overwhelming majority of Canadians live in cities, many of which are larger than some of our provinces.[5] Cities have elected municipal governments that deliver a wide range of services and enact by-laws and regulations that relate to many important aspects of everyday life. In constitutional terms, however, Canadian municipalities are creatures of our provincial governments. Section 92.8 of CA 1867 assigns each provincial legislature sovereign authority over "municipal institutions in the province." That language means that provinces have pretty much the same authority over municipal governments that Ottawa has over the territorial governments. Each province will determine what powers its municipalities will have, how their councils are elected, and even what geographic shape the municipalities will take.[6] Municipalities and provinces engage in ongoing dialogue over which governments should take responsibility for which services—and who should pay for them. Municipalities will also seek financial support from the federal government for expensive investments in things such as sewage and transit infrastructure. Generally, municipalities are restricted to property taxes and licence and user fees as forms of revenue and are unable to raise sufficient funds for many of the projects and improvements that they need and thus rely on the senior levels of government to help fund these initiatives.

First Nations. Contemporary claims to self-government by First Nations are attempts to reclaim the status and independence of Aboriginal peoples recognized by the Crown in the Royal Proclamation of 1763 and the treaty system. When the British asserted sovereignty over the lands of North America acquired from the French, they also assumed a duty to First Nations to protect and recognize their claims to the land they historically occupied. In addition, the Crown signed myriad treaties with First Nations groups, some to realize transfer of title to land and others for the securing of peace and friendship. The very term "treaty" implies a recognition of solemn obligations between parties with some form of sovereign status.

Section 91.24 of CA 1867 assigns to the federal government authority over "Indians, and Lands reserved for Indians." This is hardly the recognition of sovereignty implied in the Royal Proclamation. Through most of Canadian history, Ottawa has overseen services and obligations to Aboriginal communities,

---

5   Six cities are larger than the Province of New Brunswick. Eight are larger than Newfoundland and Labrador, and approximately 35 are larger than Prince Edward Island.

6   It has been common in recent years for provinces to try to achieve savings and improve services by amalgamating smaller municipalities into larger "regional" municipalities.

particularly those communities based on reserves throughout the country. A legacy of mismanagement and neglect, as well as a political resurgence of Aboriginal peoples, has led to efforts to re-establish self-government for these communities. In some instances, that goal has been realized, so First Nations government is a reality in some parts of Canada. Yet the extraordinary diversity of Indigenous communities throughout the country in terms of population, size, location, and economic standing has a considerable impact on how close to self-governing any particular community might be.

For much of Canadian history, First Nations communities have been governed through provisions of the Indian Act, which mandates default forms of governance and administration. Off-reserve communities are less clearly governed by the statute, though the federal government still has service obligations to many communities, either through the status given to their members by the Indian Act or as a result of other guarantees and programs. Even under the Indian Act, reserve-based communities can enjoy some degree of self-government depending on the devolution of power granted to the community under community-specific or regional self-governance agreements. Where comprehensive agreements have been reached with individual First Nations, those communities may be entirely self-governing in regards to policing, land use, and many of the typical services delivered in other communities by federal programs. The failed Charlottetown Constitutional Accord had contemplated the recognition of what it called "Aboriginal self-government" as a third order of government alongside the provinces and the federal government. Those communities that have settled comprehensive land claims and self-governance agreements with federal and provincial governments certainly approximate that vision, though they still may be financially dependent on government transfers. The reality of First Nations governance in most communities today is much more akin to that of municipal government in terms of political autonomy and fiscal independence. Although land-based First Nations have a presumed entitlement to self-governance, implementation has been uneven, and, constitutionally, those communities enjoy self-governance only because the federal government devolves its authority to individual communities. The resolution of outstanding land claims and the development of more comprehensive agreements may one day mean that First Nations in Canada (particularly those associated with territory) are wholly self-governing.

4.7 The Challenge of Canadian Federalism

The Fathers of Confederation imported the federal element of the Canadian regime from the constitutional design of the United States. To be sure, significant modifications were made to the American model of federalism. For instance, our

Constitution lays out (at least on paper) a more centralized division of powers than is to be found south of the border. Still, the basic principle of federalism is the same in the Canadian and the American regimes—two levels of government, each supreme in its own areas of jurisdiction, and both subordinate to a constitutional law.

Given this fundamental similarity, it is at first somewhat surprising to see how strikingly different our experience with federalism has been from the experience of our southern neighbours. To put the matter simply, federalism is not as important an issue in American political life. The Constitution of the United States established a relatively decentralized form of federalism. Over time, the American regime has evolved into a much more centralized federation in which Washington plays the dominant political role, and the governments of the states are clearly less important. The current pre-eminence of the American federal government is relatively uncontroversial, and there is no interest in undertaking significant reform of the status quo.

In Canada, on the other hand, just the opposite is true. Almost from the beginning, Canadian political life has been dominated by quarrels over the nature of our federal arrangements. The point should be obvious if one considers for a minute only a few of the semi-permanent issues that plague our political agenda, all of which are problems of federalism: Quebec separatism, Western alienation, responsibility for funding health care and other services, regional economic development, Senate reform, and constitutional reform. Canada is probably the only country in the world where issues of federalism are something of a national political obsession. The "Quebec question" has always been, at bottom, a dispute over the division of jurisdiction between the government of Quebec and the federal government. Rightly or wrongly, a majority of Quebeckers believe that the current division of powers does not give the "state of Quebec" sufficient control over those matters that are essential to the protection and development of the Quebec "people." Over the past 40 years, this dispute has been at the centre of six major constitutional conferences, as well as the 1980 referendum on sovereignty association, CA 1982, the Meech Lake Accord, the Charlottetown Accord referendum, and a referendum on Quebec sovereignty in 1995. The underlying issue throughout this process has been whether Quebec can acquire the powers it believes are necessary to govern itself within the bounds of some federal form of political union, or whether that objective can be achieved only by becoming a sovereign state. Sovereignty or "renewed federalism"—for most Quebeckers, these are the only serious options; the status quo is generally considered to be simply unacceptable.

There can be little doubt that Quebec's presence in Confederation is a large part of the reason federalism has been so much more of a problem or question in

Canada than it has been in the United States. Yet the role of Quebec does not fully account for this. Even if Quebec had never been a part of Canada (or, alternatively, if Quebec were to someday secede from Canada), federalism would still be more controversial here than it is in the United States.[7] The reason, in one key respect, is that federalism does not work as well with responsible government as it does with separation of powers. The crux of the issue is representation within the national government.

The citizens of a federal regime will, by definition, have dual loyalties, feeling themselves to be both citizens of a province or state and citizens of the country as a whole. By extension, they will also, of necessity, have a dual view of the union itself: on the one hand, it will be seen as a union of individual Americans, Canadians, or Australians; on the other hand, it will be seen as a union of states or provinces. To the extent that we are democrats and respect the principle of equality, this duality leads to a dilemma: should political representation within the national government be based on the principle of the equality of all individual citizens or on the principle of the equality of all the states or provinces?

The Founding Fathers of the United States resolved this dilemma by adopting **bicameralism**. In a bicameral legislative body, power is shared by two separate chambers so that neither can act without the agreement of the other. The Founding Fathers created a legislature (Congress) in which representation in one chamber was based on the principle of the equality of all individual citizens (the House of Representatives) and representation in the other was based on the principle of the equality of the states (the Senate). In the House of Representatives, states with larger populations have more seats, and states with smaller populations have fewer seats. In the Senate, however, all states have the same number of seats—two—regardless of population. The American Congress thus gives equal voice to the two visions of union—the United States as a union of individual Americans (in which all Americans are equal) and the United States as a union of states (in which all states are equal). This bicameral solution was essential to the adoption of the Constitution of the United States. If legislative power had been assigned only to a chamber based on equality of the states, the small states would have dominated the national government—something the large states would never have accepted. If legislative power had been assigned only to a chamber based on equality of individual citizens,

---

7   In his 1968 separatist manifesto *An Option for Québec*, René Lévesque claimed that separatism would be good for English Canada because once Québec had left, the rest of the country would no longer have any disputes about federalism. On this point, at least, Lévesque certainly misunderstood political life in English Canada.

the large states would have dominated the national government—something the small states would never have agreed to. Bicameralism allowed the Founding Fathers to give fair weight to both claims, so neither the small states nor the large states would dominate. Over time that vision has only strengthened the legitimacy of the national government. Americans do not commonly regard the Senate as a "states' house," but it does insulate Congress somewhat from the critique that state interests are not represented in national decision making.

The Fathers of Confederation imitated the American model of bicameralism but kept a healthy dose of Westminster in the mix. Canada's Parliament includes both a House of Commons and a Senate. Representation in the House of Commons is based on the principle of the equality of all Canadians, so provinces with larger populations have a larger number of seats. Representation in the Senate, on the other hand, is based on the principle of the equality of the regions, with each of the four main regions of the country receiving about the same number of seats. The problem in the Canadian case, however, is that responsible government makes it difficult, if not impossible, for the two chambers to be equal in power. The House of Commons is not merely a legislative body; it is also the chamber from which the executive is drawn and to which the executive must be responsible. To the extent that this role cannot be shared with the Senate, the House will of necessity dominate Parliament, and the Senate will always have a peripheral role. This means, however, that the principle of representation embedded in the Senate—the equality of the regions—is not really given meaningful expression within our national government. The chamber with real power is the one in which the two largest provinces possess nearly 60 per cent of the seats. Not surprisingly, this leads citizens in the other eight provinces to believe they have little control over their national government. (This sense of alienation has been powerful in the four Western provinces.) Accordingly, the eight smaller provinces must look to their provincial governments to champion their causes, and these provincial governments typically court public favour by "running against Ottawa"—by blaming the federal government for all their province's woes. Instead of being dealt with *within* the federal legislature, regional concerns are thus funnelled through the federal-provincial division of powers, which has the effect of making federalism our country's main battleground. Canadian premiers and prime ministers routinely face off in the media over different visions for the economy or on issues such as health care. **First ministers' conferences**, at which the premiers and the federal prime minister wrangle over financial and jurisdictional questions, though rare in recent years, have been a routine feature of Canadian politics. Since 2003, the premiers have had their own **Council of the Federation**, which for the most part serves as a vehicle for promoting the view that Ottawa should transfer more money to the provinces and allow them to decide for themselves how it will be spent. This political dynamic does not prevail in the United States, for the Senate ensures that the interests of the small states are at least assumed to be protected *within* Washington.

4.8 Current Controversies: The Pressure to Decentralize

Through much of the twentieth century, Ottawa has used its spending power to ameliorate regional·disparities and to influence public policy in areas of provincial jurisdiction. For most political leaders in Quebec, these federal "intrusions" are unacceptable since they effectively transfer decision-making authority in some areas from the Assemblée nationale in Quebec City to the English-Canadian–dominated government in Ottawa. Nationalist politicians in Quebec believe that the division of powers developed in 1867 is already too centralist; for Ottawa to "invade" jurisdictions that are supposed to belong exclusively to the provinces is intolerable.

Yet many Canadians have powerful reasons for steadfastly opposing the call for a more decentralized federal system. It is often argued that a strong federal presence in key provincial jurisdictions is essential for the defence of national standards of service in health care, welfare, and education. Many Canadians fear that if Ottawa retreats from these areas, Canadians will end up with dramatically different levels of services in the different provinces. Those who live in wealthier provinces would receive first-class health care, for example, while those in the less prosperous provinces would have to settle for something substantially worse. Political parties often advocate for programs such as national daycare or pharmacare to promote equal standards across provinces. According to opponents of decentralization, then, a federal retreat from provincial jurisdictions would make Canada less of a country and something more akin to a patchwork quilt.

One way to "square the circle"—to combine centralization and decentralization—would be to engage in **asymmetrical federalism**, an approach to federalism in which different provinces could have somewhat different powers. We might then allow Quebec to take greater control of its own affairs while maintaining a more centralized form of federalism in the rest of the country. Baier and Boothe[8] point out that Canadian federalism is already asymmetrical in a number of respects: the Constitution provides special guarantees for a

---

8   Gerald Baier and Katherine Boothe, "What Is Asymmetrical Federalism and Why Should Canadians Care?," in *Braving the New World: Readings in Contemporary Politics*, ed. Thomas Bateman and Richard Myers, 4th ed. (Toronto: Thomson-Nelson, 2008) 206–16.

number of provinces in the House and the Senate; our constitutional amending formulas treat different provinces differently; and many federal-provincial agreements typically involve only the nine provinces outside of Quebec, as Ottawa and Quebec negotiate separate agreements of their own. On a more symbolic level, in 2006, Canada's Parliament adopted a significant asymmetry in recognizing the "Québécois" as a "nation" within Canada.

Yet asymmetrical federalism is unlikely to provide a solution to the problem of Canadian federalism. To begin with, the institutionalization of special rights, special deals, or special status is offensive to the egalitarian sensibilities of most Canadians. It is therefore unlikely that the idea of asymmetry could be pushed very far without sparking a backlash. Moreover, it is not clear that a more decentralized arrangement for Quebec would not lead to similar demands from Canada's wealthier provinces. In Alberta and British Columbia, the intrusions of the federal government into areas of exclusive provincial jurisdiction (and the concomitant transfer of tax dollars from the West to the East) have also become unpopular. These two provinces routinely feel a sense of "alienation," and their view of provincial rights suggests that their dissatisfaction with Canadian federalism is only slightly less than that of Quebeckers.[9] Their sense of grievance against central Canada is expressed in terms of demands that Ottawa remove itself from areas of provincial jurisdiction and that federalism take a more decentralized form in the future. In other words, Alberta and British Columbia have a perspective on Canadian federalism that is, in some ways, not all that different from the perspective of Quebec nationalists.

The opponents of decentralization were able to carry the day in their fight against the Meech Lake and Charlottetown Accords. Those accords would have placed restrictions on new federal initiatives in areas of provincial jurisdiction and, in the case of Charlottetown, would have seen the federal government withdraw entirely from a number of the less important provincial jurisdictions. Oddly enough, however, today's federal system is perhaps becoming far more decentralized than anything contemplated in either of the accords. One of the catalysts for this transformation was the near victory of the separatist side in the 1995 referendum on sovereignty in Quebec. That close call with disaster has led our national politicians to take more seriously the traditional Quebec demands for limits to Ottawa's use of federal spending power. Under the 1999 **Social Union Framework Agreement**, for example, Ottawa consented not to introduce any new shared-cost programs in provincial jurisdictions without first obtaining the approval of seven

9   See Doug Owram, "Reluctant Hinterland," in *The Canadian Political Tradition: Basic Readings*, 2nd ed., ed. Ron S. Blair and Jack T. McLeod (Scarborough: Nelson Canada, 1993) 153–68.

provinces that, taken together, have 50 per cent of the total Canadian population. Ottawa also agreed that any province that chooses not to participate in such a program will be provided with equivalent federal dollars to run a program of its own.

A second (and perhaps even more important) catalyst of decentralization has been the federal debt and deficit. By the early 1990s, it was evident that the federal debt was getting out of control and that continuing deficits each year were seriously threatening the long-term fiscal health of the nation. A large part of Ottawa's spending came in the form of long-term commitments to the provinces, so the solution was to scale back its spending in areas of provincial jurisdiction such as health care and post-secondary education—in effect, to offload its fiscal problems on provincial governments. The decline in federal financial contributions in these areas naturally led to a decline in the federal government's influence on provincial policies and standards. For instance, provincial politicians now ask why they should be forced to make their health-care policies conform to the Canada Health Act when federal contributions to health care have slipped from historic highs of 50 per cent to somewhere in the 20–25 per cent range.

Will this new trend to decentralization be sufficient to satisfy the politicians and voters in Quebec, Alberta, and British Columbia? On the other hand, will it be so strong that it unravels the fabric of Canadian nationhood? These sorts of questions reveal how Canada's future will, in large part, be tied to the development of our federal system. When we consider whether the present federal system works, how it might be reformed, and whether Canadians can ever agree on the constitutional changes required for such reforms, the fundamental issue of federalism comes to light: to what extent do Canadians believe there should be a powerful national government that rules them from the centre of the country and is controlled by a national majority, or, asked in another way, to what extent do Canadians believe that Canada should become more of a confederation of ten largely independent provinces for whom the federal government is merely a coordinator, not a leader? Federalism is a system of divided loyalties: each of us is a citizen of both a province and a country, ruled by two different governments. Canadians are being forced to confront the question of which government they believe to be the most important and why.

Key Terms

unitary	executive federalism
federal	fiscal federalism
section 91	direct tax
section 92	indirect tax

residual power

disallowance

reservation

centralized

decentralized

quasi-federalism

classical federalism

emergency federalism

"cooperative" federalism

Social Union Framework Agreement

tax room

federal spending power

conditional grant

unconditional grant

equalization payments

bicameralism

first ministers' conferences

Council of the Federation

asymmetrical federalism

Discussion Questions

1. Is federalism good for Canadian democracy? Does its complexity hinder or confuse governmental accountability? Are there ways that federalism improves democracy?

2. Should the areas of provincial jurisdiction be identical for every province, or should some provinces have control over some jurisdictions that other provinces do not—for instance, immigration, agriculture, or broadcasting?

Chapter Five

The Canadian Charter of Rights and Freedoms

5.1 What Is a Charter of Rights?

With the adoption of CA 1982, Canada acquired a constitutionally entrenched charter of rights. For reasons that will become evident later in this chapter, the introduction of the Charter marked a profound transformation of the Canadian regime. But there are many other questions that must be addressed before we can discuss its impact. The first of these is the most obvious: what is a charter of rights?

The basic idea behind a charter of rights is best understood by thinking back to Chapter One and our discussion of Canada's regime principles. Because Canada is a democracy, one of our regime's central principles is majority rule. Yet, because Canada is not just a democracy but a *liberal* democracy, we may also say that our regime is devoted to the protection of fundamental rights. The great problem in liberal democracy is that these two fundamental principles—majority rule and fundamental rights—are not always in harmony. In the 2006 *Multani* case before the Supreme Court of Canada, the issue was whether an observant Sikh could wear a kirpan (a ceremonial metal dagger) while attending public school. Education authorities administered a reasonable no-weapons policy on school property but this clashed with young Multani's religious freedom. The court reconciled the two interests by upholding an accommodation allowing the boy to wear the kirpan as long as it was contained in an inaccessible cloth sheath. Many Quebeckers reacted angrily to the decision, claiming the rights of minorities were overtaking the interests of the majority.

The purpose of a charter of rights is to prevent democratic majorities from using political power[1] to violate rights, especially the rights of minorities. A charter does so by entrenching those rights in the text of a constitution. The rights are articulated as individual rights, and it is almost always individual persons who claim that a law or the conduct of a public official has violated their rights. But individuals are often members of groups and these groups' interests may be limited or impaired by the state. You will recall from Chapter Two that CA 1867 and CA 1982 are the supreme laws of the regime. It therefore follows that any statute that is inconsistent with the Constitution can have no force or effect. Thus, a constitutional charter of rights will put those rights identified in it beyond the reach of the majority and its elected representatives by incorporating them into the supreme law of the regime.

5.2 How the Charter Works: *Gosselin v. Québec*

To see how the Charter works, it is useful to work through a Supreme Court case, *Gosselin v. Québec*, as an example. In the 1980s the Quebec government dealt with the problem of chronic unemployment by fashioning social assistance

---

1   It is important not to confuse constitutional charters of rights with statutory **human rights codes**. A human rights code is a statute that protects rights in the private sphere. A human rights code provision prohibiting racial discrimination would thus prevent one private individual (a landlord) from discriminating against another private individual (a tenant) on the basis of race. A constitutional charter of rights, on the other hand, is meant to protect rights from violations in the public sphere, that is, violations by the government. A charter provision prohibiting racial discrimination would thus prevent a government from passing a law that was itself racially discriminatory (for example, not providing welfare for Asians) or permitting others to behave in a discriminatory fashion.

policy to encourage young people to upgrade their skills and join the labour force. Unemployed persons under 30 years of age were eligible for social assistance at about a third of the rate available to those over that age. If, however, an under-30 individual engaged in community work, education, or labour force training, he or she would get the full benefit. The government's reasoning was obvious. Social assistance rates that are relatively generous will discourage people in general and young people in particular from obtaining gainful employment. The longer a person remains unemployed the harder it will be for him or her to enter the workforce. That person will then be dependent on welfare; this will mean limited opportunities for the welfare recipient and a long-term, unsustainable drain on government revenues. So the program sought to arrange the incentives to encourage young people to get off welfare and into the workforce.

Louise Gosselin did not see it this way. She brought a Charter claim before the courts on behalf of herself and thousands of other unnamed persons, arguing, among other things, that the program discriminated against her and the others on the basis of age. Section 15 of the Canadian Charter is the equality provision; it prohibits discrimination on the basis of a number of group characteristics, including age. In general terms, in order for a law to be found in violation of section 15, it must make a distinction between people on the basis of age or some other enumerated group characteristic (such as sex, religion, race, or ethnicity) and that distinction must work to the disadvantage of the Charter claimant. For Ms. Gosselin, the program self-evidently distinguished social assistance recipients as to age and unfairly assumed that young people are particularly lazy. It harmed young recipients by providing them with social assistance cheques on which they were unable to live.

A majority of the nine-judge Supreme Court panel hearing her appeal disagreed with Gosselin. On behalf of the justices in the majority, the Chief Justice wrote that, although the program made age-based distinctions, these were to help, not hurt, young people:

> notwithstanding its possible short-term negative impact on the economic circumstances of some welfare recipients under 30 as compared to those 30 and over, the thrust of the program was to improve the situation of people in this group, and to enhance their dignity and capacity for long-term self-reliance. The nature and scope of the interests affected point not to discrimination but to concern for the situation of welfare recipients under 30.[2]

---

2   *Gosselin v. Québec (Attorney General)*, 2002 SCC 84 at para. 66.

The dissenters did find a section 15 violation. They argued that the under-30 claimants' "dignity was adversely affected" and that the low social assistance rates invited other harms to recipients. The program, they argued, was based on a faulty assumption that young people have fewer needs than older people and are particularly given to laziness.

Louise Gosselin failed in her bid for a declaration that the Quebec program was unconstitutional and for a court order that she be paid monies she would have received had the age-based rate structure not been in place. But her case is a good example of the kinds of Charter issues that come before the courts. It is also important to note that appeal courts sit in panels of three to nine judges and that, at the end of the day, a case is decided by a majority vote of the panel. On many Charter questions, reasonable people can and will disagree. And judges are reasonable people: learned in the law, experienced, highly intelligent, and equally immersed in the facts of a given case. Yet they often disagree with one another about how a Charter case should be decided.

5.3 Remedies

According to the old common law rule, where there is a right, there is a remedy. Something effectual must attend the possession of a right. What happens if courts declare a law to be in violation of a constitutional right? What are the possible "remedies"? Section 24(1) of the Charter addresses this matter as follows:

> Anyone whose rights or freedoms, as guaranteed by this Charter, have been infringed or denied may apply to a court of competent jurisdiction to obtain *such remedy as the court considers appropriate and just in the circumstances* (emphasis added).

In most cases, if the courts find a law in violation of the Charter, they employ what is called a **section 52 remedy**. Section 52(1) of CA 1982 states that any law that is "inconsistent" with the Constitution is "of no force or effect." In a section 52 remedy, the legislation (or more often, the specific section of the legislation at issue) is declared to be "of no force or effect," which means that the government no longer has the authority to act in the way the law provided. The judiciary restricts itself to determining whether the law in question is consistent with the Charter, but it is up to Parliament (or the relevant provincial legislature) to decide if and how to amend the legislation so as to make it consistent with the Charter as interpreted by the courts. In some countries, for example the United Kingdom, the judiciary is explicitly restricted to declaratory remedies. This means that a court can declare that a law is contrary to a fundamental right, but it cannot then render it inoperative. It leaves it to the politicians to respond. Notice, however, that the wording of section 24(1) gives Canada's courts leeway to determine for themselves what remedies are available to them when they find legislation in violation of the Charter. The courts have interpreted section 24 to include a variety of remedies.

First, a court can strike down a law, as explained above. If the law is void, then a Charter claimant cannot be found to have breached it.

Second, if a law is generally sound but for the absence of language that would fix a constitutional flaw, a court may, instead of striking it down, merely add the right words to the law to solve the problem. For example, in the 1998 *Vriend* case, a person alleged that he was discriminated against by a college on the basis of sexual orientation. Alberta's human rights law prohibited discrimination of the basis of a number of grounds but not sexual orientation. But section 15 of the Charter was by then interpreted by the Supreme Court to prohibit discrimination on the basis of sexual orientation. Human rights laws can be challenged for failing to conform to the protections of section 15. That is what Vriend did. In response, the Supreme Court, instead of striking down Alberta's human rights law, merely "read in" sexual orientation to its list of prohibited grounds of discrimination. This **reading in** approach is used when a law fails to extend protection of rights to those who have a legitimate constitutional claim.

Third, the judiciary can strike down a law but delay the effect of that declaration so as to allow the government to revise legislation. In some cases, an impugned law covers a complex, important area of public policy, so striking down the law means that the regulated activity would now go unregulated. Often, this is not considered a problem. But in the 2015 case of *Carter v. Canada*, the issue was a challenge to the constitutionality of Canada's criminal prohibition on assisted suicide. Lee Carter suffered a debilitating, painful disease and wanted to end her life on her terms. The Supreme Court agreed, but if it struck down the law, assisted suicide would go unregulated with potentially catastrophic consequences for many vulnerable Canadians. So the court declared the law unconstitutional for very specific reasons and suspended the effective date of that invalidation for one year, during which time Parliament was given the opportunity to produce a new law in conformity with the court's ruling.[3]

---

3   In early 2016, it granted the federal government another extension of four months to craft a new law consistent with its 2015 ruling.

Fourth, in many criminal cases in which evidence against an accused was collected by police in a manner that violated his or her Charter rights, a court may, in accordance with section 24(2), exclude that evidence from trial. This exclusion may or may not mean that the accused will be acquitted; the trial's outcome depends on what other evidence the Crown is able to introduce. But such exclusion of evidence does work to the advantage of the Charter claimant and also deters police misconduct.

Very occasionally, the courts will decide that a person's rights have been violated but order no substantive remedy. In *Canada v. Khadr* (2010), the Supreme Court considered Omar Khadr's claim that his section 7 Canadian Charter rights were violated because Canadian authorities were complicit in the torture to which he was subjected while in US custody at Guantanamo Bay. (Khadr, a Canadian citizen, was captured by American troops in Afghanistan in 2002 after allegedly throwing a grenade and killing one soldier. Khadr confessed to the act.) The Supreme Court agreed that his rights were violated but did not order his release from US custody. The court deferred to a longstanding principle that foreign affairs are a prime area of executive prerogative in which courts should not heedlessly meddle: "In this case, the evidentiary uncertainties, the limitations of the Court's institutional competence, and the need to respect the prerogative powers of the executive, lead us to conclude that the proper remedy is declaratory relief."[4]

5.4   The Adoption of the Charter

It is sometimes suggested that the adoption of the Charter in 1982 marked the introduction or creation of a new set of rights. This suggestion is misleading. Although a number of the rights set down in it might be thought of as new, the Charter was primarily a new mechanism for the protection of rights that were already well established in the Canadian political tradition.

To see that the protection of rights does not necessarily depend on the existence of a charter of rights, we need only look at the example of Britain. Britain has never had a constitutionally entrenched charter of rights, but certain fundamental rights and freedoms have long been as well respected there as they are in regimes that have constitutional charters. In some cases, those rights have been codified in organic statutes, but for the most part they exist merely as traditions (or, in some cases, as constitutional conventions). The British Parliament is

---

4   *Canada (Prime Minister) v. Khadr*, 2010 SCC 3 at para. 46.

legally able to pass legislation that violates those rights, but the inescapable necessity of keeping the support of the voters, coupled with the presence of an official opposition in the House of Commons, makes it difficult for any government to go very far in terms of violating rights.

For most of its life, the Canadian regime took the British approach to the protection of rights. Rights such as freedom of religion and freedom of speech were seen to be part of the liberal democratic tradition we inherited from Britain,[5] and Canadians generally thought it possible and desirable to trust our parliamentarians not to violate those rights.

On the whole, this approach worked reasonably well. Compared with most countries, Canada had a decent human rights record. Yet there were important exceptions to this general trend. Provincial governments were sometimes not as careful about respecting rights as they should have been. In the 1930s, the Aberhart government in Alberta enacted legislation that clearly violated freedom of speech. In the 1950s, the Duplessis government in Quebec passed a number of measures that were inconsistent with freedom of speech and freedom of religion.[6] In all of these cases, the offending measures were struck down by the Supreme Court, but only because the legislation in question was *ultra vires*: the court held that, under the division of powers, only the federal government could regulate speech and religion so as to limit the right to free speech or religious freedom.

But it was not clear that the federal government was an entirely trustworthy guardian of human rights either. During World War II, Ottawa had confined Canadians of Japanese origin in detention camps, alleging that their Japanese ancestry made them potential security threats. Though the government had widespread public support for this policy at the time, it was later recognized to have been a clear violation of the right to liberty and the right not to be detained or imprisoned arbitrarily. Indeed, the atrocities of World War II themselves produced momentum for entrenched rights protections, in Canada

---

5   Some members of the Supreme Court of Canada flirted with the thesis that the reference to a constitution "similar in principle to that of the United Kingdom" in the preamble to CA 1867 contained an "implied bill of rights" granting constitutional protection to all those rights that formed part of British constitutional traditions. See, for example, *Switzman v. Elbling* (1957). This thesis was never endorsed by a majority of the court.

6   The Aberhart government in Alberta passed a law requiring that province's newspapers to print government responses to all articles critical of the government. The Duplessis government in Quebec enacted legislation designed to suppress communist ideas and to curtail the activities of Jehovah's Witnesses.

and abroad. Perhaps the most emblematic abuses of rights by the Canadian state have been in its treatment of Aboriginal peoples. Even after the public mood was more receptive to better recognizing rights, Aboriginal peoples were still denied the right to vote, and the federal Indian Act prevented Aboriginal people from exercising other basic political rights like organizing to lobby governments or to hire legal counsel to pursue land claims. First Nations women (and their children) would lose their Aboriginal status under the Indian Act if they married non-status men. Male status holders lost no such rights if they married non-status women. And, as the Truth and Reconciliation Commission has helped Canadians to better acknowledge, thousands of young Aboriginal people were forcibly taken from their families to be educated at residential schools where they were violently discouraged from using their languages or practising their cultural traditions.

By the end of the 1950s, then, many Canadians came to be dissatisfied with our traditional, political approach to the protection of rights and freedoms. At that same time, the Supreme Court of the United States was just beginning to use that country's Bill of Rights to take bold steps in the fight for racial equality, striking down discriminatory legislation as unconstitutional. Rights activists in Canada began to argue that Canada should abandon its traditional British approach to the protection of rights and embrace the American idea of a constitutionally entrenched and judicially enforceable bill or charter of rights. The ground for such an innovation was already well prepared by our experience with federal judicial review; as a result of our interminable litigation over the division of powers, attentive Canadians were quite used to the idea that courts might tell parliaments and legislatures what they were permitted to do and what they were not.

In 1960, the Diefenbaker government moved to address the human rights issue by adopting the Canadian **Bill of Rights**. This document recognized and declared the existence of a number of "human rights and fundamental freedoms" including freedom of religion, freedom of speech, freedom of assembly and association, the right to the enjoyment of property, and a number of procedural legal rights, such as the right to retain legal counsel upon arrest. But there was a fundamental flaw in this document: it was merely an organic statute. This created two problems. The first was that this Bill of Rights, as a *federal* statute, did not apply to acts of the provincial governments and legislatures. Moreover, it was not even clear that it could be used to annul federal legislation. Courts are able to strike down one type of law only by applying or appealing to some higher law. Since the Canadian Bill of Rights was itself merely a statute, however, there was no logical reason to give it precedence over any other statute. Thus, the Canadian Bill of Rights presented the courts with a constitutional dilemma they never resolved. In the case of *The Queen v. Drybones*, a divided Supreme Court did use the Bill of Rights to invalidate a federal law that discriminated against Aboriginal Canadians. But in the other cases it heard involving the Bill of Rights, the Supreme Court always found some reason for upholding whatever legislation was being challenged.

By the 1970s, then, human rights activists came to argue that what Canada needed was a constitutionally entrenched charter of rights—a charter that would apply to all levels of government and that would be manifestly superior in status to ordinary legislation. These activists found a keen ally in Prime Minister Pierre Trudeau, who saw a constitutional charter as an excellent device for entrenching his particular vision of a bilingual Canada. Within a decade, Trudeau succeeded in effecting the adoption of a much broader document, the Canadian Charter of Rights and Freedoms.

From the point of view of its development, the Charter may be said to have three elements. First, it entrenches, in expanded form, most of the basic rights that were included in the Canadian Bill of Rights.[7] It guarantees fundamental freedoms such as freedom of speech and freedom of religion (section 2), basic democratic rights including the right to vote (sections 3–5), basic legal rights like the right not to be subjected to any cruel or unusual punishments (sections 7–14), and the right to non-discriminatory treatment under the law (section 15). Second, the Charter includes a number of language rights that entrench Trudeau's vision of a bilingual Canada (sections 16–23). Beyond these first two elements, the Charter includes various specific provisions for which there was no precedent in the Canadian Bill of Rights. Section 6 creates a regime of "mobility rights," including the right to enter, remain in, and leave Canada, and the right to pursue the gaining of a livelihood in any province. Section 27 provides an explicit recognition of the "multicultural heritage" of Canadians. Sections 1 and 33 (each of which will be discussed in detail below) establish principles and mechanisms for limiting the application of the rights enumerated in the Charter.

5.5 Opposition to the Charter

From the day the Charter was adopted, an overwhelming majority of Canadian citizens has supported it enthusiastically. Indeed, many Canadians see it as the fullest and clearest expression of the moral foundations of our regime. Yet for years there was a powerful undercurrent of opposition to it. During the

---

7   One exception is the right to the "enjoyment of property," which is protected in section 1(a) of the Bill of Rights but is not mentioned in the Charter.

negotiations that ultimately produced CA 1982, Manitoba's Premier Sterling Lyon attacked the idea of an entrenched charter of rights as an unacceptable departure from the principle of parliamentary sovereignty. Lyon argued that, in a parliamentary regime, the final responsibility for public policy should rest with the democratically elected representatives of the people in Parliament. This, he feared, would no longer be true once the Charter gave the judiciary the power to invalidate federal and provincial legislation.[8] From a social democratic perspective, Saskatchewan NDP premier Allen Blakeney worried that a Charter would be used to assert individual rights against important "collectivist" legislation that forms the basis of Canada's welfare state. Though these criticisms did not derail the adoption of the Charter, they have been taken up by some of Canada's leading constitutional experts, and skepticism about the Charter remains strong in some academic circles.

At the heart of the matter is the question of democracy. Charter skeptics argue that the adoption of an entrenched charter has effectively transferred a great deal of political power to the judiciary (especially the Supreme Court of Canada). This transfer is said to be a profoundly undemocratic development because it means that an unelected and unaccountable judiciary can use the Charter to impose its own policies on the rest of the country in a host of areas, including matters such as abortion, Sunday shopping, euthanasia, capital punishment, and the use of marijuana.

Those who defend the Charter do not deny that it has certain undemocratic effects. Indeed, they retort, that is precisely the point of having an entrenched Charter of Rights. Canada is not simply a democracy; it is a *liberal* democracy. And this means that the democratic principle of majority rule

---

8   Lyon may, in some respects, have been trying to lock the barn door after the cows had left. The noted nineteenth-century British constitutionalist A.V. Dicey once wryly remarked that the drafters of the BNA Act should have said in its preamble that Canada was to have a constitution similar in principle to that of the United States, not the United Kingdom. His point was that Canada's federal system, modelled on that of the United States, required a division of powers established in constitutional law. The adoption of a constitutional law logically meant that Canada's Parliament was not supreme, for the courts would have to possess the authority to determine whether a particular matter was *intra vires* or *ultra vires* (within or beyond the powers of, in this case, Parliament's authority). To the extent that the courts have been placing limits on the scope of Parliament's actions since Confederation, parliamentary supremacy has always been something of a misnomer, and the step from judicial review on the basis of federalism to judicial review on the basis of a charter was not, conceptually, a difficult one.

must always be tempered by a respect for the rights of the minority. Further, it is commonly argued that democracy is only intelligible and viable when it is accompanied by rights such as freedom of speech and association. Democratic government depends vitally on the enjoyment and exercise of these sorts of liberties. As the example of our treatment of Japanese-Canadians during World War II shows, the rights of the minority are sometimes subject to flagrant violation by Canada's democratically elected leaders. It is therefore not only reasonable but necessary to empower a judicial elite to correct the illiberal excesses of the democratic majority.

On its face, this rebuttal appears impressive, yet Charter skeptics claim that it loses its force when one looks at how the Charter is used by the courts in practice. Charter cases rarely, if ever, involve a blatant violation of clear-cut rights comparable to what happened in the case of the Japanese-Canadians.[9] The typical Charter case will focus instead on what Peter Russell has called the "periphery" of the rights it guarantees, the grey area where the precise meaning of the right is in doubt and where there can be reasonable differences of opinion as to what does or does not constitute a violation of the right.[10] Canadians agree, for example, that the right "not to be subjected to any cruel or unusual treatment or punishment" (section 12) includes, at its core, the principle that punishment must be proportionate to the crime. We would therefore find it reasonable for a judicial minority to use section 12 to overturn an act of a parliamentary majority imposing a minimum prison sentence of ten years on jaywalkers. But would a law permitting capital punishment for serial killers be a violation of section 12? On a question like this, there would be profound disagreement among Canadians, and it is not obvious why the nine judges of the Supreme Court should have the final say on the matter. Their legal training provides them with no special expertise for deciding a moral-political question about capital punishment. Why, then, should they, a very tiny minority, have the right to impose their moral or political views on the democratic majority?

Critics of Charter review point to a recent decision, the **PHS Community Services Society case** (2011) concerning the operation of a provincial government-sanctioned

---

9   And even when they do, it is not clear that a charter will make much difference. Charter skeptics often point out that the American Bill of Rights did not prevent the government of the United States from taking the same action against Japanese-Americans that our government took against Japanese-Canadians.

10   Peter H. Russell, "The Political Purposes of the Canadian Charter of Rights and Freedoms," *Canadian Bar Review* 61 (1983): 30–54.

and -financed safe drug-injection facility in Vancouver. Producing, trafficking, and possessing narcotics such as heroin and cocaine are prohibited under the federal government's Controlled Drugs and Substances Act (CDSA). A provision of that act gives the federal Minister of Health the discretion to exempt certain persons from the application of the act if "in the opinion of the Minister, the exemption is necessary for a medical or scientific purpose or is otherwise in the public interest" (section 56[1]). Acting on the assumption that drug addiction is an illness requiring medical intervention and that illicit drug use contributes to several collateral diseases such as HIV and hepatitis, community groups, with the support of provincial health authorities and a five-year exemption from the terms of the CDSA, opened the Insite safe injection facility in 2003.

When the federal government in 2008 signalled its unwillingness to renew the exemption, the courts were asked to order the federal Minister of Health to issue another exemption. Insite's supporters argued that the failure to renew the exemption violated section 7 of the Charter, which the courts have said requires any law that infringes the right to security of the person to be rationally, logically connected to a valid government objective and to operate in a manner that does not disproportionately burden an individual.

The Supreme Court's 2011 decision hinges mainly on an assessment of social fact evidence that drug addiction is an illness to which medical intervention is the most appropriate response, that Insite's operations have reduced collateral health effects of drug addiction in downtown Vancouver, and that they have had no discernible effect on increased drug abuse or crime. As the court pithily put it in its unanimous decision, "Insite saves lives."[11] It gave little weight to arguments that legitimate criminal law objectives in the control of illicit drug abuse are impaired by the operation of such facilities and that the use and abuse of drugs are decisions for which users are properly held criminally responsible. (The court did not consider an implication of its ruling: that the potential ill-health effects of contraband drugs imply a government role in regulating the strength and quality of illicit drugs that users consume.) More important, it considered that such determinations are not properly the subject of normal democratic debate, creating the impression that reasonable people reading the Charter could not but conclude that a ministerial refusal to authorize the operation of the injection facility violates users' rights to "security of the person" under section 7 of the Charter. Charter critics contend that such policy issues are precisely the sorts of matters on which reasonable people can and do disagree, and that these matters

---

11   *Canada (Attorney General) v. PHS Community Services Society*, 2011 SCC 44 at para. 133.

should be left to the cut and thrust of democratic electoral debate rather than to the decisions of nine jurists.

5.6 The Notwithstanding Clause

Though objections to the Charter did not block the adoption of that document, they were not without impact. Prime Minister Trudeau was able to get the Charter passed only by agreeing to an important concession: the inclusion of section 33, the **notwithstanding clause**.

Section 33 provides that Parliament or a provincial legislature may pass a law and declare it to be valid "notwithstanding" (i.e., in spite of) the guarantees offered by sections 2 and 7–15 of the Charter. Such a declaration renders the legislation immune to judicial review under those sections for a period of five years. At the end of that period, the declaration may be renewed for another five years, and Parliament or a legislature may renew such a declaration as many times as it wishes. The provision is not without precedent. The 1960 Bill of Rights contained a similar clause.

The notwithstanding clause has vigorous partisans and equally vigorous detractors. For those who share Sterling Lyon's reservations about the Charter, section 33 is a flexible instrument that allows us to combine judicial review with parliamentary supremacy: the courts may use the Charter to invalidate legislation, but when Parliament or a legislature think the judges' decision is wrong, they may use section 33 to reserve the final word for themselves.[12] From the point of view of those who oppose the notwithstanding clause, however, section 33 is a regrettable measure because it seriously compromises the efficacy of the Charter and thus weakens the protection of human rights in Canada. Brian Mulroney once expressed this view in its extreme form when he claimed that section 33 meant that "the Charter is not worth the paper it's printed on."[13]

Mulroney's claim is certainly an exaggeration. The historical record suggests that the notwithstanding clause has had little impact on the effectiveness of the Charter. Section 33 has been invoked only three times. In 1982, the Parti Québécois government of René Lévesque applied it to all Quebec legislation

---

12   Note that section 33 may be used pre-emptively to forestall judicial review rather than simply to react to an adverse court ruling.

13   Peter H. Russell, "The Notwithstanding Clause: The Charter's Homage to Parliamentary Democracy," *Policy Options*, February 1, 2007, http://policyoptions.irpp.org/issues/the-charter-25/the-notwithstanding-clause-the-charters-homage-to-parliamentary-democracy/.

as a means of showing its disapproval of CA 1982, an act that the Quebec National Assembly has still not endorsed. Several years later, the government of Saskatchewan applied the notwithstanding clause to a piece of labour legislation. Then, in 1988, after the Supreme Court declared the French-only sign provisions of Quebec's Bill 101 unconstitutional, the government of that province passed a new version of that legislation, Bill 178, and shielded it from subsequent judicial review by invoking section 33.

The use of the notwithstanding clause in this third case met with hearty approval among francophone Quebeckers, but many anglophone Canadians thought it scandalous that the Quebec government could use section 33 to do something the Supreme Court had declared a violation of rights. Though English Canadians had been almost completely indifferent about the notwithstanding clause when it had been used by the government of Saskatchewan, they now came to see it as a serious defect in the Constitution. As a result, it is now extremely difficult for a government to use section 33 because Canadians (especially English Canadians) tend to interpret such an act not as an assertion of parliamentary supremacy but as an attack on their beloved Charter. In 2005, for instance, opponents of same-sex marriages called on politicians to use section 33 to prevent the judiciary from using the Charter to legalize such marriages. Though most members of the Conservative Party opposed same-sex marriage, party leader Stephen Harper was careful to rule out the use of the notwithstanding clause. While not personally opposed to the principle of section 33, Mr. Harper recognized that a stated willingness to use it would, rightly or wrongly, allow his political rivals to paint the Conservatives as enemies of the Charter—a portrait that might be disastrous for his party. For better or for worse, then, it appears that Canadians are unlikely to see federal parliamentarians use the notwithstanding clause, at least in the foreseeable future.

Indeed, given the high regard Canadians have for the courts and the Charter, a constitutional convention may have developed against the use of section 33. In *R. v. Daviault* (1994), the Supreme Court declared that extreme intoxication akin to automatism could render someone unable to form the mental intent necessary for conviction in a serious sexual assault prosecution. Many Canadians were outraged, thinking that getting drunk before committing sexual assault would be a way to escape criminal justice. Many, including former NDP leader Ed Broadbent, called for Parliament to pass a law to reverse the decision and protect it from further Charter challenge by use of section 33. Even in these propitious circumstances, section 33 was not used. Like the powers of reservation and disallowance discussed in Chapter Three, section 33 may now be a dead letter.

5.7 Section 1

Canadians who are concerned about preserving the sanctity and integrity of Charter rights have relatively little to worry about in section 33. Yet rights can be limited in another way. **Section 1** of the Charter reads as follows:

> The *Canadian Charter of Rights and Freedoms* guarantees the rights and freedoms set out in it subject only to such reasonable limits prescribed by law as can be demonstrably justified in a free and democratic society.

Section 1 appears to be at odds with itself. It begins by "guaranteeing" the rights set down in the rest of the Charter, but it then concedes that the enjoyment of those rights shall be subject to such limitations as are "demonstrably justified in a free and democratic society." That concession has the effect of enabling the courts to permit limitations on the rights guaranteed by the Charter, and experience has shown that the courts are willing to do this on a regular basis. It may seem odd that our Charter should include such a mechanism for limiting rights, but the framers of that document had good reasons for writing section 1 the way they did. It is generally accepted that no right is absolute. Rights conflict, and decisions must be made about their order of value. Moreover, in any political order, rights must sometimes be limited for the sake of the common good. For instance, though we believe we have a right to freedom of speech, we recognize that in a free and democratic society it is perfectly reasonable to pass laws prohibiting speech of a libellous or slanderous character, or to prohibit false advertising. We would therefore not want our Charter of Rights to entrench a freedom of speech so general or absolute as to make libel and slander laws unconstitutional. Section 1 was included in the Charter to resolve this type of problem.

Negotiating these "reasonable" limits is all the more necessary in the case of some of the modern rights contained in the Charter. Modern rights such as mobility rights, language rights, and robust equality rights pose difficulties for courts not only because they are novel but because it is hard to hold that they ought to be enjoyed absolutely. For example, section 6 of the Charter says that "Every citizen of Canada has the right to enter, remain in and leave Canada." Does this mean that a citizen hiding in Canada to escape a murder he or she committed in the United States cannot be extradited to face justice in that country? Of course not. Mobility rights may be good things, but they cannot be enjoyed absolutely. They are properly and reasonably subject to limitation. Section 1 effectively turns most Charter cases into a two-stage process. In the first stage, the courts must decide whether the legislation in question violates one of the rights guaranteed by the Charter. If it does, the courts must then ask whether that violation is a reasonable limitation of the right in question under the terms of section 1. If the section 1 question is answered in the negative, then the legislation is deemed unconstitutional. If it is answered in the affirmative, however, the legislation is "saved" by section 1, despite the fact that it violates a Charter right.

In the 1986 case of *R. v. Oakes*, the Supreme Court of Canada developed a systematic procedure for adjudicating section 1 questions. A brief examination of *Oakes* will provide an excellent introduction to the meaning and significance of this section of the Charter.

David Edwin Oakes was arrested by police officers who found eight one-gram vials of hashish oil in his possession. Section 8 of the Narcotic Control Act stipulated that, once a court has determined that an individual was in possession of illegal narcotics, the burden of proof would then be on that individual to demonstrate that he or she was not in possession of them for the purpose of trafficking. Thus, if Oakes could not prove that he had no plans to sell the narcotics found in his possession, he would have been found guilty not merely of possession but of the far more serious offence of drug trafficking. Oakes protested that it should have been up to the Crown to prove him guilty of trafficking and not up to him to prove his innocence. To make his case, he argued that section 8 of the Narcotic Control Act was unconstitutional because it violated section 11(d) of the Charter, which guarantees the right to be "presumed innocent until proven guilty." The court had little trouble concluding that this section of the act was in violation of section 11(d) of the Charter, but it was then obliged to consider whether the Narcotic Control Act might not be "saved" as a reasonable limitation of section 11(d) by virtue of section 1.

In order to tackle this question rationally, the court began by establishing a general procedure for section 1 questions. The court argued that a law in violation of some Charter right could be saved under section 1 only if it met two tests. The first concerned the purpose or objective of the law: a law must be a response to a "pressing and substantial" problem in order to justify overriding a Charter right. The second concerned "proportionality," that is, the suitability of the means used to pursue the law's objective. The court said it would use three criteria when applying that test. First, are the means rational and non-arbitrary? Second, do the means impair the right in question as little as possible? Might there be other ways of achieving the same objective without limiting Charter rights? Third, is the good that will be achieved by these means sufficient to outweigh the deleterious effects they will have on those individuals or groups whose rights are being set aside?

With this framework in place, the court was able to consider Oakes's claim in a reasonable and systematic fashion. The judges easily concluded that section 8 of the Narcotic Control Act met the first test. The purpose of the provision was to allow the government to suppress the illicit drug trade, and the court accepted that this was a "substantial and pressing" concern, one of "sufficient importance to warrant overriding a constitutionally protected right." When it came to the second test, however, they were not as indulgent. Writing for the majority, Chief Justice Brian Dickson argued that the means for fighting the drug trade contemplated in section 8 of the Narcotic Control Act could not meet the first criterion of being rational and non-arbitrary. According to the court, the Criminal Code provision suggests that possession of an amount of drugs was a basic fact from which the presumed fact of possession for the purposes of trafficking was inferred. But it is not rational to infer a trafficking intent from the possession of *any* amount of drugs. Such an inference is rational only in cases of possession of large amounts. As it is structured, the law provides no rational connection between its objective and the means Parliament uses to achieve this objective. The court therefore concluded that section 8 of the act could not be saved under section 1, and they declared it to be unconstitutional. Oakes was thus innocent of the charge of drug trafficking.[14]

Although in *Oakes* the Supreme Court decided that section 1 could not be used to save section 8 of the Narcotic Control Act, the interpretive framework developed in that case has been applied in many others with the opposite result. A number of laws that violate some Charter right have been able to pass the **Oakes test** and have thus been upheld under section 1 as "reasonable limitations" of the Charter. In the 2001 case *R. v. Sharpe*, for example, the Supreme Court held that, although criminal code restrictions on the distribution of child pornography constitute a limitation of freedom of expression (section 2[b]), most of the law could be upheld as a reasonable limitation on that section. Using the *Oakes* test, the court ruled that it is important to protect children from exploitation and that the measures in the law restricting distribution of child pornography were a suitable means for achieving that end.

Experience has shown that over the years it is the "minimal impairment" branch of the proportionality step of the *Oakes* test that has done most of the rights–limitation work. Courts have often invalidated laws not because the goals of the laws were illegitimate but because the means the legislature chose to attain those objectives limited rights to a degree in excess of what was necessary to do so.

---

14   See *R. v. Oakes*, 1986 1 SCR 103.

5.8 The Political Impact of the Charter

The adoption of a constitutionally entrenched charter of rights has substantially altered the structure of the Canadian regime. The most obvious change is the fact that courts now decide many questions that were formerly decided by governments and legislatures. In other words, the Charter has made judges more powerful and more active political players. Numerous examples of this change could be cited. We shall limit ourselves here to a few of the most celebrated.

In 1988, the Supreme Court of Canada handed down one of its most famous Charter decisions, *R. v. Morgentaler.* This case dealt with the politically explosive issue of abortion. Parliament had legislated what it thought was a compromise solution to the abortion issue: abortions were made an offence under the Criminal Code unless they were performed in accredited hospitals for medical reasons as determined by a therapeutic abortion committee. The law was challenged by Dr. Henry Morgentaler, who sought an unrestricted right to perform abortions in his own clinics. In *Morgentaler*, the Supreme Court held by a 5–2 vote that Parliament's law was a violation of section 7 of the Charter and that it could not be sustained under section 1. Significantly, the court's position was quite fragmented. Four separate opinions were written. One claimed that the law should be struck down on the grounds that section 7 made it unconstitutional to restrict abortions except, perhaps, in the latest stages of pregnancy. Two other opinions suggested that the law was unconstitutional but only because its specific regulations were in one way or another procedurally unfair. Contrary to the first three opinions, the fourth claimed that the law should be upheld. In this opinion, it was argued that the government had every right to regulate abortion and that the specific terms of the law in question were not tainted by a lack of procedural fairness.

Though the judges had difficulty agreeing on how to apply the Charter to abortion law, there was no ambiguity about the effect of their decision: the law was struck down, and Dr. Morgentaler was free to perform abortions in his clinics. It is worth noting that the decision in *Morgentaler* did not preclude the introduction of a new abortion law, as the majority of the judges had indicated that they would not oppose a law that was "procedurally fair." The Mulroney government proposed to Parliament a bill it thought would satisfy the judges, but it was narrowly defeated in the Senate. The Supreme Court's decision in *Morgentaler* has thus turned out to be the decisive factor in the decriminalization of abortion.

Our judges have had a significant impact on many other policy questions. In the 1988 case of **Ford v. Québec**, the Supreme Court struck down Quebec's law prohibiting signs in languages other than French. The court's decision touched off a political storm, culminating in the adoption of Bill 178 and, some would say, in the defeat of the Meech Lake Accord. In the 1985 case of *Singh v. Minister of Employment and Immigration*, the Supreme Court declared that Canada would have to change its policy on the handling of refugee claims, despite the fact that this policy had been praised by the United Nations as a model for the rest of the world. On the basis of section 7 of the Charter, the judges held that all persons claiming refugee status must be given a full hearing. The federal government was forced to introduce new regulations to comply with this judicial order, thereby creating the most open and liberal procedures in the world for the handling of refugee applications. In the 2001 case of *United States v. Burns*, the court declared that prisoners may not be extradited to states that use the death penalty unless the Minister of Justice receives assurances that the death penalty will not be sought. In so doing, the court appears to have closed the door to any future reintroduction of capital punishment as a violation of section 7 of the Charter.

When the government of Prime Minister Paul Martin contemplated legalizing same-sex marriage in 2004, it first submitted to the Supreme Court a set of questions inquiring into whether same-sex marriage is consistent with the terms of the Charter. The government also asked whether the opposite-sex requirement of marriage is consistent with the Charter, which in terms of Charter rights is the more important question. It is one thing for the Court to say that it is fine for the legislature to change the definition of marriage; it is another for a court to declare that the traditional definition is unconstitutional. The Court replied that same-sex marriage is consistent with the Charter but declined to answer the second question. The government essentially had the Court provide constitutional cover for its change of policy on marriage, highlighting how the existence of the Charter can allow politicians to disclaim responsibility for controversial policy decisions.

These cases demonstrate how the adoption of the Charter has entailed a substantial transfer of policymaking power from elected bodies to judges. The student of Canadian government is therefore compelled to pay ever closer attention to the role and conduct of our judiciary. As we shall see in Chapter Eight, some scholars now speak of the emergence in our regime of a "Court Party," a collection of interest groups who work with the judiciary to use the Charter in order to win through the courts changes they would be unlikely to win in the political arena.[15] More generally, the new policy power of courts in the Charter

---

15   F.L. Morton and Rainer Knopff, *The Charter Revolution and the Court Party* (Toronto: University of Toronto Press, 2000).

era has created pressure for a more open, accountable mechanism of judicial appointment. For generations, judicial appointment has been the secret preserve of senior government officials. As discussed in section 8.5 of this book, changes have been made, but many observers worry about whether opening up the judicial appointment process will further politicize the courts.

The adoption of the Canadian Charter of Rights and Freedoms has thus introduced a whole new range of questions for the student of Canada's regime to ponder.

Key Terms

charter of rights	*PHS Community Services Society* case
human rights codes	notwithstanding clause
Gosselin v. Québec	section 1
section 52 remedy	*Oakes* test
reading in	*R. v. Morgentaler*
Bill of Rights	*Ford v. Québec*

Discussion Questions

1. Should the notwithstanding clause be deleted from the Charter?

2. Given what you know about the Charter of Rights, what qualities would you seek in a Supreme Court justice? What sort of appointment mechanism would you recommend to ensure judges possess these qualities?

INSTITUTIONS

THE CROWN AND ITS SERVANTS

Have you ever noticed how experts speak of the Obama "administration" but of the Trudeau "government"? The source of this difference in terminology lies in the distinction between the principle of separation of powers and the principle of responsible government, as described in Chapter Three. A constitutional order that divides power into formally distinct legislative and executive "branches" will have an executive branch that can be called the "administration" because its constitutional authority is limited to "executing" (i.e., administering) the laws. In regimes based on the principle of responsible government, however, there are no "branches." Instead, we have a "government" that exercises both legislative and executive power. This government is a complex web of interrelated institutions and offices: the Crown, the prime minister, the cabinet, and the civil service. Our purpose in this chapter is to explain what those institutions are and how they are related.

6.1 The Crown

We have seen that the preamble to CA 1867 stipulates that Canada is to have "a Constitution similar in principle to that of the United Kingdom." This implies that, in Canada as in Britain, governmental power is technically in the hands of the "Crown" and that our head of state is the reigning queen or king. To understand this fact, we should keep in mind the peculiar evolution of British constitutional practice. Centuries ago, when Britain was a full-fledged monarchy, all governmental power was vested in the Crown. Over time, in response to the demands of their people for a more democratic regime, British monarchs began to delegate certain of their powers to other officials or bodies. Legislative power was delegated to the body that came to be known as Parliament. Today, Parliament is the real seat of legislative power. Yet even today Parliament's decisions do not have the force of law until they have received royal assent, which indicates that the legislative power is still technically, in part, a power of the Crown. The same is true of executive power. As early as the seventeenth century, British monarchs began to delegate the Crown's executive power to a prime minister and cabinet. Today, the prime minister and cabinet have virtually complete control of executive power. In principle, however, this power remains a power of the Crown, and those who exercise it are deemed to do so as servants of His or Her Majesty. Their executive decisions are, in principle, merely "advice" to the Crown and have no force or effect until they receive royal assent. The British regime is thus described as a **constitutional monarchy**, a regime that is monarchical by law but democratic by convention. The Canadian Constitution is very much like the British Constitution on this point.

Section 9 of CA 1867 stipulates that "The Executive Government and Authority of and over Canada is hereby declared to continue and be vested in the Queen." Of course, the Queen would no more exercise this executive power of government here in Canada than she does in Britain. By constitutional convention, she delegates her executive power to certain elected representatives of the people—the prime minister and cabinet. In law, however, the executive power of government is a power of the Crown. In other words, all executive decisions must have the assent of the Crown and must be carried out in the Crown's name. This explains why those who prosecute criminals in Canada are called "Crown Attorneys" and why the cases they prosecute have names such as *R. v. Oakes* (the "R" here stands for *Regina*, Latin for "Queen"). Queen Elizabeth was not personally involved in the trial of David Oakes; rather, when the officials of the Department of Justice prosecuted him, they were exercising executive power that had been delegated to the department by the Queen.

A similar pattern is evident in the way the Canadian Constitution deals with legislative power. Section 17 of CA 1867 establishes that Canada shall have a Parliament consisting of "the Queen, an Upper House styled the Senate, and the House of Commons." The Constitution does not spell out the role of each of these three elements in the legislative process; these are covered by the preamble's reference to British constitutional practice. In the case of legislative power, the Queen asks Her parliament to send Her bills for Her consideration. These bills do not become law until they have obtained royal assent and are "proclaimed" by the Crown. Royal assent is still necessary for any bill to become law, but in order to guarantee the triumph of the democratic principle, a convention has evolved stipulating that royal assent cannot be withheld.

These constitutional arrangements appear to be exceedingly complicated. Yet, as we shall explain in section 6.3 below, there are important reasons for constructing our regime this way.

6.2 The Governor General

The powers, rights, and privileges of the Canadian Crown are vested in the queen or king of Canada. Our monarch is by law the same person who serves as monarch of Britain, but it is important to note that this person is serving in two distinct positions. One might say that Elizabeth II wears a number of different crowns: a British crown, a Canadian crown, an Australian crown, and so on. She is a monarch with many dominions. The important point is that, with respect to Canada, she is the **Queen of Canada**.

Now because Canada's monarch is also a British monarch who resides principally in Britain, it is practically impossible for her (or him) to reign actively here in Canada. Therefore, section 10 of CA 1867 provides that the monarch shall have a permanent representative in this country, the governor general.[1] Given that the governor general is the monarch's representative in Canada, she or he is technically the one who appoints this official. The term of office is generally five to seven years.

In the early years of Confederation, when Canada was not yet entirely independent of Britain, the governor general was seen as the British government's representative in this country. Our first governors general were therefore always British nobles, appointed by the queen or king on the recommendation of the British government. After World War I, the advice of the Canadian prime minister

---

1 The role of the governor general is played by the lieutenant governors in the provincial governments.

was sought as well. Only in 1952 did the Crown begin to appoint Canadian citizens to the position. At first, our prime ministers recommended non-political figures such as diplomats Vincent Massey (1952–59) and Jules Léger (1974–79) or the distinguished military leader Georges Vanier (1959–67). There followed a period in which the tendency was to appoint retired politicians, including Ed Schreyer (1979–84), Jeanne Sauvé (1984–90), Ray Hnatyshyn (1990–95), and Roméo LeBlanc (1995–99). More recently, the trend has been to appoint media celebrities such as Adrienne Clarkson (1999–2005) and Michaëlle Jean (2005–10). Governor General David Johnston, appointed in 2010, is a former university president.

There are obvious advantages in appointing former politicians: because the governor general is responsible for some potentially significant political decisions, it makes sense to appoint people with political experience. On the other hand, there are also some disadvantages to nominating politicians for the office. Three of the four governors general who had been politicians—Sauvé, Hnatyshyn, and LeBlanc—had served as cabinet ministers with or under the prime minister who nominated them. The danger in such appointments is that they may be perceived as partisan, or even "patronage," appointments. Such a perception is prejudicial to the dignity and independence of the office.

6.3 The Functions of the Governor General

In terms of constitutional law, the governor general, as the Crown's representative in Canada, has very extensive powers. By constitutional convention, however, most of that power is exercised by other officials. Though the Crown has to assent to any exercise of legislative power, it is well established that the governor general must approve any bill that is passed by Parliament. And although executive power is explicitly granted to the Crown in section 9 of CA 1867, section 11 stipulates that the governor general shall have certain official "advisers"—the prime minister and cabinet. By constitutional convention, the Crown's executive power is used only on the "advice" of these democratically elected officials.[2] Because cabinet decisions are in legal terms "advice" to the Crown, the governor general

---

2   The governor general would refuse to follow the advice of a prime minister on the exercise of executive power only if the prime minister attempted to offer advice after having lost the confidence of the House. After his clear defeat in the 1896 elections, Prime Minister Charles Tupper tried to take advantage of his last few days in office to have the Governor General, Lord Aberdeen, appoint a number of senators and judges. The Governor General refused on the grounds that Tupper did not have the confidence of the House and therefore had no mandate to offer such advice.

must always be kept well advised of cabinet's activities and intentions. On behalf of the cabinet, the prime minister meets regularly with the governor general to keep him or her abreast of the government's plans. Although in theory it is the governor general who is being advised by the prime minister, it is sometimes true that the prime minister will take advantage of these sessions to seek advice privately on matters that cannot be discussed with cabinet colleagues or other advisers. As the Crown's representative in the regime, and one whose impartiality cannot be questioned, the governor general is occasionally a useful sounding board for a prime minister with a difficult problem.

Because the Crown no longer has any meaningful legislative or executive power, the office of governor general is sometimes referred to in colloquial terms as a mere "rubber stamp." While it is true that he or she normally exercises no legislative or executive power of any great consequence, the governor general nonetheless plays two important roles in the Canadian regime: guardian of responsible government and representative for the Queen, our **head of state**.

We saw in Chapter Three that our system of responsible government is rather complicated. We do not directly elect anyone to run our governments; we elect parliaments out of which democratically accountable governments must be constructed. Those governments do not simply construct themselves. The one indispensable role of the governor general is to serve as the **guardian of responsible government**, the official who ensures that we have a government that enjoys the confidence of the House. Governors general carry out this function through the use of various **reserve powers** (powers they reserve the right to use on their own initiative).

One reserve power is the power to appoint the prime minister. Because the voters do not elect a prime minister, it is essential to give someone the authority to appoint one when the position is vacant. In Canada, that person is the governor general. We must remember that the governor general's choice is governed by one single criterion: the prime minister will be the person whose government has the best chance of commanding the confidence of the House of Commons. Historically, that choice has been so easy that almost anyone could be entrusted to make it. Canada has highly disciplined political parties and an electoral system that usually gives one of those parties a majority of seats. If a prime minister resigns because the electorate has given a different party a majority of seats, the leader of that other party is the obvious choice for prime minister. And even where no party has a majority, if a prime minister resigns, it has thus far in our history always been obvious who the alternative is. Still, it is conceivable that parliamentary elections could produce a fragmented House of Commons in which no party has a majority of seats and it is not evident which party is most likely to lead a minority government. In such a situation, the governor general's power to name the prime minister would be essential to the smooth functioning of responsible government.

A second reserve power is the power to dismiss a prime minister who attempts to govern without the confidence of the House of Commons. This power has never been used at the federal level and has not been used by a lieutenant governor at the provincial level since the beginning of the twentieth century. Still, the power does exist and is essential to the proper functioning of responsible government. Without it, there would be no way to prevent a prime minister and cabinet from clinging to office when, under the rules of responsible government, they are supposed to resign or ask for elections. The fact that this second reserve power is used so infrequently is more a proof of its efficacy than its irrelevance. If the governor general did not have it, we would quickly regret its absence.

A third reserve power is the power to prorogue Parliament or to dissolve Parliament and call elections. Normally, the governor general accepts whatever advice is given by the prime minister in these matters, yet there have been occasions when such advice has been refused. In 1926, Prime Minister Mackenzie King, realizing that his minority government was about to be defeated on a motion censuring the government for corruption, asked Governor General Lord Byng to dissolve Parliament and call new elections. Byng refused, instead calling upon Arthur Meighen, the Conservative leader, to form a new ministry. There is a great deal of disagreement as to whether Byng's decision was a good one,[3] but there is no doubt that the governor general needs the reserve power to refuse dissolution when a prime minister is about to lose Parliament's confidence and there is, in the judgement of the governor general, a clear alternative choice for prime minister in the House.

This relatively obscure point of constitutional procedure came to the country's attention in a major parliamentary controversy in December 2008. When the Liberals, NDP, and Bloc announced their intention to vote non-confidence in the Conservative government and offer a Liberal-NDP coalition to replace it, there was some speculation that Mr. Harper might attempt to prevent such a move by asking Governor General Michaëlle Jean for a dissolution (and therefore an election) if the House expressed a lack of confidence in his government. Because a general election had been held a mere two months earlier and the Liberal leader Stéphane Dion would obviously have the confidence of the House, the Governor General would almost certainly have been correct to refuse any request from Mr. Harper for

---

3   See J.R. Mallory, *The Structure of Canadian Government* (Toronto: Gage Publishing, 1984), 52–55.

a dissolution. Instead, Mr. Harper blocked the opposition's strategy by asking the Governor General to prorogue Parliament (i.e., declare a temporary recess) for six weeks. Some observers argued that the Governor General should have refused this request on the grounds that Mr. Harper was merely trying to prevent the opposition from exercising its right to express non-confidence. The Governor General ultimately granted this request to prorogue, probably because Mr. Harper was merely postponing the vote, not preventing it.

An interesting question about the reserve powers arose in 2015. A number of officials—including senators—are appointed by the governor general on the advice of the prime minister. Frustrated at his inability to reform the Senate, Prime Minister Harper adopted the tactic of simply refusing to recommend the appointment of any new senators. At one point, approximately one-fifth of the Senate's seats had become vacant. Mr. Harper's strategy appeared to be to force action on Senate reform by slowly rendering that body inoperative. At least one constitutional scholar argued at the time that the governor general has the reserve power to make appointments to the Senate independently if a prime minister continues to refuse to carry out this constitutional duty and provide the governor general with recommendations.[4]

Although wielding the reserve powers is the most essential function of the governor general, the most common functions of the office are ceremonial. As the official representative for the Queen, our head of state, the governor general represents the Crown in a number of ways. First, the governor general must preside over important political ceremonies, such as the opening of Parliament, and represents Canada at a wide variety of events where official representation is necessary—welcoming certain foreign dignitaries, presenting awards, and attending state funerals in foreign countries. Of particular note is the fact that the governor general is the official head of our armed forces.

The governor general's role as de facto head of state frees the prime minister to concentrate more fully on the business of governing. More important, however, is the symbolic value of having someone other than the prime minister serve as the highest representative of our regime. In his influential book *The Crown in Canada*,[5] Frank MacKinnon argues that the Crown strengthens democracy insofar as the ceremonial work of the governor general is a constant reminder to politicians that they are servants of the Crown (and hence servants of

---

4   Adam Dodek, "Harper's Constitutional Disobedience a Dangerous Game to Play," *Globe and Mail*, July 27, 2015.

5   Frank MacKinnon, *The Crown in Canada* (Calgary: Glenbow-Alberta Institute, 1976).

the people) rather than political masters. Because the office of governor general stands above party politics, it represents all the people of Canada rather than just those who voted for the party in power. This gives the citizens of the regime (and its military) a non-partisan focus for their loyalty. They can be loyal to the regime, as embodied in the governor general, without necessarily supporting the politicians who run the government at any given point in time.

6.4 The Cabinet

As we saw in Chapter Three, the real seat of government power in a system of responsible government is a body known as the "cabinet." In constitutional practice (as opposed to constitutional law), this cabinet exercises executive power. The cabinet also has decisive control over legislative power, especially in situations of majority government. But what, exactly, is the cabinet, and what is the constitutional basis of its power?

To answer these questions, we must turn, once again, to the text of the Constitution. Section 11 of CA 1867 creates a body called the **Queen's Privy Council for Canada**, which is given the all-important right to "advise" the governor general in the exercise of his or her powers. As "advisers," the privy councillors are, strictly speaking, mere servants of the Crown. As we have seen, however, under the rules of responsible government, "advice" given to the governor general is the equivalent of an order. The Queen's Privy Council for Canada is thus a very powerful body, for it controls virtually all those powers granted by the Constitution to the Crown or the governor general.

Section 11 states that the privy councillors are appointed by the governor general, but constitutional convention stipulates that the governor general will make these appointments on the "advice" of the person he or she has asked to serve as prime minister. Although the Constitution does allow for the possibility that the governor general might "remove" a member of the Privy Council, appointments to that body are, in practice, appointments for life. This means that the Privy Council includes every living person who has ever been named to that body. Privy councillors nominated by former prime ministers Chrétien, Martin, and Harper are thus still members of the Privy Council.

Of course, in a democratic regime, it would be unthinkable to have privy councillors who had been nominated by a defeated government continue to exercise political power. We therefore have a convention stipulating that the power to "advise" the governor general will be exercised only by a small subset of privy councillors: those who have been nominated by (and have maintained the confidence of) the current prime minister. It is this subset of the Privy Council that we call the "cabinet," and we may therefore define the cabinet as those privy councillors who have the power to advise the Crown. The size of the cabinet is determined by the prime minister. Mulroney's cabinet had as many as 40 ministers, and Chrétien's had as few as 28. The cabinet appointed after the 2015 election had 30 members in addition to the prime minister.[6] A number of MPs will also be appointed **parliamentary secretaries** to these ministers. A parliamentary secretary will sometimes answer questions in the House on behalf of a minister and generally serves as a kind of assistant or even apprentice to the minister. Indeed, the position of parliamentary secretary is frequently used as a way of auditioning newer MPs for subsequent promotion to cabinet.

Though it is technically correct to refer to the members of the cabinet as privy councillors, it is more common to call them "ministers." This is because most members of the cabinet will spend most of their time "advising" the Crown on the work of one of its "ministries" or departments. For instance, the Minister of Natural Resources will spend most of his or her time developing new policy for that ministry and ensuring that existing policy is being executed effectively and efficiently. (More will be said about this work in section 6.8 below.)

But the cabinet is much more than a collection of individual ministers. An essential element of our system of responsible government is the principle of **collective responsibility**—the idea that cabinet must function *as a team* to develop, implement, and take responsibility for public policy. This principle follows logically from the conventions of responsible government: it is not individual ministers who must maintain the confidence of the House or resign; it is the cabinet (including the prime minister) as a whole. To the extent that it is the cabinet that has the mandate to govern, rather than a collection of individuals, responsibility for the exercise of power must logically rest with the cabinet as a team rather than with individual ministers.

The principle of collective responsibility means that whenever ministers have an idea for new legislation in their area, their proposal must win the approval of the cabinet before it can be taken to Parliament. It also means that certain important executive decisions (e.g., which of several companies should be awarded a lucrative contract to build fighter jets) will be made by the cabinet as a whole rather than by the single minister in charge of that area. For reasons outlined in sections 6.5 and 6.7 of this book, it is increasingly the case that executive and legislative decisions requiring cabinet approval are, in fact, being made by cabinet committees or even by the prime minister. Under the principles of

---

6   The membership of the current cabinet is listed on the website of the prime minister: http://www.pm.gc.ca.

responsible government, such practice is legitimate only to the extent that those making the decisions have a mandate to speak for the cabinet.

Under the doctrine of collective responsibility, any decision made by the cabinet as a whole must be defended by each and every one of its members, and, by convention, a cabinet minister who is not prepared to defend a position taken by cabinet must resign. This explains why cabinet discussions must always be confidential and secret. Ministers have to be able to debate proposed measures freely and vigorously before they decide on them, but they would not be able to defend a cabinet decision in public if it were revealed that they had spoken against it in the course of cabinet deliberations.[7]

Because the cabinet plays such a central role in the exercise of political power, it is essential that it be as representative of the country as possible. By tradition, it will have at least one member from each of the country's ten provinces, with the possible exception of Prince Edward Island. The various regions of the country are normally represented in some sort of proportion to their population, but deviations will occur if particular regions have elected few government members. There must be a representative number of French Canadians. It is also important to ensure strong representation for women and at least some representation for those Canadians who are visible minorities. The formation of the cabinet must, in the final analysis, take into consideration the way in which Canadians identify the fundamentally important political distinctions of provinces, regions, ethnicity, and gender. Prime Minister Justin Trudeau appointed a cabinet in 2015 that includes representation from every province and from one of the territories. He also made a point of trying to select a cabinet that would "look like Canada" in that it included record numbers of MPs who are either Indigenous Canadians or members of visible minority groups. Finally, Mr. Trudeau has made history by having the first cabinet to achieve gender parity: 15 of his 30 ministers are women. Some critics pointed out, however, that 5 of the 15 women were merely **ministers of state**, that is, ministers who do not head a ministry themselves but have responsibility for a specific area of policy within a ministry headed by someone else.[8]

---

7   In an attempt to appear more "democratic," BC Premier Gordon Campbell occasionally held televised cabinet meetings when he was first elected. The kindest interpretation one can give to this kind of exercise is to characterize it as token. No meaningful cabinet decision could ever be made publicly because cabinet ministers could not make serious criticisms of proposals during the meeting and then defend them publicly afterwards.

8   All of the men in the Trudeau cabinet are full ministers.

6.5 The Cabinet Committee System

In Canada's first century, the cabinet could handle its business by meeting once a week, usually on Friday afternoons. By the 1960s, however, the growth of the welfare state had expanded the workload of governments dramatically. This expansion was reflected in the fact that the cabinet had grown from 12 ministers under Sir John A. Macdonald to over 30 under Pierre Trudeau. Because of the volume of business to be conducted, as well as the number of participants involved, the traditional cabinet meeting was no longer an adequate forum for making the kinds of decisions that it needed to make. For this reason, Prime Ministers Pearson and Trudeau developed a system of cabinet committees that revolutionized the way cabinet does its business.

Each prime minister has the authority to organize the cabinet committee system however he or she likes, and since the Pearson/Trudeau years, a number of substantially different models have been used. It therefore makes little sense to describe any particular model in detail, but each of the systems we have seen thus far is characterized by a number of essential features.

The basic idea of the system is to divide the cabinet's work and assign it to a number of smaller groups—the cabinet committees. The cabinet's work is done more efficiently because five groups of six people can do five times as much work in an hour as one group of 30 people. Most cabinet committee systems will be composed of between 5 and 12 such committees, which are usually organized around a particular policy area (for instance, economic development or social policy). Each committee will study all of the problems or questions that arise in its particular area and make recommendations to the full cabinet. For the system to function, the cabinet must normally approve a committee's recommendations without too much debate; otherwise, it would end up doing the committee's work all over again. Still, individual ministers who are not members of the committee have every right to raise questions and objections at the cabinet level and sometimes succeed in having questions sent back to the committee for further study. Most cabinet committee systems have contained one "super-committee," usually called the Priorities and Planning Committee. Chaired by the prime minister, this committee is usually responsible for determining the broad lines of government policy.

Justin Trudeau's cabinet has nine committees. Priorities and Planning has become the "Agenda and Results Committee." There are new committees focused on areas such as diversity and inclusion, world and public security, environment and climate change, growth and innovation, and parliamentary affairs. As always, the **Treasury Board** is a cabinet committee that oversees personnel, administrative, and expenditure management.[9]

6.6 The Prime Minister

Canadians know that the prime minister is the most powerful political figure in our regime, yet very few of us understand the basis for this power. Our written Constitution gives us little help in this regard. The office of prime minister is not mentioned in CA 1867, and it is mentioned only in passing in CA 1982. Thus, the powers of the prime minister are all based on constitutional convention. Let us think for a minute about the title of the office: the "prime" minister is literally the "first" minister. This title makes sense because, in seeking out a group of advisers, the governor general first names a prime minister, who then offers advice on the appointment of the other ministers.

It is this right to advise the Crown on the assignment of cabinet posts that constitutes the core of the prime minister's power. We have seen that, in a regime based on responsible government, the cabinet is the centre of legislative and executive power. The office of prime minister carries with it no specific departmental responsibilities (although prime ministers will sometimes reserve a specific ministry for themselves).[10] The fact that they control the membership of the cabinet gives prime ministers a tremendous amount of influence over all the other members of that most powerful body. Ministers who prove to be a thorn in the side of their prime minister may well be demoted to a less attractive portfolio or dropped from the cabinet altogether. Conversely, ministers who support the prime minister's views may improve their chances of promotion to a more important cabinet post. As a result, few ministers are willing to resist a prime minister when he or she has strong opinions on some question.

Prime ministers chair the meetings of the cabinet, and this function provides them with an important opportunity to exercise their leadership. Because the

---

9   The organization of the cabinet and its committees is at the discretion of the prime minister. For the latest organization of the cabinet and its committees, see the website of the prime minister: http://www.pm.gc.ca/sites/pm/files/docs/Cab_committee-comite.pdf.

10   Reserving a ministry for the prime minister was done frequently in the first century of Confederation. Prime Minister John A. Macdonald, for example, was also the Minister of Justice. Justin Trudeau assigned himself ministerial responsibility for intergovernmental affairs and for youth.

cabinet has to act together as a team, its decisions must be based on consensus. One of the prime minister's tasks is to cultivate this consensus. In order to succeed at this task, prime ministers need great skill; they must know when to postpone discussion and when to continue it; when to paper over disagreements and when to have them argued out; and, above all, when and how to use their own influence to settle a particularly divisive question. Moreover, it is up to the prime minister to determine whether consensus has been reached (there is no formal voting in cabinet) and to define what the consensus is. This prerogative is another source of significant political influence.

The other major task of the prime minister is to serve as the leading spokesperson for the cabinet. Individual ministers take responsibility for public relations in most matters relevant to their particular departments. If the issue is a particularly important one, however, the prime minister will often be the person who makes the cabinet's case to the public. This is especially true during election campaigns, when the public's attention is focused almost exclusively on the prime minister and the leaders of the opposition parties.

In addition to their right to advise the governor general on the composition of the cabinet, Canada's prime ministers wield a number of other specific powers. The most important of these are the right to advise the governor general on the dissolution of Parliament and the holding of elections; the right to advise the governor general on a number of key appointments, including appointments to the Senate and to the judiciary; and the right to organize the machinery of government, including the number and composition of departments and the nature of the cabinet committee system.

Prime ministers have a number of people who help them in the performance of their duties. First are the members of the **Prime Minister's Office (PMO)**. Originally, the PMO was a small secretariat that took responsibility for organizing the prime minister's schedule, answering mail, and other routine tasks. The office was greatly expanded by Prime Ministers Pierre Trudeau and Mulroney. Today's PMO has a staff well in excess of 100; it is responsible for monitoring the general political situation and giving the prime minister political advice. The members of the staff (led by either a "Principal Secretary" or a "Chief of Staff") are for the most part partisan political activists rather than career civil servants.

Just the opposite is true of a second secretariat, the **Privy Council Office (PCO)**, which is staffed by non-partisan career civil servants. As its name suggests, the PCO serves as a secretariat to the cabinet and is thus responsible to the chair of the cabinet, the prime minister. The PCO facilitates the collective work of the cabinet by organizing and providing logistical support for its meetings and its committees. It has also, since the 1970s, served as an agency that can give policy advice to the prime minister and cabinet (as distinct from the political advice that emanates from the PMO). The PCO is headed by the Clerk of the Privy Council, who is the highest ranking civil servant in the country.

Prime ministers are usually assisted in their duties by a **deputy prime minister**, a member of the cabinet who has a portfolio of his or her own but who also serves as a kind of second in command to the prime minister. Through most of our history, being deputy prime minister conferred little real power. At most, it meant filling in for the prime minister when he or she was absent or indisposed. Under Prime Minister Mulroney, however, the position of deputy prime minister became more significant. Mr. Mulroney actually delegated much of his day-to-day work to his deputy, Don Mazankowski, in order to free himself to concentrate on two or three particularly important issues, such as the Constitution and free trade. Prime Ministers Chrétien and Martin used the role in a similar way, but Mr. Harper moved in the opposite direction, appointing no deputy prime minister at all. Mr. Trudeau has followed Mr. Harper's lead in this respect.

6.7   Prime Ministerial Government?

It is sometimes argued that the Canadian regime is moving away from cabinet government and toward "prime ministerial" government.[11] There can be no doubt that the office of prime minister has grown substantially more powerful in recent years. In this television age, the prime minister's role as the chief spokesperson for the government gives him or her a public profile that dwarfs the profile of the cabinet. Moreover, the decentralizing tendencies of the cabinet committee system have had the effect of fragmenting the collective power of the cabinet. To a large extent, the prime minister, with the assistance of the PMO and PCO, has stepped into the gap. In recent years, a series of prime ministers have used their authority to transfer more and more of the cabinet's power into their own hands. The trend is now so strong that Jean Chrétien could make the astonishing comment that cabinet serves as a "focus group" for the prime minister.[12]

Stephen Harper's time in office suggests that he ran a government that was at least as "prime ministerial" as those of his immediate predecessors—and

---

11   For a discussion of this thesis, see Donald Savoie, *Governing from the Centre: The Concentration of Power in Canadian Politics* (Toronto: University of Toronto Press, 1999).

12   Ibid., 259–60.

probably more so. His handling of the issue of Quebec's status as a nation provides one of the most striking illustrations of the degree to which he controlled his government. In late 2006, Mr. Harper caught everyone off guard by announcing that his government would introduce and support a resolution declaring that the Québecois constitute a "nation" within a united Canada. No one was more surprised by this announcement than Michael Chong. As Minister of Intergovernmental Affairs, Mr. Chong was the person in cabinet responsible for policy in this area, but Mr. Harper did not even bother to inform (let alone consult) Mr. Chong before embarking on this significant change in policy. Mr. Chong subsequently resigned as a matter of principle.

There are several other indications of a strengthening of prime ministerial government under Mr. Harper. He laid down rigid restrictions about when and where cabinet ministers could speak and what they could say. He also took personal control over the appointment of the chairs of the committees of the House of Commons, something that had traditionally been left to the committees themselves.

For some, it is ironic that these extensions of prime ministerial government were taken by Mr. Harper. After all, his political roots were in the Reform Party, which originally stood for more open, democratic, and accountable government. Perhaps what the case of Mr. Harper shows is that the tendency toward prime ministerial government is a function of the regime itself rather than simply the product of a few individual prime ministers.

Still, one must be careful not to overestimate the power of the prime minister. It should never be forgotten that prime ministers are not directly elected to their position by the people. Because they are ultimately dependent on the confidence of the House of Commons, they cannot afford to alienate key sources of support such as their caucus (the team of MPs from their party) or the cabinet. Indeed, a united cabinet, through the threat of collective resignation, could probably force the resignation of any prime minister, as could a major revolt among members of the caucus. In practice, it has been rare for a prime minister to be forced out of office this way. Mackenzie Bowell's caucus compelled him to resign in 1896. It has been speculated that Jean Chrétien's resignation in 2003 was largely a result of pressure from members of the Liberal caucus loyal to Finance Minister Paul Martin. The critical point, however, is not the number of times a prime minister has been forced out of office; it is the way in which that possibility reminds all prime ministers that there are limits to how far they can push, or how much incompetence or unpopularity their supporters will tolerate. In recent years, a spate of examples at the provincial level has driven home this point. In 2010, British Columbia Premier Gordon Campbell resigned when it became clear that a large part of his caucus was prepared to repudiate him publicly. The same thing happened to Alberta's premiers Ed Stelmach in 2011 and Alison Redford in 2014. Later in 2014, the resignation of five cabinet ministers compelled Manitoba Premier Greg Selinger to call a leadership contest, giving party members (rather than the caucus) an opportunity to determine whether he should continue in office.

In the final analysis, the strength of any particular prime minister's grip on government will depend as much on political circumstances as on the rules of the Constitution. The prime minister is invited to form a government because he or she is the leader of the party that is most likely to have the confidence of the House of Commons. The prime minister's power as prime minister will therefore be directly related to the control he or she has over that party. This control of the party will be influenced by a number of factors. One is the process used by the party to choose its leader.[13] Another is party unity: the prime minister will have trouble dominating the government if the party in power is divided into factions. The most important factor, however, is the prime minister's popularity with the voters. Popular prime ministers who are poised to lead their party to victory will command greater support in their party. On the other hand, prime ministers whose personal unpopularity threatens to lead to electoral defeat may have a difficult time keeping their cabinet and caucus in line.

6.8 The Civil Service

Section 9 of CA 1867 invests the executive power of government in the Crown. We have seen that, under the terms of responsible government, the Crown exercises its executive power on the advice of a small number of servants (its ministers) who are accountable to the elected representatives of the people. But the tasks associated with the exercise of executive power are too numerous and complex to be handled by such a small group of people. The Crown therefore needs many other servants to carry out its executive tasks. These people are known as the Crown's "civil" servants (as opposed to its military servants). In 2010, the federal government employed about 180,000 of them. They are non-partisan professionals, hired on the basis of merit (rather than because of their political connections), in most cases by the politically neutral Public Service Commission (PSC).[14]

---

13   This process is discussed in Chapter Ten.

14   The public service includes both the civil service and all other employees of the national government who fall under the Public Service Employment Act. A full accounting of all these employees is provided by the Public Service Commission at http://www.psc-cfp.gc.ca.

The civil service may be divided into two branches. The majority work in what are known as **line departments**, ministries such as Transport, Health, or Foreign Affairs, which provide services of some sort to the general public. A smaller group are employed by the so-called **central agencies**, such as the PSC or the Treasury Board.[15] These are bodies that engage in the coordination of government policy rather than in the delivery of particular services to the public. Many of these civil servants wield a substantial amount of power. The civil servants who work as officers for Canada Customs, for instance, have a good deal of authority when it comes to searching the cars of Canadians returning from visits to the United States. In order to prevent abuses of that power, the government must ensure that all civil servants will be accountable for the way in which they carry out their duties. Under responsible government, this accountability is achieved through the principle of **ministerial responsibility**.

According to this principle, the minister who heads each department must be accountable to the House of Commons for the conduct of each and every civil servant working in that department. On the most basic level, such accountability implies that the ministers may be asked in the House to investigate allegations of incompetence or impropriety in their departments and to take appropriate measures. If the incompetence or impropriety is substantial and may be attributed to serious mismanagement by the minister, the convention of ministerial responsibility requires the minister to resign, but resignations for reasons of egregious mismanagement have rarely occurred at the federal level.[16] In 1985, Fisheries Minister John Fraser was compelled to resign after it became known that he personally ordered officials in his ministry to approve the sale of tuna that departmental officials had deemed unsafe for human consumption. In 2005, Immigration Minister Judy Sgro resigned amid public concerns over her department's practice of providing visas to exotic dancers.

It is common, in our parliamentary system, for opposition members to demand a minister's resignation for much less serious matters or for matters in which the minister was less directly implicated. One of our most famous controversies regarding ministerial responsibility took place in 1988 when the budget of Finance Minister Michael Wilson was leaked to the press the day before it was

---

15   The Treasury Board is a special committee of the cabinet, established by statute, which reviews all proposed expenditures and which serves as the official employer of the civil service.

16   S.L. Sutherland, "Responsible Government and Ministerial Responsibility: Every Reform Is Its Own Problem," *Canadian Journal of Political Science* 24, no. 1 (March 1991): 100–05.

due to be released. The leaking of a budget is a serious problem because those who have advance knowledge of certain changes in the government's fiscal policy can take advantage of that knowledge to make substantial profits by buying or selling stocks, bonds, currencies, or other commodities. When Wilson's budget was leaked to the press, members of the opposition immediately called for his resignation. Wilson refused to resign, arguing that he could not be held personally accountable for the actions of an unknown person or persons who may have leaked the budget for criminal or malicious reasons. Wilson's argument was a reasonable one: to take a more stringent view of the meaning of ministerial responsibility would make each and every minister the hostage of any disaffected civil servant who wanted to see the minister fired. Under the convention of ministerial responsibility, Wilson would have been required to resign had the leak occurred due to gross personal negligence on his part, but it is well established that a minister cannot be required to resign for mistakes that are not his or her own. To be sure, ministers would be *politically* accountable to the House of Commons for such mistakes—that is, they must ensure that appropriate disciplinary and corrective measures be taken—but they are not *personally* accountable for mistakes made by others.

Figure 6.1: Ministerial Responsibility

Some observers argue that it is unrealistic or simplistic to say that ministers are in charge of their departments. The civil servants in each department are divided into various ranks. At the top of the ladder in each department is an official known as the deputy minister, a career civil servant who usually has advanced technical training and a good deal of civil service experience. In most cases, the deputy minister will know far more about the business of the department than will the minister. In theory, the deputy minister is merely the minister's chief adviser; in practice, however, the deputy's superiority in knowledge can mean that he or she is really the one who runs the department. This situation is particularly likely when one has a strong and experienced deputy working for a weak or inexperienced minister.

The Commission of Inquiry into the Sponsorship Scandal (informally known as the Gomery Commission) filed its second and final report in February 2006. In that report, Justice Gomery suggested that the "sponsorship scandal" was in many respects a failure of ministerial responsibility. Responsible government is based on the principle that those who exercise the power of government (the prime minister and cabinet) are responsible to the House of Commons, that is, accountable to the House for their actions. Justice Gomery found that the misconduct that took place in the sponsorship scandal was facilitated by an absence of appropriate mechanisms to keep the prime minister and cabinet fully accountable to the House. His report recommended a number of reforms, including these:

- In order to make the civil service more independent of the prime minister and cabinet, the deputy ministers should be appointed independently rather than by the prime minister.
- Cabinet ministers should be made accountable to the House for the actions not only of their civil servants but also of their political staff (e.g., executive assistants, chiefs of staff).
- Parliamentary committees, especially the Public Accounts Committee which reviews government expenditures, should be strengthened.
- All secret contingency funds (such as the notorious "Unity Reserve" that Prime Minister Chrétien used to fund the sponsorship activities) should be placed under the direction of central agencies where they will be subject to greater transparency.

As part of its Federal Accountability Act, the Conservative government acted upon the third and fourth of these reforms, but it expressed no interest in the first two.

Key Terms

constitutional monarchy

Queen of Canada

head of state

guardian of responsible government

reserve powers

Queen's Privy Council for Canada

parliamentary secretaries

collective responsibility

ministers of state

Treasury Board

Prime Minister's Office (PMO)

Privy Council Office (PCO)

deputy prime minister

line departments

central agencies

ministerial responsibility

Discussion Questions

1. Given that Canada is a democracy, should the governor general not be elected?

2. Are prime ministers and premiers too powerful? If so, what could be done about it?

Parliament

Under the heading "Legislative Power," section 17 of CA 1867 declares that Canada shall have a "Parliament" consisting of a House of Commons, a Senate, and the Queen. Since Canada's senators are appointed and the Queen has her position by heredity, only the House of Commons can claim to be a democratic institution. By constitutional convention, then, it is the House of Commons that takes the predominant role in the exercise of Parliament's powers. This in turn explains why people commonly equate "Parliament" with the House of Commons.

Sections 91 and 94 of CA 1867, as we have seen, spell out the areas in which Parliament (as opposed to provincial legislatures) has the authority to legislate. Sections 18–57 of CA 1867 set forth rules that govern the composition of the

Senate and the House, along with a few rules in relation to votes, quorum, and some other procedural matters. But to understand fully the role of Parliament in the Canadian regime, we have to go back to the statement in the preamble of CA 1867 stipulating that Canada is to have "a Constitution similar in principle to that of the United Kingdom." This statement establishes that, unless otherwise specified, our Parliament is to be a Canadian version of the British Parliament at Westminster. Of course, we have seen that the British Constitution is one that has been in continual evolution. This means that the place of Parliament in the British regime has changed greatly over the years. Before we begin to describe the specific workings of Canada's Parliament, it will be necessary to explain briefly the general role of that institution in modern times.

7.1 The Role of Parliament

British constitutional history is the history of the development of parliamentary democracy. Originally, Parliament served as a body that advised the Crown in its exercise of legislative power. It was called a "parliament" (from the French word *parler*, to speak) because it was in essence a deliberative body, that is, a body designed to engage in speech about what should be done. Over time, Parliament's advice came to be understood as binding on the monarch so that it was in effect in control of the legislative activity of government. As democratic ideas developed further, the British adopted the principle of responsible government—the idea that those exercising executive power must have the confidence of the people's representatives in Parliament. By the early nineteenth century, Parliament was in what is sometimes called its "golden age." With full control over legislative power, and a tight grip on those exercising executive power, Parliament was the most important political institution in British politics.

By the end of the nineteenth century, however, the power of Parliament had begun to wane because of the rise of highly disciplined political parties whose members could be counted on to vote in accordance with the wishes of their party leaders. In the "golden age" of Parliament, what was said or done in that body was often of decisive importance. Great speeches might make or break legislative proposals, or force a cabinet to resign. But once Britain's parliamentarians had all joined parties that were able to control the way their members voted, real power was transferred to the cabinet; because the cabinet constituted the leadership of the party that had control of Parliament, it had effective control over that body. One might say that Parliament lost much of its influence because what was *said* there rarely affected what was *done* there. Party discipline guaranteed that the cabinet would always have enough votes to protect its own position in power and to get its legislation adopted.[1]

This is the situation that now prevails in Canada. In the Canadian regime, Parliament adopts legislation, and, formally, Parliament determines whether a cabinet has the right to govern. But the existence of highly disciplined parliamentary parties means that Parliament rarely uses its power in these matters. When it adopts legislation, Parliament is in most cases merely ratifying legislative decisions that have, in effect, been made by the prime minister and cabinet. Nor does Parliament often exercise much real power when it comes to determining whether a government should continue in office. For a cabinet supported by a party with a parliamentary majority is virtually guaranteed the "confidence" of the House of Commons.

Since 2004, Canadians have three times elected parliaments in which no party has a majority. In some respects, Parliament plays a more important role in these minority situations. Governments cannot simply legislate as they please and must sometimes work out compromises if they wish to avoid new elections. Pundits and politicians speculate endlessly about whether or when the House will vote to bring down the government. Yet even in the case of minority government, it is not the debate in the House that determines what the House will do; if the House votes to withdraw confidence in a government, it is just formalizing a decision made by two or more of the opposition parties to force a change in government or new elections.[2]

In order to understand properly the role of Parliament in the Canadian regime, we must look at that institution in light of the changes that have followed from the emergence of disciplined political parties. Though Parliament is still a legislative body and the House of Commons still has the power to make or break a government, the development of party discipline and the resulting transfer of parliamentary power to the cabinet have left Parliament with a new role. *The primary operational purpose of the modern parliament is to make the cabinet accountable for*

---

1   Gary W. Cox, *The Efficient Secret: Cabinet and the Development of Political Parties in Victorian England* (New York: Cambridge University Press, 1987).

2   One rare exception was a vote of confidence in May 2005 when the number of votes held by the parties supporting the Martin government (Liberal and NDP) appeared to be equal to the number of votes held by the parties opposing it (Conservative and Bloc). The fate of the government therefore appeared to depend on the vote of independent MP Chuck Cadman. Cadman was very coy about which way he intended to vote, and many Canadians tuned in to watch this dramatic, but exceptional, vote on television.

its actions to the public. Parliament provides a forum in which opposition members can criticize the government, offer constructive alternatives, and perhaps succeed in pressuring the government to make changes to a bill or even withdraw it. The opposition cannot prevent a cabinet with a parliamentary majority from doing as it pleases, as the party in power will, by definition, be able to outvote the parties in opposition. But effective criticism of a government's policy in a high-profile setting such as Parliament can be very damaging to the governing party's chances in the next elections. By allowing opposition members to scrutinize and criticize the cabinet's conduct or policy, then, Parliament plays an essential role in keeping the government sensitive to the concerns of the voters.

7.2 The Parliamentary Calendar

To understand how Parliament works, one must begin with some basic information about the parliamentary calendar.

Parliament is not an institution that works in accordance with a permanent and unchanging schedule. Its schedule is determined first by the timing of the general election. Each time general elections are held, a new contingent of MPs is elected to the House of Commons, and a new Parliament will be convened. These Parliaments are thus numbered in tandem with the country's elections. In 1867, Canada's first national election gave rise to the first Parliament. Our forty-second Parliament was elected in 2015.

Following the election, the prime minister will decide when the new Parliament will be convened. The governor general, upon the advice of the prime minister, will then convene Parliament, and it will begin its first **session**. That session has no set length, and the end of the session will be decided by the government. When the government decides that the session should be brought to an end, the prime minister will advise the governor general to end the session by way of a formal process known as **prorogation**. Any legislative work begun in one session (for instance, the adoption of new youth crime legislation) has to be completed in that session. If it is not, and those sponsoring the legislation wish to try again in a new session, they must start all over from scratch.

For most of our history, sessions have typically been about a year in length. Because elections are normally held about every four years, this means that each Parliament usually has four sessions. There is no fixed rule on this matter, however; the first session of the thirty-second Parliament, in which Prime Minister Pierre Trudeau's government proposed a number of controversial pieces of legislation (including the National Energy Policy and the plan for CA 1982), lasted almost four years.

The sessions of Parliament are divided into **sittings**. Each time the House of Commons meets is a sitting. It may be a very brief meeting or a very long one, sometimes lasting longer than a year. At the end of the sitting, the House of Commons stands adjourned, until the next sitting. An adjournment might last overnight, or it might last for weeks to accommodate a holiday season for example. A session will thus consist of consecutive days when the House of Commons is sitting, and then periods of time when it is adjourned. These periods are set throughout the calendar year so that MPs have extended periods of time to travel to their constituencies and conduct other business of Parliament.

Each session of Parliament begins with a **throne speech**, delivered to the members of both the House and the Senate, plus selected dignitaries, assembled together in the Senate chamber. This speech is read by the governor general, but it is prepared by the Prime Minister's Office (PMO). The speech outlines the legislative program that the government is proposing to Parliament. That program and the government's general performance are then debated for a few days in the House of Commons and voted on. The vote on the throne speech is a **confidence vote**, meaning a vote that the government must win in order to maintain the confidence of the House and stay in office. A government that loses a confidence vote must either resign or seek a new mandate from the electorate.

When the prime minister decides that it is time to terminate a session, he or she will request that Parliament be prorogued. After a number of sessions of Parliament, the prime minister will conclude that it is time to seek a new mandate by way of a general election. He or she will formally request that the governor general proclaim a **dissolution** of Parliament. Dissolution automatically entails the holding of general elections to select another Parliament. The cycle then begins again.

7.3 The House of Commons: Membership and Officers

The House of Commons currently consists of 338 Members of Parliament (or MPs). Each MP has been elected to represent one territorially based constituency known formally as an **electoral district** and informally as a **riding**. In general, ridings are constructed in accordance with the principle of representation by population, so that the percentage of "seats" each province has in the House will be roughly equivalent to its percentage of the national population. There are some institutionalized deviations from this principle. Some of the smaller provinces (especially Prince Edward Island) are overrepresented in the House because of section 51A of CA 1867, which guarantees every province at least as many seats in the House as it has in the Senate. The three territories are also overrepresented in the House in that their modest populations are all less than the average population of a Canadian riding. These deviations serve to improve dramatically the representation of the smaller partners in Confederation, yet do not seriously weaken the influence of the larger provinces. The number of seats per province is adjusted after each decennial census in order to ensure that the distribution of ridings keeps pace with changes in population[3]

In constitutional terms, the primary distinction among MPs is that those who serve in the cabinet are **government members** while those who do not—even if they represent the same party as the government—are **private members**. In political terms, however, we categorize MPs somewhat differently. Those who form and support the government are referred to as **government MPs** and all others are referred to as **opposition MPs**.

Within the ranks of the opposition, there is a further distinction: the largest of the opposition parties becomes the Official Opposition, or, to use the formal title, "Her Majesty's Loyal Opposition." The formal title is meant to convey the notion that the role of this group is to provide criticism of Her Majesty's government, while remaining loyal to Her Majesty (and, by extension, to the regime). Under parliamentary rules, the Official Opposition is entitled to certain privileges that are not extended to the other opposition parties. Its leader is granted special speaking privileges in the House and must be consulted by the prime minister in relation to certain key appointments and other critical matters. The Leader of the Opposition even has a special residence provided at taxpayers' expense (Stornoway). The conferral of these privileges and titles on a politician who, in effect, lost the election, is indicative of how vital a role the opposition plays in Parliament. Because the central task of the modern parliament is to make the government accountable to the public, the opposition is an extremely important component of that body. Opposition parties will name a **shadow cabinet**, a team of **opposition critics** for each of the government's ministries. For instance, in the forty-second Parliament, Conservative MP Lisa Raitt was asked by her party's leader to serve as the opposition critic for finance. As such, she has the responsibility of studying and criticizing the work of Minister of Finance Bill Morneau.

The layout of the House reflects the importance of the adversarial government-opposition relationship in a regime based on responsible government. While most legislative chambers in the world seat all members together, facing a central podium, the Canadian House of Commons (like the British House in Westminster) has the government and opposition members facing

---

3   The process governing the redistribution of seats is discussed in detail in section 9.4.

each other like the offensive and defensive lines of a football team. Moreover, the prime minister and cabinet are always seated directly opposite the leader of the Official Opposition and his or her shadow cabinet. Members of the cabinet and the shadow cabinet normally occupy the first few rows, known as the **front benches.** Those MPs who are not in the cabinet or shadow cabinet sit behind and have come to be known, informally, as **backbenchers.** Figure 7.1 provides a sketch of the layout of the House.

Figure 7.1: Plan of House of Commons, 42nd Parliament

Because the House of Commons is by design an adversarial legislative assembly, it necessarily requires a number of "parliamentary officers" who are neutral officials of Parliament as a whole and who ensure that the business of Parliament is conducted in a timely fashion and in accordance with the rules. The most important parliamentary officer of the House of Commons is the **Speaker.** The Speaker is an MP elected by the House at the beginning of each Parliament to preside over its debates and to take responsibility for its administration. The person chosen as Speaker will, of course, have been elected to the House as a partisan politician—usually as an MP for the governing party. Once installed in office, however, the Speaker must maintain a strict impartiality. Speakers do not take part in parliamentary debate and are permitted to vote only when it is necessary to break a tie.

The House has a number of other officers. The **Clerk of the House**, who sits at a table in the middle of the floor directly in front of the Speaker, takes responsibility for doing the official paperwork of the House and provides procedural advice to the Speaker when this is necessary. The **Sergeant-at-Arms**, usually a distinguished military figure, is responsible for the security of the House.[4] Recording secretaries are also present in the House to keep an official record of its debates (commonly known as *Hansard*).

There is another category of officers who report to Parliament in order to ensure its ability to perform independent administrative and "watchdog" functions. Among them are the Auditor General, the Parliamentary Budget Officer, the Chief Electoral Officer, the Commissioner of Official Languages, and the Privacy Commissioner.

The primary responsibility of the **Auditor General** is to review government spending. The importance of this particular position became quite evident to Canadians in February 2004 when Auditor General Sheila Fraser released a report suggesting that the Chrétien government had seriously mismanaged the Canada Unity Fund, set up in the wake of the 1995 referendum to raise Canada's profile in Quebec. Among other things, it appeared that up to $100 million of the money had been given to advertising firms with strong connections to the Liberal Party for work of little or no value. The ensuing "sponsorship scandal" led to the removal of several prominent Liberals from their top management positions in Crown corporations and to criminal charges against the civil servant who managed the sponsorship dossier. It also played a key role in turning what had appeared to be an easy Liberal majority victory in the June 2004 elections into a mere minority government—a stinging rebuke from the electorate. In 2015, Auditor General Michael Ferguson filed a report detailing questionable expense claims made by a number of members of the Senate, most of them appointed by Conservative Prime Minister Stephen Harper. This report also

---

4   While the office is very much a ceremonial one, it is not merely so. In October 2014, an armed gunman killed a ceremonial guard at the War Memorial, and then gained entry to the Parliament Buildings where he wounded a constable. Sergeant-at-Arms Kevin Vickers was one of those involved in the ensuing gun battle with the attacker, who was shot and killed in the halls of the Parliament Buildings.

appeared to have played a role in the defeat of the Conservative government in elections held that fall.

Since 2006, Canada has had a **Parliamentary Budget Office** (PBO). Reporting to the Speakers of both houses, the Parliamentary Budget Officer provides Parliament with independent assessment of the government's financial position, of its budget estimates, and of broader economic trends that may have an impact on the government's finances. He or she may also provide independent estimates of the cost of any particular proposal under consideration by the government. A striking example of the usefulness of the PBO occurred in 2011 when a report it had commissioned showed that the real cost of acquiring F-35 fighter jets was likely to be almost three times what the Ministry of National Defence had projected it would be. Parliament also has a **Conflict of Interest and Ethics Officer**, reporting to the Speaker, to deal with conflicts of interest that may arise between members' private interests as citizens and their public duties as MPs as defined in the Conflict of Interest Act of 2006 and the Conflict of Interest Code for Members of the House of Commons.

7.4 The Business of the House of Commons

The work of the House is complex and varied, but four main elements of its business may be identified.

The first and most important business of the House is the adoption of **bills**. Bills are legislative proposals. Any MP has the right to introduce a bill for the consideration of the House, but, for reasons discussed in section 7.6, **private members' bills**, though numerous, are rarely adopted. Most of Parliament's legislative activity is focused on **government bills**, legislative proposals presented to the House by a minister. These proposals have, in most cases, been generated by some combination of civil service, minister, and cabinet, and they are referred to as government bills because they normally will have received cabinet approval before they are brought to the House. Only a minister can introduce legislation that entails new taxes or the expenditure of public monies.

Parliament has an elaborate procedure for considering bills, but the complexities of the procedure are there for good reasons. A bill is adopted only after it has passed three "readings." In order to discourage hastiness, the rules stipulate that each of these readings must take place on different days.[5] Moreover, in

---

5   The House of Commons may, on occasion, vote to suspend this rule if it deems immediate action on a bill necessary.

order to facilitate an orderly consideration of bills, each reading has a distinct focus or purpose. The point of the **first reading** is merely to introduce the bill to the House and to give its members (and the public) a chance to acquaint themselves with its provisions. Some time later, the minister sponsoring the bill will move that it be given **second reading**. The second reading focuses on the basic purpose or principles of the bill. This reading gives the House an opportunity to endorse the general thrust of the proposal without getting bogged down in debate about details. Once a bill passes second reading, it is sent to one of the House's committees for careful study of its specific provisions. At the **report stage**, the committee presents the House with the results of its study. The report normally includes proposals for amending some of the bill's provisions, and these amendments are voted on by the House. The bill is then presented to the House for final approval in a **third reading**. From here, the bill proceeds to the Senate, where it must go through the same stages. Once the bill has passed all three readings in the Senate,[6] it is presented to the governor general for **royal assent**, which is a constitutional formality. Only then, at the **proclamation** stage, may the bill be proclaimed, that is, transformed from a legislative proposal into a binding law or "statute."

A second type of business conducted in the House is the adoption of **resolutions**. A resolution differs from a bill in that it simply expresses the opinion of the House; it does not result in the adoption of a new law or policy. When a resolution is debated and voted on, that is the end of the process. What, then, is the point of a resolution? Resolutions are essentially a means of allowing for public debate on issues. The opposition might move a resolution that "this House condemn the government's handling of the economy" in order to try to persuade the public that the government's economic policy is inadequate. The government, on the other hand, might propose a resolution designed to test the public's reaction to some course of action it is considering.

A third type of business conducted in the House is the **scrutiny of public expenditure**. This scrutiny comes in two stages, before and after the expenditure. Before any money is spent by a governmental department, the department must present its **estimates** (its proposed expenditures for the coming year) to whichever of the House's standing committees has jurisdiction in that area of government. This process presents MPs with an opportunity to examine any detail in relation to proposed government spending, and not a penny of public money may be

---

6   On occasion, the government may introduce a bill in the Senate, in which case consideration by the House of Commons follows consideration by the Senate instead of preceding it.

spent by a department without prior approval by the House. Public expenditures are also scrutinized after the fact. The House's Standing Committee on Public Accounts, which is usually chaired by a member of the opposition, examines the finances of each department to ensure that the public's money has been spent wisely. The committee is assisted in its efforts by the Auditor General.

The fourth major type of business conducted in the House is the provision of information. In order to hold government accountable for its work, MPs must have access to relevant information. The procedures of the House allow members to submit written questions or requests for information. The government tables its responses to such questions or requests with the clerk, and they are subsequently recorded in *Hansard*. MPs also have the chance to pose impromptu questions orally in "Question Period." As most Canadians will know, however, the questions asked in this forum are rarely asked in good faith. Opposition members often ask questions that are designed not to elicit information but to embarrass the government; indeed, the "questions" that are posed are often not questions at all but barely camouflaged speeches. The ministers to whom the questions are directed therefore respond in kind: questions are frequently evaded or used as an opportunity to attack the opposition.

Many Canadians have a negative impression of Question Period because of the highly partisan and frequently hyperbolic character of the exchanges that take place during it. Yet, while there are good reasons to be critical of some of the excesses of Question Period, no other forum allows for such intense and powerful criticism of government policy; it is no coincidence that almost all the footage of parliamentary debate one sees on the television news is drawn from that source. For all its faults, then, Question Period is an essential device for allowing Parliament to perform its crucial role of keeping the government accountable to the House, and thus, to the public.

7.5 The Rules of Procedure of the House of Commons

The proceedings of the House of Commons are governed by two types of rules. First, Parliament has codified basic regulations concerning the organization of its business and the conduct of its debates in a body of rules known as the **Standing Orders**.[7] The House may amend these by a simple majority vote, and there have been numerous changes to them over the years. In addition to its

---

7   There is also a Parliament of Canada Act that governs a number of important administrative matters, including salaries and pensions.

Standing Orders, the House also recognizes a large number of rules that derive from British (or in some cases, Canadian) parliamentary tradition. It is useful to think of these rules as something like the parliamentary equivalent of constitutional conventions: though not carved in stone, they are respected because years of experience have shown them to be useful.

To the outside observer, many of the rules of procedure followed by the House may seem somewhat quaint. But rules that at first glance appear arbitrary or even whimsical often turn out, on closer inspection, to be both rational and valuable. The House of Commons is meant to be an adversarial chamber. In one way or another, most parliamentary rules are designed either to facilitate or to regulate the adversarial relationship between government and opposition. As mentioned previously, the seating arrangements in the House of Commons promote an adversarial mentality: government and opposition members are seated facing each other, ready to do battle. At the same time, however, the House follows certain rules that are designed to ensure that the battle between the two sides remains civil: comments must always be addressed to the Speaker, rather than directly to one's opponent; and to prevent disagreements from becoming personal, colleagues are addressed by title, position, or constituency name (as "the prime minister" or "the Honourable Member from X," for example) rather than by name.

Among the most important rules are those governing the use of House time. In the House of Commons, time is a precious commodity for it takes a good deal of time for the government to get its program through. Though the opposition rarely has enough votes to block government measures, it can exert great pressure on the government by tying up House time and stalling the government's legislative agenda. The House therefore has a number of rules regarding the use of time that are carefully designed to strike a reasonable balance between the government's need to get its business through the House and the opposition's role as a check on the government. Speeches are normally limited to 20 minutes, and each member may speak only once on a given motion. Twenty minutes per member per motion is enough to allow the opposition members to cause substantial headaches for the government but not enough time to stall legislation indefinitely. There is also a rule under the Standing Orders known as **closure**, which permits the government to cut off debate if it decides that the opposition is taking too much time. On paper, the closure provision would seem to deprive the opposition of a fair share in the control of the House's time. One must keep in mind, however, that closure is a suppression of debate. When the rule was first developed, it was assumed that governments would resort to it only in extreme cases, for suppressing debate might be perceived by the public as anti-democratic.

During Canada's first century, the closure rule was indeed used rarely and often at great cost to the popularity of the government. More recently, however, it seems that a decline in public attention to Parliament has permitted governments to invoke closure more indiscriminately.

7.6   The Backbencher

Government members focus most of their time and attention on overseeing the ministries for which they are responsible and participating in the collective work of the cabinet. Even those private members who serve as opposition critics have the important responsibility of following the work of a particular ministry, and they take every opportunity to speak either in the House or to the media about that work. Simple backbenchers, on the other hand, serve in relative anonymity. Indeed, they are often dismissed as "trained seals" whose only job is to vote when and how their leaders tell them to.

Yet it would be a mistake to think that backbenchers are without influence. Parliament provides three major opportunities for them to voice their concerns. The first is the weekly caucus meeting, held on Wednesday mornings whenever the House is in session. These meetings are held behind closed doors, so caucus members may speak frankly but without damaging party unity. In opposition caucus meetings, the backbenchers wield a great deal of influence. In government caucus meetings, the backbenchers are less powerful; to a large extent, these meetings are used by the prime minister and cabinet as a means of informing the backbenchers of what they have already decided to do. Still, the prime minister and cabinet can remain in office only as long as they have the confidence of the House, and this gives the government backbenchers a certain amount of leverage; concerted opposition on their part to cabinet proposals will force the cabinet to reconsider.

A second venue in which backbenchers may exert influence is the House of Commons committees. Chief among these are the "standing" (i.e., permanent) committees, each of which focuses on some particular area of public policy. The members of these committees, almost all of whom are backbenchers, may thus develop expertise in various policy areas. The committees are responsible for the clause-by-clause examination of bills that takes place after second reading and for the examination of departmental estimates. They may also take responsibility for carrying out studies or investigations on topics relevant to their jurisdiction, sometimes holding hearings across the country. Standing committees have 12 members, assigned by party affiliation in proportion to each party's strength in the House. Each committee has a chair who runs its meetings and decides all questions of order and procedure. On most committees, the chair is one of the government members. A few, however—the Standing Committee on Public Accounts and the Standing Committee on Access to Information, Privacy and Ethics, for instance—are always chaired by an opposition member because the role of those committees is to serve as a check on the actions of the government. Party discipline is normally much less rigid in committees than it is in the House itself, giving committee members an opportunity to exert some personal influence on the business of Parliament.

The third means for backbenchers to voice their concerns is the private member's bill. Any member of the House may introduce a bill for first reading on any topic, provided that the proposal does not require the expenditure of public money. The rules of the House allot little time for discussion of private members' bills, but these bills do afford backbenchers an opportunity to put their ideas before the public, and it is not uncommon for some of those ideas to be picked up by the government and reintroduced later in the form of a government bill. The forty-first Parliament passed 43 private members' bills (versus 117 government bills), an unusually high number. These included a bill to amend the criminal code to cover mischief relating to war memorials; a bill to address concerns of victims of violent offenders; a bill pertaining to the protection of employees' voting rights; and bills to recognize Purple Day (a day to increase public awareness about epilepsy), National Philanthropy Day, World Autism Awareness Day, Trapping and Fishing Heritage Day, Health and Fitness Day, and even National Fiddling Day.

7.7 House of Commons Reform

One of the most common complaints by Canadians about their government is that their elected representatives do not effectively represent them. MPs are routinely criticized for being too subservient to their party leaders. They seem to do a better job of representing the party in Parliament than of representing their constituents. This criticism has been the underlying cause behind numerous attempts to reform the rules and structure of the House of Commons. Attempts at reform have focused on three areas in which the power of individual members might be increased: the standing committees, private members' bills, and free votes.

With respect to the standing committees, reform proposals generally focus on providing the committees with more substantial research resources and increasing the prestige of committee chairs. In a 2008 study of the subject, for example, Tom Axworthy of Queen's University advocated giving committee chairs the same salaries and perks as cabinet ministers and providing each committee with five or six full-time research officers rather than the one they typically have now.[8]

A second reform that is often discussed is the idea of allowing greater opportunities for the introduction and consideration of private members' bills. Providing more time for the debate of such bills would increase the power of individual MPs to bring forward issues relevant to their particular constituents.

Finally, it is proposed that MPs should be given more opportunity to vote against their own party. This freedom could be accomplished by relaxing the fairly strict rule governing confidence. Canadian parliamentarians have traditionally worked from the understanding that the defeat of any government bill amounts to a withdrawal of the House's confidence in the government itself. Though it is clear that items such as the government's budget or the throne speech must be treated as matters of confidence, it is not obvious why every government bill has to be. One way to provide backbenchers with greater freedom would be to make it clear, perhaps in the rules of Parliament, that the government loses the confidence of the House only if it is defeated on its budget, the throne speech, or through an explicit motion of non-confidence. That would allow government backbenchers to vote against (and even defeat) a specific government bill but then vote to continue their support of the government on a separate non-confidence motion. Such a change in voting procedures would certainly give backbench MPs a more active role in the management of public affairs. On the other hand, like most proposals for reforming the House of Commons, there are potential drawbacks. Relaxing the confidence rule will encourage MPs from the government side to vote with the opposition. It is unlikely, however, that such a change would alter the way the opposition MPs vote. We could therefore find ourselves frequently confronted by an apparently divided government party and completely united opposition parties, a situation that might turn out to be a recipe for weak government.

In the final analysis, one has to ask whether the defects of parliamentary government are not outweighed by its advantages. Parliamentary government runs smoothly and efficiently because it is, in the main, cabinet government and not a government of 338 individual MPs. Cabinet government allows us to establish clearly who is responsible for government legislation and current public policy. The prime minister, the cabinet, and, ultimately, the governing party will be held accountable by the electorate at the next election. Parliamentary

---

8   Tom Axworthy, *Everything Old Is New Again: Observations on Parliamentary Reform* (Kingston: Centre for the Study of Democracy, Queen's University, April 2008).

government may not be ideal in every respect, but its advantages should not be taken lightly.

7.8 The Senate

The purpose of the Senate is to serve as a chamber of "sober second thought," which reviews legislative proposals emanating from the House of Commons. It was originally hoped that in performing this function, the Senate would look at legislation from a perspective that differed from that of the House of Commons in two distinct ways. First, the Fathers of Confederation worried that a House of Commons elected on the democratic principle might fail to respect the rights of property; the poor majority might use its democratic power to despoil the rich minority. Thus, the Senate was meant to be a body that would stand up for property rights. This history is reflected in the fact that section 23 of CA 1867 specifies that senators must possess real property valued at a minimum of $4,000 in the province they represent, and they must also have a net personal worth of at least $4,000. The sum of $4,000 does not seem like much today, but in 1867 a relatively small proportion of Canadians could have claimed to be that wealthy.

Second, the Senate was intended to pay special attention to the concerns of the less populous regions of the country. While the principle for allocating seats in the House of Commons was representation by population (making the larger provinces of Ontario and Quebec dominant in that body), the principle for allocating Senate seats was equality of the regions. CA 1867 originally granted 24 seats to each of the three regions that first formed the country: Ontario, Quebec, and the Maritimes. The subsequent entry of other provinces into Confederation led to some minor deviations from the principle of regional equality, but Senate representation is still, in essence, based on that principle.[9] The regional nature of Senate representation is further underscored by the requirement that senators reside and possess property in the province they represent.[10]

---

9   The Senate currently has 105 seats: Ontario and Quebec have 24 each; the West has 24 seats (6 per province); the Maritimes still have 24, but Nova Scotia and New Brunswick each gave up 2 to Prince Edward Island when that province entered Confederation in 1873. Newfoundland was granted 6 Senate seats when it joined Canada in 1949. This is the primary deviation from the principle of regional equality. The Yukon, Nunavut, and the Northwest Territories have 1 Senate seat each.

10   MPs are not required to own property or even to reside in the ridings they represent. Most do, of course, because it would be a political liability to be seen as an "outsider."

In law, the powers of the Senate are almost the same as those of the House of Commons.[11] In practice, however, the Senate almost never makes full use of its powers because senators are not elected. Section 24 of CA 1867 provides that senators are to be "summoned" to that body by the governor general; in practice, this means that they are appointed by the prime minister. From the very beginning of Confederation, it was recognized that an appointed body like the Senate would have to defer to the leadership of the elected House of Commons. Over the course of our history, the prestige of the Senate has declined steadily, in part because Canadians, whose political ideas are increasingly democratic, have become less tolerant of non-elected officials. However, the decline is also a result of the fact that so many of the appointments made to the Senate by our prime ministers have been patronage appointments designed to reward service to the prime minister's party. By the middle of the twentieth century, it had become a convention of our Constitution that the Senate must not oppose a bill that has the support of the House of Commons. Though senators still carried out their responsibilities for reviewing legislation, they restricted themselves to making recommendations for minor improvements to the bills sent to them by the House. Occasionally such "recommendations" can have major effects. In recent years, for example, government efforts to adopt new legislation in relation to cruelty to animals have been repeatedly stalled as the Senate sends each bill back to the Commons with amendments the government deems unacceptable.

The Senate has also, on occasion, demonstrated a willingness to confront the House of Commons more directly. When the PC government came to power in 1984, the Liberals had been in office for 16 years. In that period, the vast majority of Senate appointees had been card-carrying Liberals, and the Liberals thus had a comfortable majority there. When the PC-dominated House adopted a bill implementing the controversial Free Trade Agreement with the United States, the Liberal-dominated Senate refused to go along. By withholding their approval of the bill, the Liberal senators forced the PCs to call a general election, thereby giving the voters an opportunity to express their views on the issue. Shortly after the PCs won that election, they introduced legislation in the House to create the controversial Goods and Services Tax (GST). Again, after the legislation was passed by the House, the Liberal senators threatened to deny the bill their

---

11   There are two exceptions. Section 53 of CA 1867 specifies that the House of Commons is to take the leading role in the adoption of "money bills" (legislation raising or spending public funds). Section 47(1) of CA 1982 specifies that the Senate has only a suspensory veto over constitutional amendments proposed by the House of Commons.

approval. Prime Minister Mulroney responded by using section 26 of CA 1867, which gives the government the authority to appoint four or eight additional senators (one or two per region) when this is necessary to break a deadlock between the two houses of Parliament. Mulroney appointed eight new senators, all of them PCs, enough to ensure that the upper house passed the government's bill.

These episodes provide an interesting illustration of how constitutional conventions work. We saw in Chapter Two that conventions depend for their enforcement on public reaction. In these cases, the Liberal senators gambled that public opinion would support them. They argued that their actions were consistent with the spirit, if not the letter, of the convention in question, for the purpose of the convention subordinating the Senate to the House of Commons was to ensure that power would be exercised democratically, and the polls indicated that the majority of voters wanted an election on free trade and the defeat of the GST. Whether the argument was good or not, the Liberals got away with it. The only way to enforce a convention is for the voters to punish those who violate it. In the 1993 elections, however, the voters gave the Liberals a strong majority.

7.9 Senate Reform

Canadians have long been dissatisfied with the Senate. Senate reform is thus a perennial topic of Canadian political discourse. It includes ideas about changing the way one becomes a senator, about revising the powers of the Senate, and about reforming the relationship between the Senate and the House of Commons.

A substantial body of opinion suggests that the best way to reform the Senate is to abolish it. Many Canadians believe that senators do little or no productive work and that the institution is nothing but a great waste of money.[12] This is an overly simplistic view, but it is a popular one nonetheless. A more sophisticated case for abolition is made by those who point out that, to the extent that senators have an influence on legislation, it is often an undesirable influence. The Senate was intended to be a body that would represent the interests of property. Although the vast majority of today's Canadians would be able to meet the Constitution's requirement that senators possess $4,000 in property, that body is still not representative of the socio-economic majority; even today, many (if not most) senators are very closely linked to Canada's business elite. Colin Campbell has argued that the Senate has operated as a "lobby" for big business, reworking

---

12   The spate of inappropriate expense claims uncovered by the Auditor General also created perceptions among some that the Senate is not merely unproductive but also corrupt.

legislation to the advantage of banks and other large corporations.[13] It is because of the close link between the Senate and corporate Canada that the NDP traditionally supports Senate abolition.

Most advocates of Senate reform prefer to keep the Senate but seek to restructure it so as to give more effective parliamentary representation to Canada's less populous regions. The most common proposal along these lines is to transform the upper house into an elected legislative body. Drawing inspiration largely from the Senate of the United States, reformers argue that, in a federal union, the legislative body of the national government should have one house based on representation by population and a second, equally powerful house based on the principle of the equality of the provinces or regions of the country. According to this view, the key to making Canada's Senate effective is to elect its members so that they will have as much democratic legitimacy as the members of the House of Commons.

Other observers argue that the Senate should be left pretty much as it is. These analysts reject the proposal for electing senators on the grounds that it could lead to parliamentary paralysis when the two chambers are dominated by different parties. They also reject abolition, arguing that the Senate is more useful than people realize: it cleans up errors or oversights in bills passed by the House of Commons; it serves as a source of cabinet ministers when a prime minister has no MPs from a particular province;[14] and it serves as a convenient place to which a prime minister might "promote" cabinet ministers whose services are no longer required. Defenders of the status quo argue that because the operation of the Senate costs each Canadian only about a dollar a year, it would make more sense to make minor improvements to the institution than to abolish it.[15]

Senate reform has long been an issue dear to the hearts of many Western Canadians who see a more powerful Senate as a vehicle for better protecting Western interests against a House of Commons that is heavily dominated by

---

13   Colin Campbell, *The Canadian Senate: A Lobby from Within* (Toronto: Macmillan, 1978).

14   After winning the 1979 election with almost no seats from Quebec, Prime Minister Joe Clark used the Senate to strengthen his cabinet's representation from that province. After the 1980 election, which left incoming Liberals with no seats west of Winnipeg, Prime Minister Pierre Trudeau did the same thing. With a relatively small pool of MPs from Quebec in 2006, and none from Montreal, Prime Minister Harper appointed Michael Fortier to the Senate and named him to the cabinet.

15   Darcy Wudel, "A Job Description for Senators," *Policy Options* 7, no. 3 (April 1986); Jonathan Lemco and Peter Regenstreif, "Let the Senate Be," *Policy Options* 6, no. 4 (May 1985).

central Canada. It was an especially important issue for the old Reform Party, of which Mr. Harper was once a member. When Mr. Harper became prime minister, he attempted to move the Senate reform agenda forward incrementally. Having gained a majority in the 2011 election, Prime Minister Harper introduced new legislation—the Senate Reform Act—during the forty-first Parliament. The proposed legislation would have changed the Senate in two important ways. First, it would have limited the terms of senators to nine years, while maintaining the mandatory retirement age of 75. Second, the act would have allowed for the provinces to hold elections for recommendation to the Crown. The prime minister would be obligated to consider these recommendations before advising the governor general on new appointments. In 2014, however, the Supreme Court of Canada ruled that Parliament does not have the authority, on its own, to implement the reforms proposed by the Harper government. Section 24 of CA 1867 stipulates that senators are appointed and section 42(1)(b) of CA 1982 stipulates that changes to the "method of selecting Senators" requires a constitutional amendment according to the "7/50 formula": resolutions of acceptance from at least seven provincial legislatures representing at least 50 per cent of Canada's national population. And since the Constitution explicitly states that senators may serve until the age of 75, the same formula would have to be used to establish limits to the terms of individual senators. Finally, the court noted that the more extreme approach to Senate reform—abolition—would require the agreement of all ten provincial legislatures. Following the Supreme Court's decision, Prime Minister Harper simply stopped recommending candidates to fill vacant seats in the Senate, presumably in order to put pressure on the provinces to negotiate some kind of deal. At the time of the 2015 election, 22 Senate seats were vacant.

These vacant Senate seats have presented Prime Minister Justin Trudeau with an interesting opportunity for incremental change of his own. While in opposition, Mr. Trudeau's position was that the functioning of the Senate would be improved if senators did not have direct party affiliations. He therefore took the extraordinary step of removing all senators from the Liberal caucus, forcing them to sit as independents. Shortly after becoming prime minister, Mr. Trudeau reformed the appointment process, creating an Independent Advisory Board on Senate Appointments to recommend to him worthy nominees for vacant Senate seats.[16] The theory is that, over time, the appointment of high-profile and

---

16   This advisory board will have three national members plus two ad hoc members from the province for which a senator needs to be appointed. The members are appointed by the prime minister, who receives their recommendations, but is not bound by them.

non-partisan senators—rather than of prominent Liberals or Conservatives—will both improve the performance of that chamber and enhance its standing with the public. The large number of vacancies left by Mr. Harper provides the perfect opportunity to put this theory to the test.

Yet the kind of incremental reform pursued by the Harper and Trudeau governments has been criticized by long-time advocates of more profound reform. In both cases the argument being made is that piecemeal reform is inadequate and may entrench even more deeply some of the problems associated with the Senate. For instance, a more democratically legitimate (and hence more powerful) Senate is not a good thing from the point of view of those provinces or regions that believe they have less than their fair share of senators. In 2015, British Columbia Premier Christy Clark criticized the Trudeau government's plan for just that reason. Yet provinces such as Prince Edward Island, which are strongly overrepresented in the Senate, would surely block any attempt to change the allocation of Senate seats by province. Moreover, although public support for abolition has increased substantially in the wake of revelations about inappropriate expenses charged by a number of senators, PEI's Premier Wade MacLauchlan has made it clear that his province has no interest in permitting the abolition of an institution that serves his province well. And so the conundrum of Senate reform, which has been with us almost since Confederation, is unlikely to be resolved any time soon.

Key Terms

session	Auditor General
prorogation	Parliamentary Budget Office
sitting	Conflict of Interest and Ethics Officer
throne speech	bills
confidence vote	private members' bills
dissolution	government bills
electoral district/riding	first reading
government members	second reading
private members	report stage
government MPs	third reading
opposition MPs	royal assent
Speaker	shadow cabinet
Clerk of the House	opposition critics
Sergeant-at-Arms	front benches
Hansard	backbenchers

proclamation
resolution
scrutiny of public expenditure
estimates

Standing Orders
closure
Senate reform

Discussion Questions

1. Should parliamentary procedure be altered so that governments lose the confidence of the House only when defeated on the budget, the throne speech, or an explicit motion of non-confidence?

2. Is it more important for MPs to be in Ottawa carrying out the business of the House or to be in their ridings working for their constituents?

8.1   The Role of the Judiciary

The first thing that students of the Constitution should notice about the provisions of CA 1867 governing "the judicature" is the location of those provisions. As we have seen, the sections governing executive and legislative power occupy a prominent position close to the beginning of CA 1867. Judicial power, on the other hand, is not discussed until Part VII, three-quarters of the way through the act. To some extent, this is because Canada's judicial system has a federal dimension to it, a fact that makes it reasonable to outline the provisions governing judicial power only after the provisions governing federalism have been laid down. But the relatively late discussion of judicial power is also a reflection of the fact that the Fathers of Confederation viewed judicial power as substantially less important than the legislative and executive powers.

Such a view would be untenable today, for the role of the judiciary has expanded far beyond its modest origins. In 1867, most observers would have ascribed to the judiciary two basic tasks: the adjudication of legal disputes between private parties and the adjudication of cases in public law. Today's judges regularly engage in two additional activities: the supervision of inquiries and commissions and judicial review of the Constitution. Judicial review, in particular, has magnified the importance of the judiciary far beyond anything the Fathers of Confederation had expected. These four tasks can be summed up as follows.

1. Adjudicating legal disputes between private parties. According to the liberal philosopher John Locke, the primary reason human beings create political regimes is that they need someone to settle their disputes in a peaceful, authoritative, and impartial manner. Locke believed in certain universal and permanent principles of justice, which he called natural laws, and he thought that all human beings could in principle understand the validity of those laws. But Locke doubted that human beings would respect those laws consistently. He also doubted their ability to apply and enforce them impartially. In their natural state of freedom, then, people would inevitably be drawn into an ever-escalating cycle of injustice and vengeance. Reasonable human beings are therefore willing to renounce their natural freedom and put themselves under the command of a political regime that will be able to resolve disputes before they turn violent.

In order to accomplish this objective, the political regime will adopt laws to govern the most common private disputes and establish courts to settle such disputes according to the principles laid down in those laws. The regime will still permit, and may even encourage, individuals to employ a number of private mechanisms to settle their disputes. The most common of these are negotiation, mediation (a process in which a third party is brought in to facilitate negotiations between the disputants), and arbitration (in which the disputants agree to allow a third party to impose a settlement on them). But the effectiveness of these three mechanisms is largely dependent on the fact that disputants know that unresolved disputes can, and normally will, be taken to the courts for decisive resolution.

At the time of Confederation, it was deemed necessary to put responsibility for "private law"—laws governing matters such as property rights, contracts, and torts—in the hands of the provincial governments. Section 92.13 of CA 1867 thus reserves "property and civil rights" as an exclusive jurisdiction of the legislatures of the provinces. The reason for this was that New Brunswick, Nova Scotia, and Ontario embodied their private law in one format while Quebec used another.

Private law in Quebec is embodied in a statute called the civil code, a detailed, comprehensive, and massive compendium of all the rules governing matters of property and civil rights. This practice, used by most legislative jurisdictions in the world today, was one that Quebec had adopted when it was a French colony, and, in 1774, the British government guaranteed Quebeckers the right to retain their code. The other colonies, more British in heritage, had always followed the British practice of embodying much of their private law in a form known as "common law." Common law is judge-made law, as opposed to statutes adopted by legislative bodies. In late medieval England, royally appointed judges slowly began to take control of what hitherto had been a patchwork system of justice. In order to impose some order and consistency on that system, they adopted the practice of deciding cases involving matters such as property or contracts on the basis of **precedents** (previous judicial decisions on the same point of law). If no precedent existed, judges were free to decide cases in the manner that seemed most consistent with the underlying principles of the case law that did exist. By virtue of the principle of *stare decisis* ("to stand by what has been decided"), however, judges were required to respect any precedent that had been endorsed by courts of authority superior to their own. By following these basic rules, England's judges were able, over time, to develop a single system of private law "common" to the whole country.

2. Adjudicating cases in public law. Judges also have substantial authority in matters of "public law." The difference between public and private law is that while private law governs relationships between two or more private parties, public law creates and regulates relationships between private parties and the government. This difference is reflected in the names of the cases heard under each type of law: a typical case in private law might be titled *Jones v. Smith*, but cases in public law will feature the Queen (often abbreviated as "R") or some officer of the Crown in their titles—*Russell v. The Queen* or *Ford v. Québec (Attorney General)*.

The two main areas of public law are criminal law and administrative law. Section 91.27 of CA 1867 declares criminal law to be an exclusive jurisdiction of Parliament (i.e., Ottawa). Our criminal law is contained primarily in the Criminal Code of Canada, which prohibits a wide variety of actions by declaring them to be criminal offences—assault, sexual assault, fraud, murder, and hateful speech, to name but a few. In addition to offering a legal definition of these crimes, the Criminal Code establishes appropriate ranges of punishment for each of them. It is the judges of Canada's courts, however, who decide on the specific sentence, and in most cases the Criminal Code grants them a good deal of latitude. This constitutes a very substantial form of power over individual liberty.

The term "administrative law" refers to any regulatory legislation that does not involve the application of criminal sanctions. Administrative law thus covers a very wide range of topics at both levels of government, from traffic regulations (a provincial matter) to old age pensions (a federal jurisdiction). Because of the tremendous number of administrative law decisions that need to be made by today's governments, a good deal of administrative law is now applied by administrative tribunals (e.g., the Workers' Compensation Board) rather than courts. However, the judiciary still hears many types of administrative law cases and will often have the power to overrule decisions made by administrative tribunals.

3. Judicial inquiries. In recent decades, it has become increasingly common for governments to ask judges to take charge of independent investigations and commissions looking into problematic areas of public policy or alleged misconduct in some part of the public sector. Judges have been asked to lead inquiries into the "sponsorship scandal," alleged racism in the justice system of Nova Scotia, alleged illegal activities by the Royal Canadian Mounted Police (RCMP), and Canada's medicare system, among other subjects. These exercises may be relatively focused and discrete investigations of particular incidents or alleged wrongdoing, or more discursive, wide-ranging, or even speculative inquiries into how public policy can be improved in particular fields.

Governments are not obligated to place the direction of inquiries in the hands of judges. In fact, many such investigations or commissions have been led by non-judicial figures. There are two reasons governments frequently look to the judiciary for their leadership, though. First, judges have professional experience in organizing hearings in which parties are able to present evidence in a procedurally fair manner. In order to find facts and even assign blame, inquiries find these procedural skills very valuable. Second (and probably more important), judges have a reputation for impartiality. The recommendations of these investigations often carry a good deal of weight with the governments that create them, and have an equally high level of public legitimacy. Judges are seen as working at an arm's length from the government of the day and appear to have no partisan or political interest in any particular outcome. The individual judges who head such commissions are thus able to exert a substantial amount of influence on specific political issues.

4. Judicial review of the Constitution. We have seen in Chapter Two that the terms of the Constitution require interpretation and that it is the courts that take responsibility for this task. We have also seen, in Chapters Four and Five, that this function of judicial review has given Canada's judiciary substantial political power. Judges now decide, or decisively influence, a number of important questions of principle and policy: How extensive are the powers of the federal and provincial legislatures? Is it permissible for either level of government to restrict access to abortions? Are laws prohibiting the use of marijuana acceptable? These types of issues are now routinely decided by the courts rather than by legislatures.

It is important to note, however, that the judiciary does not become involved in such questions on its own initiative. Most of the time, judicial review of the Constitution is triggered by specific cases in private or public law when a ruling on the meaning of some part of the Constitution is necessary for the adjudication of the dispute in question. Let us take as an example the case of *R. v. Big M Drug Mart Ltd.* (1985). In this case, Big M Drug Mart was charged with violating a federal statute, The Lord's Day Act, which prohibited commercial establishments like Big M from doing business on Sunday. In court, Big M did not deny that it was open on Sundays in violation of the law, but it argued that it should not be punished because the law itself was in violation of section 2(a) of the Charter of Rights and Freedoms, which guarantees "freedom of religion." In order to determine whether Big M should be punished, the courts that heard this case (including, in the end, the Supreme Court of Canada) were required to make a ruling on the meaning of section 2(a). Does the right to freedom of religion make it unconstitutional for governments to prohibit shopping on "the Lord's day"? If it does, Big M is innocent. If it does not, Big M must be punished in accordance with the law.

The second mechanism for triggering judicial review of the Constitution is the **reference procedure**. When the federal government created the Supreme Court of Canada, it provided that the court could be called on to give its opinion on the constitutionality of specific decisions or statutes referred to it by the governor in council. Originally, the government's intention was to use this reference procedure to help it decide whether specific provincial statutes should be disallowed. Eventually, however, the reference procedure came to be used as a means of obtaining quick rulings on the constitutionality of proposed legislation. (Waiting for the constitutionality of a law to be challenged by private parties and appealed through the judicial system might take as long as ten years.) In the 1930s, for example, the government was able to refer the "New Deal" legislation proposed by R.B. Bennett to the courts and to learn in relatively short order that most of the legislation was *ultra vires*—beyond the jurisdiction—of the federal government. The provincial governments soon recognized the value of the reference procedure and established comparable mechanisms in their own courts. Today, most judicial review of the Constitution arises from the adjudication of cases rather than from reference questions, but the reference procedure is the source of some of the more interesting and important cases—the patriation reference, for example (discussed in section 2.3).

8.2 The Fundamental Principles of the Canadian Judiciary

There are three fundamental principles that govern the Canadian judiciary in its efforts to carry out the tasks described above: impartiality, independence, and equality before the law. Each of these principles has been inherited from British constitutional tradition. Indeed, it is plausible to argue that the authoritative status of these three principles is implied by the statement in the preamble to CA 1867 that Canada is to have "a Constitution similar in principle to that of the United Kingdom." As we shall see, however, the Constitution entrenches these principles in other places as well.

1. Impartiality. Section 11(d) of the Charter of Rights and Freedoms guarantees that any person charged in Canada with some offence has the right to a "fair" trial before an "impartial tribunal." There is nothing surprising in this, for the requirement that judges be impartial is more or less implicit in the very concept of adjudication.

The general meaning of the principle of **impartiality** is relatively straightforward: judges must be free from prejudice for or against any party appearing before them. It may, of course, be impossible for human beings to refrain from showing at least some prejudice in their judgement about things, but our regime assumes that its judges will be reasonably impartial and, for the most part, leaves it up to individual judges to police themselves in this regard. It does, however, attempt to promote impartiality by means of three specific provisions.

The first is the potential to appeal a judge's decision to a higher court. The right to seek an appeal promotes impartiality in two ways: knowing that their judgements may be subjected to the scrutiny of a higher court gives individual judges an incentive to be fair and objective, and parties who think they have been victims of judicial bias get a second hearing. It is important to note, however, that the right to appeal is not unlimited. In the first place, it is not usually automatic. One generally has to ask the court to which one seeks to appeal for permission (or "leave") to appeal. Not every aspect of a case is subject to appeal.

When judges adjudicate disputes, they engage in two distinct processes: they must first decide the facts of the situation in dispute—what exactly happened—and they must then determine what the law says about these situations. Appeal courts will grant leave to appeal if there appear to be problems in what a judge has said about the law or perhaps if the judge has made procedural errors, but, as a rule, they do not hear appeals of a judge's decision about the facts of a case.

Another feature of Canada's judicial regime that serves to promote impartiality is its "adversarial" character. In many countries, judges will play a very active role in the judicial process, taking responsibility for fact-finding and then settling the disputes in accordance with their understanding of the law. Such arrangements are not consistent with our regime's suspicion of public power and its emphasis on individual liberty and responsibility. In Canada, we follow the British practice of giving judges a more passive role. We place the responsibility for establishing facts and presenting arguments with the adversaries themselves, and our judges serve as referees rather than inquisitors. Instead of seeking out facts and arguments, they restrict themselves to making rulings on the basis of the facts and arguments presented to them by individual litigants. This has the effect of minimizing judges' latitude for imposing their own views on the contending parties.

The third provision is the doctrine of political neutrality. This doctrine, which we also inherited from Britain, decrees that judges must keep silent about political matters. They may not be members of political parties, they may not speak on political topics, and they must not display public preference for any particular political views. The reason for this doctrine is not hard to see. Judges will often be called upon to hear cases in which they will make decisions of political importance. If a judge has taken a public stand on a particular issue, if, for instance, a judge proclaims herself to be an ardent opponent of abortion, it will be difficult to persuade the public that both sides in a case involving abortion will get a fair hearing from her. Moreover, as Peter Russell points out, if judges start attacking politicians, politicians will fight back. This would only serve to undermine the authority and independence of the courts.[1]

In 1981, Canadians witnessed an interesting example of the doctrine of political neutrality. Justice Thomas Berger of the BC Supreme Court publicly attacked the constitutional accord that formed the basis of CA 1982 because it did not contain a veto for Quebec and because it did not entrench certain rights for Aboriginal Canadians. A committee of the Canadian Judicial Council, which investigated Berger's conduct, reported that his comments might serve to undermine the public's perception of the judiciary's impartiality:

> It is apparent that some of the native peoples are unhappy with s.35 of the Canadian *Charter of Rights and Freedoms*. If Justice Berger should be called upon to interpret that section, for example, the meaning to be given to the word "existing" in "the existing aboriginal and treaty rights of the aboriginal peoples of Canada," would the general public have confidence now in his impartiality? After Justice Berger spoke

---

1   Peter H. Russell, *The Judiciary in Canada: The Third Branch of Government* (Toronto: McGraw-Hill Ryerson, 1987), 88–89.

publicly on the necessity for Quebec retaining a veto, his brother judges in Quebec were called on to determine whether such a right existed.[2]

The committee found that Berger's remarks were sufficiently indiscreet to justify removing him from the bench but thought that a warning would be more appropriate. Berger rejected these findings but resigned from his position a year later.

It is sometimes alleged that the judiciary is not truly impartial because it tends, on the whole, to be moderate or even conservative in its politics. Numerous observers argue that courts draw their members from the established centres of power and privilege in Canada and rarely concern themselves with the distribution of wealth and power. The governments that appoint judges are generally satisfied with the economic status quo. Finally, the judicial function is to enforce the law, not reform it along progressive lines. Ultimately, on this account, courts are conservative institutions.[3]

It is certainly important for students of Canadian politics to understand the political implications of judicial decision making, and it is possible to argue that the judiciary's political impact is in a sense conservative. Yet to claim that this constitutes a lack of impartiality is unfair to our judges. In the Canadian regime, the primary task of the judiciary is to apply the law, not to make it. In those cases where they in effect "make the law" by giving concrete meaning to imprecise legislative language, it is entirely reasonable to expect them to formulate their interpretations in light of the basic principles of the existing regime. It is perfectly legitimate for Canadians to seek modifications to the existing regime by pressuring their politicians to introduce the appropriate legislative changes, but it would be inconsistent with the principle of responsible government to expect the judiciary to act as agents of radical political change.

2. Judicial independence. In addition to guaranteeing a right to a trial before an "impartial" tribunal, section 11(d) of the Charter of Rights and Freedoms also guarantees that the tribunal shall be "independent." Although the terms "independent" and "impartial" sound alike, they do not mean the same thing. Impartiality is essentially a value or ethic that judges aspire to live up to as professionals with a commitment to professional ethics. **Judicial independence** is a set of structures or rules that help judges live up to the principle of impartiality.

---

2   *Report of the Committee of Investigation to the Canadian Judicial Council,* May 31, 1982, quoted in F.L. Morton, *Law, Politics, and the Judicial Process in Canada* (Calgary: University of Calgary Press, 1990), 111.

3   In the contemporary era, the classic statement of this position is Michael Mandel, *The Charter of Rights and the Legalization of Politics in Canada* (Toronto: Wall and Thompson, 1989). See also Allan C. Hutchinson, *Waiting for Coraf: A Critique of Law and Rights* (Toronto: University of Toronto Press, 1995).

When we say that the judiciary must be independent, we mean that it must be independent of the executive branch of the regime. The reason is quite simple. In many, if not most cases before the courts, the executive will be a party to the dispute. To reuse our earlier example, *R. v. Big M Drug Mart Ltd.* is actually a dispute between Big M and the Attorney General of Alberta (a member of the provincial executive) who, in taking Big M to court, is attempting to execute his duties under the law by prosecuting a party alleged to have violated a federal statute. The judiciary would have difficulty being impartial if it were subject to the control of an executive that, of necessity, frequently appears before it as a litigant. The principle of judicial independence thus entails certain conditions to guarantee that judges will be free of pressure from the political executive.

In a 1985 case entitled *Valente v. The Queen*, the Supreme Court of Canada had an opportunity to articulate those conditions in an authoritative fashion. The first is that judges must have security of tenure. In other words, the executive must not be able to fire judges merely because it dislikes their rulings. Second, the salaries of judges must be fixed by law, for, if the judiciary is not financially independent of the executive, the executive might try to influence judges by increasing or decreasing their salaries. The third and final condition is that judges must have control over those aspects of the administration of their courts that have an impact on judicial decision making (the scheduling of cases, for example).

Using those three conditions as a standard, we can say that Canada's judiciary is highly independent. Section 99 of CA 1867 explicitly guarantees the judges of our superior courts security of tenure until the age of 75 "during good behaviour." This is a traditional way of saying that judges may be removed from office only if they are physically or mentally incapable of performing their duties or if they have engaged in activities that might bring the administration of justice into disrepute (e.g., selling drugs or driving under the influence of alcohol). In other words, judges may not be fired for making decisions that the executive does not like or even for making mistakes. The tenure of the judges of Canada's other courts is protected by similar provisions in the statutes creating those courts.

Section 100 of CA 1867 entrenches the principle that the remuneration of the judges of our superior courts shall be fixed by law. This protects the salaries of individual judges from manipulation by the executive. Once again, the judges of our other courts are protected by similar provisions in the statutes creating those courts.

The third condition of judicial independence set down by the Supreme Court in *Valente* is not entrenched anywhere in the Constitution. For the most part, however, Canada's judges have ample authority over those aspects of court-room administration that are essential to their adjudicative work.

The importance Canadians attribute to the principle of judicial independence may be seen in an incident known as "The Judges Affair." In March 1976, the Chief Justice of the Quebec Superior Court, Jules Deschênes, wrote to the federal Minister of Justice to complain that on separate occasions three of Prime Minister Trudeau's cabinet ministers had contacted judges concerning cases they were hearing. None of the ministers resigned over the allegations, but the prime minister made it clear that similar conduct would not be tolerated in the future. Two years later, when it was reported that Labour Minister John Munro had contacted a judge to discuss the sentencing of one of his constituents, he was forced to resign. A decade later, Jean Charest was forced to resign from the Mulroney cabinet for having called a judge on behalf of a constituent from his riding.

3. Equality before the law. The third fundamental principle of Canada's judicial regime is that everyone is equal before the law. This principle is explicitly entrenched in section 15(1) of the Charter of Rights and Freedoms. It is also implicit in the preamble to the Charter, which stipulates that "Canada is founded on principles that recognize the supremacy of . . . the rule of law." One aspect of "the rule of law" is the principle that the law must be applied to all people equally.

Though Canada's courts are in principle committed to such equality, problems arise from the fact that legal proceedings are often very costly for those engaged in them. Provincial governments maintain legal aid programs to ensure that defendants in criminal cases who cannot afford to pay a lawyer will be provided with one. In non-criminal cases, however, the assistance offered under such programs is spotty. As a result, people who are entitled to some kind of redress under the law often are not able to pursue their claims because they cannot afford to. Moreover, even those who can pay a lawyer may find that they cannot afford full justice. In a judicial system that relies almost exclusively on the adversarial process for the presentation of facts and the articulation of arguments, the quality of one's legal representation can make the difference between winning and losing one's case. It is often true that the more money one has for legal fees, the better one is represented. This is not simply because high-priced lawyers are sometimes more effective than less expensive lawyers. It is also a function of the fact that the litigants with more money can afford expensive legal research and can drag cases on so long with appeals or procedural disputes that their adversaries can no longer afford the fight.

8.3 Canada's Courts

At first glance, Canada appears to have a bewildering array of courts, some of which have odd or even quaint names. But there is a logic to the structure of Canada's court system that is easily understood if one keeps in mind a small number of basic principles.

The first of these principles is hierarchy. Court systems are almost by definition stratified into different layers with some courts deemed superior to others
and one court labelled "supreme." There are several reasons for this structure.
One is the division of judicial activity into trials (where a case is heard for the first
time) and appeals (where the decision reached in the trial stage is re-examined).
Logic dictates that, if an appeal court is going to have the authority to overturn a
decision reached by a trial court, it will have to be of higher status. Moreover, if
litigants are to have a right to appeal the decision of the appeal court, there must
be a court of higher authority than the appeal court—hence, at some point, there
must be a final court of appeal, which is "supreme."

Another reason court systems are organized in hierarchical fashion is that
some subjects of adjudication are inherently more important than others. Murder
cases are very important, for example, because those found guilty of murder are subject to very severe penalties. Traffic violations, on the other hand, generally involve
relatively light sentences and are thus not as important as murder cases. It therefore
makes sense to divide a judicial system into **superior courts**, which will in theory
have the most able judges, and **inferior courts**, which may have more informal procedures, depending on the type of case they handle.

One may thus sketch a simple, hypothetical hierarchy of courts something
like the diagram in Figure 8.1. Here we find inferior courts specializing in traffic
violations or small claims, "superior" trial courts to handle crimes such as murder
or assault and battery, a court of appeal to hear appeals from both the inferior
and superior trial courts, and a "supreme court" to hear appeals from the court
of appeal.

Figure 8.1: Hierarchy of Courts in Canada

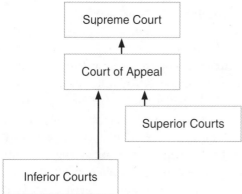

The second principle we must keep in mind in order to understand Canada's court system is federalism. The system sketched in Figure 8.1 would work well in a unitary regime like that of Britain. In a federal regime, however, the design of a court system becomes more complicated because one has to accommodate the claims of two layers of government. As we saw in Chapter Four, the United States was the first great model of a federal regime. In planning a judicial system for their federation, the Americans thought it best to create what is called a "dual" system. In this approach, there are two distinct networks of courts: a federal network for the adjudication of cases under federal law and a separate network in each state for adjudicating cases involving state law. The sole unifying feature in this dual system is that the Supreme Court of the United States sits in appeal of cases from both networks. Figure 8.2 provides a simple outline of the American "dual" system.

Figure 8.2: Dual Court System of the United States

It is not surprising that the Americans opted for a dual system with a separate network of state courts, for their regime was originally designed to be a strongly decentralized federation with highly independent state governments. As we have seen, however, our Fathers of Confederation thought that the Americans had made a grave mistake in giving so much authority to their state governments. Accordingly, in planning Canada's judicial system, they sought an approach that would combine the diversity required by federalism and the uniformity that comes from a single centralized system. This led them to create what Peter Russell has called an **integrated judicial system**: a single system under the joint custody of the two levels of government.[4] This system is outlined in Figure 8.3. It is more complex than the American one, but its structure can be easily understood if one looks at it in light of the basic rules set down in the Constitution.

Figure 8.3: Canada's Integrated Judicial System

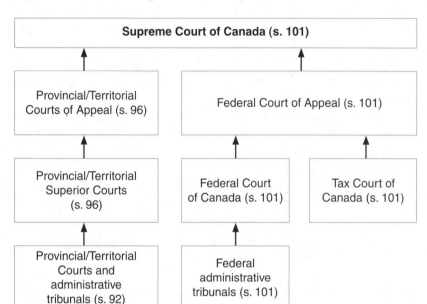

Section 92.14 of CA 1867 stipulates that the provincial legislatures are to have jurisdiction over "the Administration of Justice in the Province, including the maintenance and organization of Provincial Courts, both of Civil and Criminal Jurisdiction." In other words, provincial governments have the power to create and run whatever courts they deem necessary for the operation of a fair and efficient judicial system. This includes inferior courts (often called "provincial courts") such as traffic, family, or small claims courts. It also includes the superior courts that, as we have noted, are either trial courts for more serious offences and disputes or appeal courts.

Placing the administration of justice in the hands of provincial governments derives from the desire for local control that is common in a federation.

---

4   See Peter H. Russell, ed., *Canada's Trial Courts: Two Tiers or One?* (Toronto: University of Toronto Press, 2007).

Given the guarantee of the civil code system of Quebec and the common law system in use in the rest of the provinces, provincial control helps to deal with the different demands placed on their respective judicial systems. Provincial control also fits with the idea that different provinces may find that situational factors as mundane as size could make a system appropriate for one province but inappropriate for another: though a large province might find it necessary to have "district" courts to give service to all areas of the province, such a system might be unnecessary in a small province. In any event, the colonies that united in 1867 to form Canada already had their own distinctive judicial systems in place, each of which was tailored to meet local needs, and there was no pressing reason to replace them.

There was, however, a need to modify the rules for appointing judges. Although the federal principle requires local control over local matters, it also dictates that matters of national interest be handled nationally. The Fathers of Confederation decided that criminal law was a national matter (although the Americans had left it in the hands of the state governments) and should therefore be written by the federal parliament. But the objective of having a single criminal law for all Canadians would have been undermined had its enforcement been left in the hands of a provincially controlled judiciary. Judges have a good deal of discretion when it comes to the sentencing of offenders, and courts in one province might have consistently imposed lighter or harsher sentences than judges in other provinces. In order to ensure that Canada's criminal law would be applied with some degree of consistency, section 96 of CA 1867 stipulated that the federal government was to have the authority to appoint the judges of all superior courts (which would handle the most important aspects of criminal law). Further to this end, section 100 provides that the salaries of those judges are to be set and paid by the federal parliament. While Canada's inferior courts are completely under provincial control, then, we have a network of superior courts under shared jurisdiction: the provinces create and maintain the courts according to local need, but Ottawa appoints and pays the judges to ensure national consistency of judicial decision making. These two types of court are often referred to as **section 92 courts** (inferior) and **section 96 courts** (superior).

The Constitution also provides for a third type of court: federally created courts with federally appointed judges, sometimes called **section 101 courts**. Section 101 of CA 1867 grants Parliament the authority to establish special courts for "the better administration" of federal law, as well as a "General Court of Appeal for Canada." Parliament has made use of both branches of its powers under section 101. In 1875, it created the Exchequer Court as a special court for the "better administration" of certain areas of federal law. In 1970, this court was significantly restructured and then renamed the Federal Court of Canada. The Federal Court hears cases in specialized areas of federal law (e.g., maritime law, immigration law, and patent and copyright law) as well as appeals of decisions made by federal regulatory agencies and administrative tribunals. Appeals from the Federal Court of Canada go to the Federal Court of Appeal. Section 101 also allowed for the establishment of the Tax Court of Canada in 1983. This court hears cases involving federal income and corporate tax, the GST, and employment insurance. Appeals from its decisions go to the Federal Court of Appeal.

In 1875, Parliament also used its powers under section 101 to create the Supreme Court of Canada. The Supreme Court has the authority to hear appeals from provincial courts of appeal, from the Federal Court of Canada, and from the Federal Court of Appeal. The fact that this measure was not taken until eight years into the history of the Dominion does not mean that Canada was without a supreme court during that initial period. The Fathers of Confederation assumed that Canadians would use a British institution, the **Judicial Committee of the Privy Council (JCPC)** as their final court of appeal. The creation of the Supreme Court of Canada did not immediately change that practice: decisions of provincial courts of appeal could be appealed to the JCPC rather than to the Supreme Court. Indeed, the decisions of the Supreme Court could themselves be appealed to the JCPC. In short, the Supreme Court was at first not truly "supreme." One might say that it was the supreme court *in* Canada but not the supreme court *of* Canada. It was not until after World War II that this quasi-colonial situation was terminated. In 1949, with the blessing of the JCPC itself, Parliament abolished the right to appeal cases to the JCPC. Only then did the Supreme Court of Canada become truly supreme.

8.4 The Supreme Court of Canada

The Supreme Court now consists of nine judges, appointed by the prime minister. According to the terms of the Supreme Court Act, three of these judges must come from Quebec to ensure that the court will have at least three judges who are familiar with Quebec's civil law system. By convention, at least one judge is always from Atlantic Canada and two from the Western provinces, with the remaining three being from Ontario. There may be other expectations of representation that have risen to the level of convention as well. It would be hard to imagine a Supreme Court without female justices, and there is increasingly an expectation that most if not all judges be able to work in both official languages.

The court now hears about 80 cases a year. In some of these cases, the right to such a hearing is automatic (e.g., in certain criminal cases after the appeal court has overturned the decision of the trial court). For the most part, however, the court is now in control of its own docket. Those who wish to appeal a case to it must persuade at least two members of a three-judge panel that the case deserves to be heard. The judges will want to hear a case if it appears there has been a serious error in the lower court's decision or if that case raises an important legal or constitutional issue that needs to be settled by the country's highest court.

In order to avoid deadlock, odd-number panels of justices generally hear cases. There can be as few as five justices on a panel, though exceptionally important cases will be heard by all nine. Most, however, are heard by a panel of seven judges. After the case has been heard, the justices retire to discuss it. In the Supreme Court of the United States the most senior judges speak first in these discussions, but in Canada it is customary to have the justices speak in reverse order of seniority. This is meant to ensure that the newer justices will not feel pressured to go along with the views of their more senior colleagues. In many cases, the justices arrive at a unanimous conclusion, and one or more of them is assigned to write a "decision," which explains the ruling and the reasons for it. When the court is not unanimous, one or more justices will author the **majority opinion** while another will write a **dissenting opinion**. Occasionally, justices may agree on a disposition of the case on the basis of different reasons. In such cases, there will be a majority opinion, but individual judges may write their own **concurring opinions**.

Perhaps the most peculiar feature of the Supreme Court is the fact that it exists by virtue of an organic statute—The Supreme Court Act, 1875—rather than an entrenched constitutional law. The amending formula set out in section 41 stipulates that the "composition of the Supreme Court of Canada" may not be amended without the consent of Parliament and all ten provincial legislatures. Likewise, section 42 subjects any other changes in the Supreme Court to approval by the general amending formula. These inclusions have essentially entrenched the current format and powers of the court without formally incorporating the text of the Supreme Court Act into the entrenched constitution.

8.5 The Politics of Judicial Appointments

Canada's judiciary was designed to be professional and non-political. Our judges are not elected to their positions; they are appointed by the executive from the ranks of practising lawyers and legal specialists. Moreover, the principles of judicial independence and impartiality have served to keep our judges at arm's length from partisan politics. In recent decades, however, the process for selecting our federally appointed judges (of whom there are approximately 1,100) has become something of a political issue.

Originally, the movement to reform the process for judicial appointments was in the direction of making that process less political than it is. The target of reformers was the partisan character of the appointment process. It has always been the case that the party in power tends to appoint a disproportionate number of its own supporters to the bench. This tendency is less pronounced now than it was 50 years ago, but it is still significant. Reformers have not been able to eliminate the partisan character of judicial appointments, but they have managed to curb the most serious abuses. Since 1988, input on these appointments has been provided by a number of regional judicial advisory committees (JACs). The Federal Minister of Justice appoints three members of each JAC and chooses a further four based on recommendations from the Canadian Bar Association, the provincial government, the provincial law society, and law enforcement. The Chief Justice of the province chooses an eighth member of each JAC as a judicial representative. The JACs place applicants for judicial vacancies in one of two categories. Applicants are deemed either "recommended" or "unable to recommend." The designation of recommended really means qualified, as more applicants will be deemed recommended than there are vacancies. Without the capacity to rank candidates, the JACs really are only screening applicants and real discretion on appointments is with the federal Minister of Justice and the prime minister.

With respect to the Supreme Court, the reform movement has been quite different. While the aim of the reforms described above has been to make the appointment process less political, when it comes to Supreme Court appointments, reformers seek to make the process more political. Observers of the judiciary are quick to point out that much of the time, especially in cases involving judicial review of the Constitution, judges are making decisions that have significant political consequences. Moreover, as we saw in Chapter Five, it appears that many of these decisions are of necessity made on political (or moral-political) rather than legal grounds. This leads many observers to ask why a small number of unelected (and largely unknown) Supreme Court judges should have the power to make fundamental, and often irrevocable, political decisions for Canada. That in turn leads them to press for changes to the appointment process.

For example, it has now been conceded by all relevant parties that provincial governments ought to have some input into the appointment of

Supreme Court justices. As we saw in Chapter Four, those judges have to make rulings about the respective powers of the federal and provincial governments under sections 91 and 92 of CA 1867. In the past, it was assumed that Supreme Court judges were non-partisan professionals who could be trusted to make those rulings in an impartial manner, even though they owed their positions on the court to the federal government. Now, however, it is generally supposed that division of powers cases are at least to some extent inherently political rather than legal matters. This fact makes it necessary to alter a regime in which one of the parties to those cases—the federal government—has exclusive control over appointments to the court that has the final say on those cases. It was only logical that, in both the Meech Lake and Charlottetown Accords, Ottawa should agree to share the power of Supreme Court appointments with the provincial governments. This process would allow each level of government to veto the appointment to the court of anyone whose views on federalism were unacceptable to it.

But it is the adoption of the Charter of Rights and Freedoms that has led to the most radical calls for politicizing the appointment of the judiciary. In Charter cases, judges have decided whether Canada should have laws against euthanasia, whether Sunday shopping should be permitted, whether the government should be allowed to permit cruise missile testing, and other similar questions. Reasonable people of good faith will likely differ on the interpretation of many constitutional rights, so judicial determination seems more political than legal. If we are choosing political decision makers, goes the logic, citizens should be more aware of the politics of appointees. Thus some advocate for the American practice of subjecting nominees for Supreme Court positions to examination by the legislative branch of the regime. In theory, this practice is meant to allow the public to find out ahead of time what political views the nominee would bring to the bench and to block the appointment of nominees whose views are deemed undesirable.

As part of his response to what he called Canada's "democratic deficit," Prime Minister Martin expressed support for some kind of public review process for Supreme Court appointments. When two vacancies had to be filled in the summer of 2004, an ad hoc committee, including both parliamentarians and members of the legal community, was given an opportunity to review the credentials of the two nominees, Louise Charron and Rosalie Abella. Martin indicated that the use of this ad hoc committee was a temporary expedient and that he hoped in the future to develop a more permanent arrangement for reviewing Supreme Court appointments. When Stephen Harper became prime minister in 2006, he took a slightly different approach. He required his first Supreme Court appointee, Marshall Rothstein, to appear before a committee of parliamentarians for a three-hour televised interview. Committee members were able to express their opinions regarding the suitability of the nominee to Prime Minister Harper, but the decision to appoint remained entirely in his hands. Vacancies on the Supreme Court since then have been filled by inconsistent means. Some appointees have faced no scrutiny at all, and others were selected by Prime Minister Harper from a shortlist prepared by a parliamentary committee.

In 2013, a Supreme Court appointment became a matter of intense public controversy when Prime Minister Harper nominated Federal Court Justice Marc Nadon to the Supreme Court. Upon the retirement of Justice Morris Fish, a vacancy was created among the Quebec jurists on the Court. A parliamentary committee recommended a shortlist, from which Prime Minister Harper selected Justice Nadon. Nadon was duly appointed to the court and sworn in on October 7, 2013. Shortly thereafter, Toronto lawyer Rocco Galati challenged the constitutionality of Nadon's appointment. The argument was that, although Nadon had practised law in Quebec for many years, he was at the time of his appointment neither a member of the Quebec bar nor a member of a Quebec court despite the explicit requirement that justices appointed to fill Quebec vacancies were obliged to meet one of those two criteria. Galati's claim was that, in order to be eligible for appointment, Justice Nadon had to be *currently* a member of the Quebec bar or a member of a Quebec high court.

Apparently the federal government had long suspected a hitch in appointing a judge from the Federal Court to fill a Quebec vacancy and so obtained legal opinions from eminent authorities in Canada to ensure it was possible. Furthermore, the Harper government had Parliament hastily pass amendments to the Supreme Court Act clarifying that current membership in the Quebec bar was not required. To ensure that these changes were indeed constitutional, the government then referred the whole matter to the Supreme Court of Canada for its opinion. Justice Nadon, at that point already on the court, recused himself from this proceeding.

In March 2014, a 6–1 majority of the court declared that, to be appointed to a Quebec vacancy, one must be a current member of the Quebec bar or a Quebec court. Justice Nadon was thus deemed ineligible because at the time of his appointment he was neither a member of the Quebec bar nor a member of a Quebec court. Nadon was now off the Supreme Court. The incident was further marred by accusations from the Harper government that the Supreme Court, and in particular the Chief Justice, had interfered in the appointment of the Prime Minister's preferred candidate.[5] Shortly thereafter, Mr. Harper filled the Quebec vacancy with Justice Clément Gascon, this time without the advice or scrutiny of a parliamentary committee. The further two vacancies filled by Prime Minister Harper were done in much the same way.

Though it is generally desirable to promote openness and transparency in government, the idea of reviewing nominations to the Supreme Court is not without its problems. In the first place, it is not clear that parliamentarians will be able to find out exactly what a nominee's political views are. As the American experience indicates, potential judges are reluctant to commit themselves to specific positions in response to hypothetical questions, for they realize that this will compromise their ability to deal with particular cases in an impartial fashion. They therefore tend to be highly evasive when answering such questions before screening committees. The American approach is distinguished by the fact that the president must have the support of the Senate for a nominee actually to be appointed to the court. In our more disciplined party system, it is unlikely that a government with a parliamentary majority would allow its members to be anything other than disciplined in their support of nominees if Parliament were given the final authority to approve nominees. Finally, one has to wonder if such a process would not serve to make the judges themselves politically partisan. After all, if Parliament has examined their political beliefs and found them acceptable, why should they feel any restraint about imposing those beliefs on Canadians when they make their rulings?

8.6 Judicial Power and the Charter

One of the most interesting features of the judiciary as a political institution is that it is the only institution in our regime that has the power to decide unilaterally just how much power it will have. Under section 52(1) of CA 1982, our courts have an obligation to strike down any law that violates a Charter right. A law that prohibited Catholics from voting would clearly be a violation of both section 2(a) and section 15.1 of the Charter, and the judiciary would have a clear obligation to declare it unconstitutional. But what about a provincial law prohibiting privately funded health care? A Quebec doctor named Jacques Chaoulli argued that Quebec's ban on private health insurance infringed the

---

5   See Thomas M.J. Bateman, "The Other Shoe to Drop: Marc Nadon and Judicial Appointment Politics in Canada," *Journal of Parliamentary and Political Law* 9 (2015): 169–87.

right to "security of the person" in section 7 of the Charter because it denied people access to speedy private medical care, forcing them to spend time on long wait lists for public medical care. In the Supreme Court's 2005 *Chaoulli* decision, four justices of the Supreme Court declared that Quebec's law was an infringement of section 7—but three justices declared it was not. Significantly, one of the concerns expressed by the minority in this case was that the issue before the court was really a question of social policy. In the view of the minority, policy questions of this sort are best left in the hands of legislative bodies where the relevant cost-benefit trade-offs can be made by officials who are democratically accountable to the people.

The view articulated by the minority in *Chaoulli* might be characterized by the term **judicial restraint**. Those who favour judicial restraint argue that when courts apply an entrenched bill of rights such as the Charter, they should give the benefit of the doubt to the legislature that enacted the law in question and should use their power to strike a law down only when the infringement of the right is clear. **Judicial activism**, on the other hand, is the approach that favours pushing the power of judicial review vigorously, beyond the black-and-white issues and deep into the grey. The term "judicial activism" is frequently used in a manner that suggests the judge or judges in question are using their judicial power to advance a specific political agenda.

When the adoption of the Charter was first being debated, it was frequently suggested that Canada's judiciary would probably exercise restraint in its application of the Charter as it had always been very restrained in its handling of the Canadian Bill of Rights. What has the record shown more than three decades later? Depending on their own political perspective, experts disagree somewhat as to how activist our courts have been, but most would likely characterize the judiciary's record as at least moderately activist. This activism is abetted by a supportive legal and policy community that has a vested interest in the judiciary not restraining itself. Morton and Knopff have suggested that interest groups that have not been successful at lobbying elected politicians have turned to the courts as a more effective vehicle for advancing their agendas. To justify that approach, those same groups have to promote the legitimacy of judicial activism as well. Drawing on funding provided by governments or foundations, they pursue long-term litigation strategies designed to expand the reach of the Charter and shape its interpretation so as to promote their particular causes.[6]

---

6   F.L. Morton and Rainer Knopff, *The Charter Revolution and the Court Party* (Toronto: University of Toronto Press, 2000).

Key Terms

precedents
stare decisis
reference procedure
impartiality
judicial independence
superior courts
inferior courts
integrated judicial system
section 92 courts

section 96 courts
section 101 courts
Judicial Committee of the Privy
  Council (JCPC)
majority opinion
dissenting opinion
concurring opinion
judicial restraint
judicial activism

Discussion Questions

1. Should the House of Commons be given the authority to reject a prime minister's nominee to the Supreme Court?

2. Which is more in keeping with the principles of a liberal democratic regime: judicial activism or judicial restraint?

PART FOUR

CANADIAN DEMOCRACY IN ACTION: ELECTIONS, PARTIES, AND POLICY

CHAPTER NINE

ELECTIONS

9.1   Elections and Representation

We learned in Chapter One that the Canadian regime is not a direct democracy but a representative democracy. This means that the central democratic mechanism of our regime is elections. Section 3 of CA 1982 entrenches the most important of our democratic rights in the following language:

> Every citizen of Canada has a right to vote in an election of members of the House of Commons or of a legislative assembly and to be qualified for membership therein.

To understand the significance of these rights, it is important to consider them in light of the basic principles of responsible government. We have seen that, in responsible government, the regime obtains its democratic legitimacy by virtue of the fact that those who exercise political authority are in some way accountable to the citizens who form the electorate. Our Members of Parliament are directly accountable to us in that they must be periodically re-elected in order to remain in office. The prime minister and cabinet are indirectly accountable to us in that they must always maintain the confidence of the House of Commons, which we have elected directly. Elections to the House of Commons thus constitute the democratic linchpin of the regime because they ensure that those who make political decisions will in some sense represent the will or interests of the electorate.

But how exactly do elected representatives or MPs "represent" the voters? What exactly is meant by the term "representation"? It is important to consider these questions with some care if we are to understand properly the logic of our elections. Modern democratic states are obviously far too big to have direct democracy. The citizens cannot literally be present in a legislative assembly. Their views, opinions, interests, and even their sentiments must be presented. So we strive to make them present by way of a person chosen by the people to do just that. In this sense, then, the electorate is again made present or re-presented. But the nature of this re-presentation is a complex matter. In democratic theory, there are at least three main concepts of representation. According to the first view, elected representatives are seen as **delegates**, that is, spokespersons who faithfully transmit the views of the majority of the people who elect them. A second interpretation treats representatives as **trustees**, people to whom we "entrust" the responsibilities of government. In this view, our representatives are elected for their character and judgement and are free to decide for themselves how to vote on each issue. A third concept of representation emphasizes the role of the representative as a **party member**. According to this view, the task of our representatives is to be loyal supporters of the policies advocated by their party. It should be obvious that these three concepts of representation are to some extent at odds with each other. On any given issue, it is likely that an MP would vote one way as a loyal party member and a different way as a delegate speaking for his or her local constituents. Acting as a trustee and voting according to his or her conscience, the MP might favour yet another alternative.

Which of these models of representation do we use in Canada? This is a question for which there is no simple answer, and that perhaps explains why Canadians are often confused about it. Some will tell you that they vote for the party (or perhaps the party leader), while others claim to vote based on the personal qualities of their local candidates. Still, consideration of the logic of responsible government will allow us to draw some general inferences about how our representatives are supposed to represent us.

We know that responsible government turns out, in practice, to be government by a cabinet that is accountable to the House of Commons. Because the cabinet is not elected directly by the voters, it is important that we elect the House of Commons in such a way as to draw the strongest link possible between the voters and the cabinet. This means that our representation must, for the most part, be party representation. The idea of party representation forms the basis of the concept of a **mandate**. If it is assumed that the voters elected their MPs primarily on the basis of party affiliation, then the party that is called on to form the government may reasonably infer that the electorate has endorsed the general line of policy that it proposed in the election campaign. The party may thus claim that it has a "democratic mandate" to carry out that line of policy. If our MPs were elected primarily as delegates or trustees, there would be no such mandate. The strongest link between the electorate and its government would be severed, leaving the government less accountable to the people than we think it should be.[1]

This is not to say, however, that there is no room for the delegate and trustee models of representation in Canada. It should not be forgotten that MPs have an opportunity for full and free debate on matters within their respective parliamentary caucuses. Voters may therefore reasonably expect their MP to speak in accordance with his or her judgement (trustee model) or on behalf of the constituents (delegate model) in that setting. But they probably should not expect their MP to vote against a position taken by his or her party once the caucus has made up its mind. Canada's approach to representation should therefore be understood as a mixture of the delegate, trustee, and party member theories, but an approach that puts the heaviest emphasis on the party member theory. This view is confirmed by the fact that Canadians seldom elect an MP who runs as an "independent," or does not belong to one of the major political parties.

---

[1]   We suggested, in Chapter One, that the Fathers of Confederation would not have insisted on maintaining such a direct link between the voters and the government. It is obvious that Canadians' thinking on this point has changed. Though Canadians maintain a belief in the virtues of indirect (representative) government, we do insist that the government should be accountable to the electorate in some meaningful way.

The complexity of our approach to representation in Canada becomes evident whenever there is an incident of **"floor-crossing"** in the House of Commons. Immediately after the 2006 election, David Emerson, who had been elected in Vancouver Kingsway as a Liberal candidate, "crossed the floor" of the House of Commons to join the Conservative caucus and become a minister in the Harper government. Many voters of Vancouver Kingsway were outraged by this move. How could someone who had just been elected as a Liberal decide without consulting the voters to defect to the Conservatives? Wasn't Mr. Emerson cheating all those who had voted Liberal of their democratic rights? From the point of view of the "party member" theory of representation, he most certainly was. On the other hand, floor-crossing is perfectly consistent with the trustee theory of representation. As the "trustee" of the voters of Vancouver Kingsway, Mr. Emerson could argue that the voters had elected him as an individual and had given him the authority to do what he thought best for the riding and for the country. And that was essentially Mr. Emerson's argument: because Vancouver needed to have a voice in the cabinet and the Vancouver area had not elected any Conservatives, it would be in the best interests of Vancouverites for him to switch to the Conservatives and provide a voice for Vancouver in the corridors of power. Mr. Emerson's position was not unreasonable, but his situation was relatively unique. In general, Canadians tend to punish floor-crossers by voting them out at the earliest possible opportunity,[2] which makes floor-crossing relatively rare and which indicates that most Canadians regard *party* representation as the most fundamental aspect of representation in our regime.[3]

9.2   Representation and Diversity

Another issue that emerges when we consider the matter of representation is the question of who can represent us. According to the **microcosm theory of representation**, legislative bodies are fully representative *only* if the assembly is a microcosm of society as a whole. For example, if half of the population is female, then roughly half of the representatives ought to be female. Similarly, if the population is composed of a variety of ethnic groups, the assembly should be inclusive of that

---

2   MP Eve Adams, who quit the Conservative Party and crossed the floor to join the Liberals in 2015, could not even win a Liberal nomination five months later.

3   One obvious way to make floor-crossing more legitimate would be to create an expectation that any MP who wishes to change parties must first resign and then be re-elected in a by-election under that party's banner.

diversity. The case for the microcosm theory of representation is grounded in two arguments. The first is an argument for inclusivity as a requirement of fairness: if Chinese-Canadians constitute 5 per cent of Canada's population, it would be unfair if our legislative body did not include at least some Chinese-Canadian representatives. The second argument for diversity is that our legislative body needs to be inclusive of the wide variety of Canadian citizens to ensure that their perspectives are heard and their interests can be defended.

The microcosm theory has always played some role in the Canadian regime. As we saw in Chapter Six, the prime minister is expected to form a cabinet that reflects our country's diversity not only in geographic terms but also in terms of religion, ethnicity, language, and gender. The microcosm theory is also becoming increasingly influential in deciding who is to be selected to serve on the Supreme Court of Canada. In recent times, there has been some discussion of reforming our electoral system in order to have our Parliament mirror more closely the social composition of the country. During the negotiations leading to the Charlottetown Accord, for example, it was proposed that half the seats in any elected Senate should be reserved for women.

There are, of course, some serious questions to be considered in relation to the microcosm theory of representation. To begin with, there is a philosophical issue: when, how, and to what extent is it true that the interests of various groups can be represented only by members of those groups? There are also two practical questions. First, who would decide what the politically relevant characteristics of society are? How do we determine which groups should have defined representation and which should not? Justin Trudeau was praised for the prominent place he assigned in his cabinet for Aboriginal Canadians and Canadians from visible minorities, but those very efforts to reflect Canada's diversity brought grumbling from some of the ethnic groups he left out. Second, how is a system to be designed to ensure that those characteristics are indeed represented? It would be easy enough to guarantee that there is an equal number of men and women in Parliament: we could simply make it a rule that Canadians must elect one of each in every riding. But what about other groups?

The case of the representation of women is particularly instructive. Women are clearly a more visible political force now than they were 30 years ago. Women have been elected leaders of major political parties in most provinces and at the national level. Women have held the office of premier in most provinces and one woman (Kim Campbell) has served as prime minister. This progress is also reflected in a slow but steady increase in the percentage of MPs who are women.

Figure 9.1: Women Elected to Parliament and Percentage of MPs Who Are Women

Year	Number	Percentage (%)
1980	14	5
1984	27	10
1988	39	13
1993	53	18
1997	62	20.5
2000	62	20.5
2004	65	21
2006	64	21
2008	69	22
2011	76	24
2015	88	26

The slowness of progress in this area has led some to advocate reform of the electoral system to increase the likelihood of women seeking and winning election to public office. A system using multi-member electoral districts, for example, would probably increase the number of women elected because political parties would likely seek to balance their slate of nominees by having a man and a woman nominated in each constituency. The adoption of a party list form of proportional representation (described in 9.7) would also serve to increase the number of women in the House as parties would be able to compose lists that are more equally balanced between men and women. A different approach to the problem is to work within the existing system and to simply focus on finding more women candidates. The Liberal Party under Stéphane Dion was committed to ensuring that 35 per cent of its candidates would be women in the 2006 election. A problem with setting fixed targets, however, is that the selection of candidates is carried out at the local level. To guarantee that the party will meet an overall national target, the party leadership in Ottawa has to be ready to interfere, if necessary, with the local riding associations' right to choose their own candidates. National party influence in candidate selection would alter a long-standing principle that this function is a matter of local party democracy. Moreover, an artificially imposed target has a tendency to foster the nomination of token women candidates in ridings the party has no chance of winning. The discrepancy between the percentage of Liberal ridings with women candidates in 2008 (37 per cent) and the percentage of Liberal winners who were women (24 per cent) suggests that this happened with some frequency.

Prime Minister Trudeau's decision in 2015 to appoint a cabinet built on the principle of gender parity is probably the single most significant advance we have seen in terms of the representation of women in Canadian parliamentary democracy. It is hard to imagine the next prime minister backing too far away from the principle of gender parity in the cabinet, and should several consecutive prime ministers follow it, the principle may eventually become a constitutional convention. Also, with more women being appointed to cabinet, women will be more likely to win party nominations at the local level, producing higher numbers of female MPs. One might conclude from this example that the best way to advance the cause of inclusivity is to rely on the discretionary appointment powers exercised by our political leaders rather than on specific institutional reforms.

9.3 Canada's Current Electoral System: SMP

Political institutions are not neutral when it comes to how they structure choices and hence affect outcomes. They therefore affect the way politics is conducted. Electoral institutions, in particular, can play a substantial role in determining who wins and who loses an election, how strong different parties will be, and what types of party are likely to succeed. It is therefore important to understand what kind of electoral system Canada uses and to consider what impact that system has on the country's political life. We take up the former point in this section and the latter in section 9.6.

The design of an electoral system will depend on three main factors. The first is the question of electoral districts. Will the country be divided up into a number of electoral districts, or will the voters all vote in a single national election? Second is the number of representatives. What is the optimum number of representatives for the legislative body? If there are too few, that body may not be sufficiently representative of the population. If there are too many, it may become dysfunctional. (Imagine a House of Commons with 10,000 MPs!) Furthermore, if the electoral system is based on multiple districts, one has to ask if there will be one member elected per district or multiple-member districts. (One might want double-member districts to ensure that each district is represented by one man and one woman, for example, or by more than one party.) Finally, there is the question of the method of electing representatives. How is the actual voting to be structured? Does the person with the most votes (a **plurality**) win, or must the winner have a majority of votes? Does the elector simply choose one candidate, or does the voter rank the candidates in order of preference? Alternatively, does the elector choose only the desired party rather than a specific candidate?

The preamble to CA 1867 specifies that Canada is to have "a Constitution similar in Principle to that of the United Kingdom." In addition to this constitution, we also adopted a similar electoral system. Like Britain, then, Canada has what is usually referred to as the **single-member plurality (SMP)** system. This is an electoral system in which the country is divided into a number of electoral districts (informally called **ridings** or **constituencies**), each of which has one representative.[4] That representative is elected by a plurality of votes rather than a majority. A winning candidate will therefore often have less than 50 per cent of the votes cast in the district. For this reason, Canada is sometimes said to have a **first-past-the-post electoral system**: you don't have to have a majority to win; you only need to get to the finish line ahead of all the other candidates.

Section 37 of CA 1867 specifies how many MPs there will be from each province. By extension, this should tell us how many electoral districts there will be. Sections 51 and 52, however, provide for a readjustment of these numbers after each decennial census of the population in order to ensure that changes in population will be reflected in the distribution of seats. The results of the 2011 Census showed substantial population growth in Ontario, British Columbia, and Alberta. Parliament passed the Fair Representation Act later that year, which had the effect of adding 30 new seats to the House of Commons—almost all of them in those three provinces. Even so, the allocation of seats by province will never be strictly proportional. Section 51A of CA 1867 provides special protection for the smaller provinces by declaring that no province shall have fewer MPs than its number of senators. Because of section 51A, Prince Edward Island is guaranteed four MPs (though in terms of population, it deserves only one). Similarly, New Brunswick must always have ten MPs, though its current population would warrant only seven.[5]

---

4   Note that, at the time of Confederation, most constituencies in Britain elected two members. Such dual-member ridings were eliminated in Britain in 1885. In the early years of Confederation, Canada also had a number of dual-member constituencies, but they became less common in the twentieth century and had disappeared entirely by the 1960s.

5   Note that the effect of the amended section 51 of CA 1867 is that no province will ever have fewer seats in the House of Commons than it had in 1985, which is when this section came into force.

Figure 9.2: Distribution of Seats in the House of Commons (as of 2015)

Atlantic Canada		*32*
	Prince Edward Island	4
	Nova Scotia	11
	New Brunswick	10
	Newfoundland and Labrador	7
Central Canada		*199*
	Ontario	121
	Quebec	78
Western Canada		*104*
	Manitoba	14
	Saskatchewan	14
	Alberta	34
	British Columbia	42
Northern Canada		*3*
	Nunavut	1
	Northwest Territories	1
	Yukon	1
Total		*338*

The process for determining the specific boundaries of these electoral districts is led by a set of independent **electoral boundaries commissions** (one per province), which provide Parliament with a set of recommendations. Each three-person commission is chaired by a judge, and commission members are typically high-profile citizens who are known for their impartiality and/or expertise in law or political science. To carry out their work, the commissions must give due consideration to the principle of **community of interest** (e.g., keeping rural communities with rural communities rather than mixing urban and rural populations or keeping minority language populations together). The commissions also pay careful attention to the number of voters and the geographic size of each constituency. In order to respect the democratic principle of "one person, one vote," a province's electoral districts should be roughly equal in population. At the last redistribution of seats, the calculated average population for an electoral district, or **electoral quotient**, was 111,166. But it is impossible, and in some cases undesirable, to insist that every constituency be exactly the same size. Notice, for example, that making the electoral districts equal in terms of the size of their population will make them unequal in geographical size. One will find 111,000 people in a relatively small area in Toronto, but it may take a huge swathe of territory to create a district with that population in Northern Ontario. In addition, a constituency of immense geographical size may be too large for an individual MP to represent effectively. In order to keep the geographical size of constituencies reasonable, it is not uncommon to create electoral districts with smaller than average populations in remote areas. Finally, because the electoral districts are first allocated by province and then their boundaries are drawn with a view to districts being roughly equal in population, the smaller provinces with a guaranteed minimum of representatives will necessarily have electoral districts that are below the electoral quotient. The institution of federalism thus affects the principle of equal representation.

9.4 Voting in Canada

Although in constitutional law it is the governor general who dissolves Parliament and calls new elections, he or she does so on the "advice" of the prime minister. If the prime minister's party controls only a minority of votes in the House of Commons, the House has the ability to force an election at any time by voting a lack of confidence in the government. Such a vote would compel the prime minister either to resign or, more likely, to advise the governor general to dissolve Parliament and call elections. In the case of majority government, however, the prime minister has traditionally had a free hand to determine the timing of elections, within certain limits. Section 4(1) of CA 1982 stipulates that no Parliament is to last longer than five years. Prime ministers have rarely waited the full five years because there is a general expectation in Canada that elections ought to be held in the fourth year of a Parliament. If a prime minister waited five years to ask for a dissolution, that was usually a sign that the government was afraid to face the electorate. On the other hand, prime ministers have sometimes been tempted to ask for a dissolution after fewer than four years if their government was particularly popular or the opposition was particularly weak.

As noted in Chapter Three, the Harper government, following the lead of several provincial legislatures, passed legislation providing for a "fixed" election date: Our federal elections are now supposed to be held every fourth year on the third Monday in October. In theory, this legislation was designed both to minimize uncertainty regarding the timing of elections and to deprive prime ministers of the opportunity to use their control over election timing to the advantage of their own party. However, the very nature of responsible government makes it impossible to stick to a fixed election date in every case. Whenever the House expresses a lack of confidence in a government (which can happen at any time in a minority situation), an election is almost always necessary. If the House has no confidence in the

Crown's ministers, then our government has no democratic mandate. Unless the leader of some other party can put together a ministry that *will* have the confidence of the House (and that is usually unlikely), the only way to restore democratic legitimacy is to hold elections for a new House because electing a new House will either restore confidence in the existing government or make it clear that the prime minister must resign and make way for another leader who does have its confidence.

Mr. Harper's fixed-date legislation had to take this complication into consideration. Consequently, the wording of the legislation stipulated that the new law did not revoke the power of the governor general to dissolve Parliament and hold elections prior to the "fixed" date. Mr. Harper took advantage of this loophole to ask the governor general for a dissolution in September 2008, 13 months before the date set in the legislation. It is worth noting that the House had not actually declared a lack of confidence in the government. Most analysts agree that Mr. Harper was taking advantage of the loophole in the legislation to arrange to have the elections at the time that would be most favourable to his party—the very sort of thing that the legislation was supposed to prevent.

Once the governor general dissolves Parliament, a **general election** follows immediately. (We speak of a "general election" to describe nationwide elections. A **by-election** is held in a single constituency to fill a seat vacated midway through a Parliament by the death or resignation of an MP.) Under the Canada Elections Act, an election campaign must be a minimum of 36 days, and recent campaigns have typically been between five and seven weeks in duration. There is, however, no maximum. Many eyebrows were raised when Stephen Harper opted for a campaign of 78 days in 2015. It was widely suggested that he had done so to suppress third-party advertising that was critical of his government[6] and to take advantage of his own party's significant edge in donations.[7] Many people complained that the campaign was too long, including some candidates. On the other hand, the longer campaign likely lessened the impact of specific short-term incidents and encouraged voters to focus on longer-term considerations.

General elections are administered by a politically neutral civil servant called the **Chief Electoral Officer** who appoints a **returning officer** for each of

---

6 The amount of money spent on advertising by "third parties" (that is, non-party organizations advocating for or against some political party) is strictly limited once the election campaign has officially begun.

7 The amount of money a party is permitted to spend increases with the length of the campaign. Mr. Harper's party had much more money available than the maximum for a 36-day campaign but the other parties did not.

the 338 electoral districts in Canada. Electoral districts are divided into smaller units called **polls**, each of which has about 250 voters. The returning officer for each electoral district will appoint a deputy returning officer and a couple of poll clerks to run the election at each poll. The returning officer also appoints two **enumerators** for each poll; their task is to prepare the official voters' list for the poll. Under the Canada Elections Act, all citizens who are 18 years of age or older have the right to vote. (One notable exception is the Chief Electoral Officer, who has no vote. The returning officers are allowed to vote only in the case of a tie.) The preliminary voters list must be ready 26 days before the election. Those who have been left off the list have 10 days to get their name added to it.

To have their names put on the ballot, candidates must present the returning officer with official nomination papers signed by 100 eligible voters from the constituency. (The candidates themselves do not have to be residents of the constituency, but it is generally a political liability to be a non-resident.) Candidates must also leave the returning officer a deposit of $1,000, a sum that is returned to all those who submit in a timely manner all their financial reports to Elections Canada.

In order to minimize the influence that those with money might have on electoral outcomes, Canadian electoral laws place limits on the amount that a candidate may spend. A more complicated matter is the issue of third-party advertising. The problem is well illustrated by the 1988 election. It is widely believed that the victory of the Progressive Conservative Party, which backed free trade, was in some measure due to a massive advertising campaign conducted on its behalf by "big business." Parliament has attempted to limit this type of advertising. Its rationale has been that such advertising is inconsistent with the democratic principle of "one person, one vote" because it gives the wealthy more influence on elections than the less wealthy. Ottawa's earliest attempts to deal with third-party advertising were deemed by the courts to violate section 2 of the Charter, but a revised law met with the approval of the Supreme Court of Canada in a 2004 decision. Under this law, third parties wishing to run ads during an election campaign must register with Elections Canada and must respect mandated spending limits. For the 2015 election, the limits were $8,788 in any individual constituency and $439,410 nationally.[8]

Elections are normally held on a Monday. The polls are open for 12 hours in each of Canada's time zones. The times are staggered in order to minimize the gap between closing times. The goal is to reduce the impact that comes from having voters in Western Canada knowing the results in the East before voting

---

8   For current information on election finances, see Elections Canada, http://www.elections.ca.

is complete in the West. Lest the voters in the more westerly time zones be influenced by the results of the voting in the East, election law used to impose a blackout on broadcasters from reporting on results in jurisdictions where polls are still open. Communication technology has increasingly made those restrictions ineffective. In the 2015 election, broadcast blackouts were not enforced.

Each party is permitted to have two **scrutineers** at the poll all day long to observe the process and to keep the candidates posted on whether known supporters have voted. Upon the closing of the poll, the votes are counted by the deputy returning officer while the scrutineers look on. The deputy returning officer then seals all the votes in the ballot box and sends them to the returning officer for an official count, which takes place over the next few days. But the deputy returning officer's unofficial count is immediately communicated to the returning officer, who passes the information on to the media. The unofficial results are thus generally known within approximately half an hour.

Figure 9.3: The 2015 General Election

	Atlantic	Quebec	Ontario	West	Territories	Canada
Liberal	32	40	80	29	3	184
Conservative	0	12	33	54	0	99
NDP	0	16	8	20	0	44
BQ	0	10	0	0	0	10
Green	0	0	0	1	0	1

9.5   Polls and Electoral Choice

Polling by political parties, private corporations, the media, and governments goes on constantly and has become a pervasive aspect of our lives. Polls inform us about everything from the important to the trivial, from Canadian opinions about major policy issues to how many people believe that Elvis is still alive. The interesting question is why they have become so pervasive. One reason is that they are a useful tool of mass marketing. Mass marketing techniques for determining market demand and advertising can be used successfully in democratic politics. Interest groups, government departments and agencies, and political parties all use opinion polls in order to determine what issues are important to the public and whether a particular idea, policy, or personality could prove popular. Accordingly, one may argue that public opinion polling is an important resource in modern democracy. If governments and political parties are there to serve the people, they need to know what the people are thinking. Politicians can get a better read on public opinion and can give the people what they want by means of public opinion polls.

Polling gives rise to two concerns. First, if polls have become instruments of knowledge of public opinion, then they have reduced or replaced the MP as a source of information about voters and issues important to them. It is perhaps no accident that, as polls have become more prolific, MPs have lost prominence relative to the party leader and first minister. Second, polls contribute to conformism by promoting the view that something is good simply because a majority in a public opinion poll think it to be good. Public opinion can easily change, especially on an emotionally charged political issue. A few grisly murders and the polls may show Canadians strongly in favour of capital punishment. Moreover, we are left to wonder how informed the public may be on a particular issue, and hence, to put the matter bluntly, what the value is of knowing their opinion. One might ask 1,001 Canadians whether the Bank of Canada should lower its interest rate. How would they know what the reasons and repercussions of changes to the bank's policy are?

Polls thus exacerbate a danger that is unique to the democratic regime—granting a kind of superior status to the opinion of a majority. Tocqueville described the problem in the following terms:

> The moral authority of the majority is partly based upon the notion that there is more intelligence and wisdom in a number of men united than in a single individual, and that the number of the legislators is more important than their quality.[9]

The danger is that we come to believe something is either true or good because a majority of people believe it so. Such a danger has been all too often realized with respect to issues of racial and religious tolerance. The most common debate about public opinion polls concerns their possible effects on elections. Many argue for a ban on publication of pre-election opinion polls that attempt to measure and predict voter preference. Their argument is that, in the weeks between the time Parliament is dissolved and the election takes place, Canadians should be left to make up their own minds without the "benefit" of polls. Those who propose that the publication of public opinion polls be prohibited in the period immediately

---

9   Alexis de Tocqueville, *Democracy in America*, trans. Henry Reeve (New York: Vintage Books, 1945), 1: 265.

preceding an election argue that such polls undermine the electoral process in two important ways. First, the publication of pre-election polls turns elections into the equivalent of horse races: election coverage in the media often focuses more on who is ahead in the latest poll than on what the issues are. Politics is thus treated as the equivalent of a sporting event and to a great extent trivialized, with voters paying more attention to who is winning than who ought to win. A second problem caused by pre-election polls is their effect on voting behaviour.

Political parties and candidates who are shown to be badly trailing are often written off by voters, who then switch their votes to one of the two leading contenders. Often a bandwagon effect is created by voters who want to ensure that the winning candidate in their riding is from the party that is most likely to form the government. Whether voters switch their votes to the second-place or first-place party, the effect is the same: the SMP system's tendency to make it difficult for third parties to elect their candidates is magnified. If elections are supposed to be the average citizen's main opportunity for intelligent, public-spirited political participation, then the publication of election polls seems inconsistent with healthy democracy.

The issue of election polls points to a fundamental question for liberal democratic politics. To prohibit their publication would almost certainly be a violation of some of our most important rights—freedom of the press, for example. Yet if it can be established that polls diminish thoughtful participation in politics, then arguably they would be anti-democratic. In the final analysis, the question of public opinion polls reveals the deep tension that sometimes exists between our devotion to liberalism and our devotion to democracy.

9.6 The Effects of SMP

Our use of a single-member plurality system has important consequences for electoral politics in Canada. SMP divides our voting into 338 separate elections. It then awards seats in the House of Commons only to those who come first in each of the electoral districts. These arrangements will generally produce results marked by a wide discrepancy between a party's share of votes and its share of seats.

To see how this may be so, let us consider a hypothetical example. Imagine a Canadian election with only three parties, Parties A, B, and C. Suppose that on voting day, Party A gets 34 per cent of the total votes in Canada, Party B gets 33 per cent, and Party C also gets 33 per cent. This would appear to be the closest election in Canadian history. But what happens if the overall ratio of support (34/33/33) is consistent right across the country and replicated in every single riding? Under our SMP system, Party A would end up with all 338 seats (it would win each constituency 34–33–33) and parties B and C would get none! Under SMP, then, it is theoretically possible that one party could get 100 per cent of the seats in the House of Commons even though a large majority of the electorate (66 per cent) voted for someone else. Furthermore, the votes of those 66 per cent would, in a manner of speaking, be wasted.

The example cited above is an extreme one, but Canadian political history contains cases that are similar in principle. In the 1987 provincial election in New Brunswick, for example, the Liberal Party under the leadership of Frank McKenna received about 60 per cent of the total vote. Because that support was relatively consistent across the province, the Liberals won all 58 seats in the New Brunswick legislature. And despite winning almost 40 per cent of the votes, the Conservatives and the NDP got no seats at all. This outcome demonstrates dramatically a characteristic that is typical, in lesser degree, of all Canadian elections. SMP systematically favours the leading national party with the widest distribution of voters. Such a party will almost always receive a larger percentage of seats than its percentage of the popular vote in the "winner-take-all" format of SMP.[10]

The historical record shows that, in recent decades, the leading national party generally obtains around 40 per cent of the votes. But thanks to our electoral system, 40 per cent of the vote consistently yields the leading party a majority of the seats. This is a significant fact, for it means that it is the SMP electoral system that is responsible for the creation of majority governments in Canada. Only 3 of the 25 elections since World War I have given a single party more than 50 per cent of the votes (1940, 1958, and 1984). Yet 17 of those elections have resulted in majority governments. Both Mr. Harper in 2011 and Mr. Trudeau in 2015 won majority governments with slightly less than 40 per cent of the votes. Moreover, even if the leading national party does not receive enough of a boost from SMP to convert a minority of votes into a majority of seats, it will still find itself with a greater share of the seats than its share of the vote. In the 2008 election, for instance, the Conservative Party picked up 46.4 per cent of the seats—close to a majority—with only 37.6 per cent of the vote.

The impact of the SMP system is felt not only by the leading party. Necessarily, if the leading party benefits from SMP, it does so at the expense of the other parties. But the other parties are not all treated the same way by SMP.

---

10   It remains true that in tight two-party election races, as demonstrated in Quebec provincial politics, sometimes the party with fewer votes wins more seats.

Our electoral system favours small regional parties but works against the less popular national parties. A moment's reflection on the logic of SMP shows why. Because of SMP's "winner-take-all" approach, votes are wasted unless the party comes in first in an electoral district. Thus secondary parties will succeed only if their support is heavily concentrated in key areas so that they come in first in some ridings. If their support is spread evenly throughout the country, they are unlikely to win many seats. The 2008 election provides a good illustration of the point. The Green Party won almost 7 per cent of the vote but did not win a single seat. With slightly more than 18 per cent of the vote, the NDP received only about 12 per cent of the seats. On the other hand, the Bloc obtained far fewer votes than the NDP (9.9 per cent of the total as opposed to 18.2 per cent) but captured substantially more seats (49 to 37) because its support was concentrated entirely in the province of Quebec.

In the 2015 election, the results were again skewed in favour of the dominant party and against the other national parties. The Liberal party, with just under 40 per cent of the vote, won 184 seats, which is 54.4 per cent of the total 338. The Conservatives won 29 per cent of the seats, but had 31.9 per cent of the vote; the NDP won 13 per cent of the seats with almost 20 per cent of the vote; and the Green Party won only 1 seat, a mere 0.3 per cent of the seats although the party gained 3.4 per cent of the total vote. Smaller parties are thus clearly disadvantaged unless they have a strong regional base, like the Bloc Québécois, where that small total percentage of the vote can be concentrated to win a number of specific ridings.

SMP strengthens regionalism in Canada not only by promoting regional parties but also by intensifying regional strengths and weaknesses within our broadly national parties. Because of its "winner-take-all" rules, SMP systematically under-represents certain regions in each party caucus and overrepresents others. In the 1980 election, for example, over 20 per cent of Westerners voted for Liberal candidates. Yet because the Liberal candidates consistently came in behind the PC or NDP candidates, the Liberals ended up with only two seats in the whole region (about 3 per cent). This made it difficult for incoming Liberal Prime Minister Pierre Trudeau to give Western Canada adequate representation in his cabinet. During the same period, Mr. Trudeau would sometimes win almost every seat in Quebec, even though substantial numbers of Quebec voters did not support him. Consequently, the Liberal caucus of that period did not really reflect Liberal support in the country

Recent elections have further demonstrated this tendency to promote regionalism. For instance, in the 2011 election, the Liberal Party received 25 per cent of the vote in Ontario but only 10 per cent of the seats. Meanwhile, with

44 per cent of the vote in that province, the Conservatives won 69 per cent of the seats. Similarly, one might conclude on the basis of seats that Western Canada is overwhelmingly Conservative and has no interest in the Liberal Party. But vote totals show that this is not true. The Conservative Party won 72 of the 92 seats in the four western provinces—a stunning 78 per cent of the seats. And yet their share of the popular vote in the region was less than 60 per cent.

In the 2015 election, one again finds the magnification of regional voting into apparently huge party advantages. The most obvious example is in Atlantic Canada. The Liberal party won about 59 per cent of the popular vote, but all 32 seats. Based on this outcome, it looks as though Atlantic Canadians are by and large overwhelming supporters of the Liberal Party. But 41 per cent voted for one of the other parties, and that vote is not reflected in the total outcome. In Western Canada, the reverse effect takes place. There the Liberal party typically wins a much smaller percentage of the seats than it gets votes. And although the Liberals did better this time in Manitoba and British Columbia, the pattern continued in Saskatchewan and Alberta. In Saskatchewan, for example, the Liberals won only one seat even though they took 24 per cent of the popular vote. Again we see the magnification effect of regional voting differences.

To summarize, we may say that the SMP electoral system has four major effects on electoral politics. First, it rewards the largest national party with more seats than it "deserves," frequently converting a minority of votes into a majority of seats. Second, it handicaps smaller national parties such as the NDP and the Green Party by giving them a smaller share of seats than their share of the popular vote. Third, it encourages regionalism by fostering the growth of parties that focus on regional interests and concerns. Fourth, it encourages regionalism by magnifying the regional strengths and weaknesses of our national parties. The question that continues to present itself to Canadians is whether, in light of these effects, the electoral system should be reformed.

9.7 Proportional Representation

Political observers who are troubled by some of the effects of SMP have typically advocated the adoption of an alternative electoral system, called **proportional representation (PR)**. Proportional representation is used in many liberal democracies. (In fact, the pure SMP system that Canada inherited from Britain is relatively rare in the world.) PR exists in a variety of forms, some of them rather complicated. The easiest way to understand it is to consider what is known as the **party list system**.

In this system, each party prepares a list of its candidates in rank order. Electoral districts are abolished, so that, instead of holding 338 elections, we hold a single nationwide election. In this single election, the electorate votes for parties rather than candidates. When the results are tabulated, the number of seats each party wins is determined by the proportion of the vote it received. If, for example, Party A received 20 per cent of the vote, it would receive exactly 20 per cent of the seats available. On the assumption that we keep 338 seats, this would mean that Party A gets 68 seats. Those seats would then be awarded to the first 68 candidates on Party A's list.

Advocates of PR argue that this system is fairer than SMP. Parties get seats in proportions that mirror the preferences indicated by the voters. As opposed to SMP, this electoral system does not "distort" the electorate's voting pattern by favouring certain types of parties and disadvantaging others. For instance, if the 2015 election had been held under PR, the Liberals would have received 39.5 per cent of the seats (134) because they received 39.5 per cent of the votes.[11] SMP converted that 39.5 into 54 per cent of the seats, a solid majority. The NDP, with 19.8 per cent of the vote, would have received 67 seats under PR instead of the 44 the party got under SMP, and the Greens would have received 12 seats instead of just 1. PR is also said to be fairer in that it eliminates the phenomenon of "wasted ballots." Under PR, every vote has an impact on shaping the composition of the House of Commons.

Another point raised by advocates of PR is that it allows for more diverse representation within each party caucus. We have seen that SMP tends to magnify the regional strengths and weaknesses of each party. PR offers a solution to this problem. Because parties are free to structure their lists as they like, each party can arrange its list to ensure that all regions will have adequate representation within the caucus. Similarly, the party leadership can use its control over the composition of the list to ensure adequate representation in the House of Commons for groups that are traditionally under-represented there—women, for instance.

It should be noted, however, that PR also entails certain disadvantages. The charge most frequently levelled against it is that it leads to political instability. As we have seen, the Canadian electorate rarely gives any party a majority of

---

11   Of course, it is unlikely that voters would vote in exactly the same way under a PR system. The calculations of any individual voter are influenced by the electoral system. In an SMP system you are more likely to vote for your second choice if your preferred candidate has no chance of winning, or if doing so will help thwart the election of a candidate you particularly dislike. Such incentives to vote "strategically" do not exist in a straight PR system.

votes. It is our SMP electoral system that is responsible for transforming a mere plurality of votes (nationwide) into a majority of seats in the House of Commons. Precisely because PR gives each party seats based on its proportion of the overall vote, the adoption of PR would make majority governments extremely rare. Minority governments or coalition governments, which are generally less stable, would become the norm.

Connected with the concern about permanent minority government is the allegation that PR will lead to a more divisive politics by facilitating the emergence of small, single-issue parties and parties with non-mainstream agendas. Such parties are generally shut out of the House of Commons by our SMP system, which awards seats only to those parties strong enough to come first in some riding. Under PR, however, it is likely that an anti-abortion party or an animal rights party—or even a frivolous group such as the Rhinoceros Party—would be able to scrape together enough votes across Canada to earn a seat or two in the House of Commons. In a minority government situation, the government party might have to cut a deal with one of these minor parties in order to stay in office if it were in danger of losing a vote. The tail would then wag the dog as the minor party dictated its terms to the party in power.

A third major problem with PR is that local constituencies would no longer have an MP of their own. A well-structured party list might ensure that all regions have adequate representation, but it would not guarantee an MP for any particular area or community. Ontario, for example, would likely be dominated by representatives from Toronto. The province of New Brunswick might have two MPs from Moncton and three from Saint John, but nobody from the other two-thirds of the province. And even in those two cities, the link between the voters and the MPs would be much weaker than it is today, for the MPs would owe their positions in the House of Commons not to the support of the local electorate but to the party bosses in Ottawa who put their names high on the party list. For these reasons, the adoption of PR would mean that Canadians would no longer be able to count on having a representative in Ottawa to listen to their concerns or to help them when they have problems with the government. It would also mean that the individuals who actually form the government would never have been elected as individuals. They would be party loyalists who owed their place in Ottawa to the leaders of their party—the people with the authority to put their name on the party's electoral list. This arrangement would almost certainly make them less responsive to the electorate and even more subordinate to party bosses.

Proponents of PR have tried to address these problems by suggesting a **mixed member proportional (MMP)** system that blends a party list form of PR with SMP. Under MMP systems, only some of the seats would be elected on the basis of a party list system (usually one-quarter to one-half) and the rest would be elected using SMP. Voters could thus vote twice—once for their local candidate and once for the party list. Although this blended system may seem a bit complicated, it is used in many countries today and is the most common way of implementing PR.

9.8 Single Transferable Vote

Another alternative to the SMP is a system known as the **single transferable vote (STV)**. In this type of electoral system people do not vote for just one candidate; they rank all the candidates in order of preference.[12] When the votes are counted, if no candidate has a majority of first-place votes, then first- and second-place votes are counted. If there is still no candidate with a majority, the first-, second-, and third-place votes are counted. The process continues until one candidate has a clear majority. The aim of such a system is to ensure that the candidates who are elected have the broadest base of support and a clear title to the seat. In SMP, of course, candidates usually win with a mere plurality rather than a majority. That may often mean that the winner is not really the most acceptable candidate to the riding as a whole. For instance, a Conservative candidate might win a riding with 35 per cent of the vote, just ahead of a Liberal candidate with 30 per cent, an NDP candidate with 25 per cent, and a Green candidate with 10 per cent. It may well be that those who voted for the losing candidates would have strongly preferred any of the losing candidates to the Conservative candidate. Yet even though 65 per cent of the voters see the Conservative as the least desirable candidate, the Conservative wins, thanks to SMP. By insisting on a clear majority and by counting second, third, and fourth preferences when necessary to arrive at a clear majority, STV ensures that the candidate who is elected is the candidate with the greatest overall support.

STV is typically (though not always) used in conjunction with a multi-member district system to provide a more proportional division of seats among the political parties. In a district with five seats, then, each party would have the right to nominate up to five candidates, voters would rank all of the candidates in order of preference, and the first five to reach 50 per cent (counting down from first to second to third preference and so on) would be declared elected.

---

12   For this reason, STV systems are popularly known as "ranked voting" or preferential balloting.

A multi-member STV system is more proportional than SMP in that in a district where Party A and Party B have roughly equal support, they will likely split the five seats available, instead of having one party win the only seat available while the other party gets nothing.

9.9 Electoral Reform

For many years, electoral reform was largely an academic issue. It was raised primarily by supporters of parties that are disadvantaged by SMP, by individuals troubled by the fact that votes cast for the losing party in a given riding are "wasted," or by people who simply think it unfair that the percentage of seats a party gets does not correspond exactly to its percentage of the vote. Not surprisingly, however, calls for reform have traditionally been ignored by the parties in power because it is precisely those parties that benefit from SMP.

In the past few years, however, electoral reform has become a much more serious possibility. Oddly enough, though one might argue that the case for reform is strongest at the national level (because of the way SMP exacerbates Canadian regionalism), it was at the provincial level that serious consideration of reform first emerged. Governments in Prince Edward Island, New Brunswick, Ontario, and Quebec all expressed interest in introducing some form of MMP at the provincial level, but no change has taken place at this point. Voters in PEI actually defeated a proposal to switch to MMP in 2005, and voters in Ontario rejected a similar proposal in 2007. The voters of British Columbia considered adopting a multi-member STV system in 2005. Although 58 per cent voted in favour of the proposal, it was not adopted because the legislation providing for the referendum stipulated that major change to something as fundamental as the electoral system would require the support of at least 60 per cent of the electorate and a majority in 60 per cent of ridings. A second referendum on the question was held in 2009, and the STV proposal was again defeated, failing to even secure a majority of voter support.

The issue of electoral reform is now on the federal agenda as well. Justin Trudeau declared in October of 2015 that the election that had just made him prime minister would be Canada's last election under SMP. That may have been an overly bold claim. Even though Mr. Trudeau's party controls a majority of seats in the House of Commons, a good case could be made that such a fundamental change to Canada's electoral system would require the endorsement of the people in a referendum, and not just a legislated revision of the Canada Elections Act. As Canadians have historically been reluctant to embrace radical change in referenda, it would be rash to assume that such a proposal would necessarily win popular approval, especially if it does not have the support of all of the parties.[13] And it seems quite unlikely that any particular proposal would be supported by all of the parties because every system will work to the advantage of some of them and to the disadvantage of the others. Consider the table below:

Figure 9.4: Results of 2015 Election Using SMP, PR, and STV[14]

Party	SMP	PR	STV
Liberal	184	134	224
Conservative	99	109	61
NDP	44	67	50
Bloc	10	16	2
Green	1	12	1

It is not coincidental that Prime Minister Trudeau favours STV. As a party of the centre, and thus the party most likely to be a voter's second choice, the Liberals would benefit substantially from a system that takes second-choice votes into consideration. Note that if the 2015 election had been run under STV, the Liberal Party would have obtained 66 per cent of the seats with less than 40 per cent of the vote. More important, STV would probably make it next to impossible for the Liberals' chief rivals, the Conservative Party, to win. An STV system might make the Liberals the more or less permanent government of Canada. In contrast, PR would make it very difficult for the Liberals (or any party, for that matter) to win a majority government. Yet that too might have the effect of giving the Liberals an almost permanent hold on power insofar as it would be difficult to imagine the Conservatives and the NDP supporting each other; any minority government would therefore have to include—if not be led by—the Liberals. The Conservatives were slightly disadvantaged by SMP in the 2015

---

13   Some might argue that a fundamental change to the electoral system would require the use of the constitutional amending formula in section 42 of CA 1982. That argument is probably not convincing, but the government might wish to have the point clarified by means of a reference to the Supreme Court before proceeding with either a referendum or with legislation.

14   Calculations for results under PR are done on the assumption that the party lists used would be national lists. One could also implement a PR system in which seats were allocated on the basis of provincial lists. The results might well be substantially different. The calculations for results under STV were made by Éric Grenier of ThreeHundredEight.com, a website dedicated to political polling in Canada. http://www.cbc.ca/news/politics/grenier-preferential-ballot-1.3332566.

election, as is often the case with the major party that comes in second. Yet it was SMP that allowed the Conservatives to form a majority government from 2011 to 2015 with less than 40 per cent of the votes, and members of that party generally see SMP as essential to their chances for victory. For that reason, the Conservatives strongly oppose any change to the electoral system. The federal Greens and New Democrats, who have long suffered under SMP, have always promoted PR because it would provide them with many more seats than they typically win under SMP.[15] STV would not help the NDP as much and would do the Green Party no good at all. As a regional party, the Bloc has benefited enormously from SMP in most elections and would generally not do as well under the other two systems.[16] It seems, then, that Canadians might expect the Conservatives and the Bloc to favour SMP, to oppose PR, and to strongly oppose STV. The Greens and the NDP will likely oppose SMP and STV and favour PR. The Liberals will prefer STV, yet as none of the other parties is likely to support it, they may be willing to settle for PR. It should not be forgotten that there are variations on each system that may allow for compromise and deal making: an MMP variation of PR, or a multi-member variation of STV, for instance. But the chances that a parliamentary committee might produce a unanimous recommendation are slim because the interests of the various parties point committee members in contrary directions.

To be sure, debates about Canada's electoral system are usually couched in terms of fairness, not partisan self-interest. Champions of SMP, PR, and STV will claim that only the system they advocate is truly fair and that is why they support it. In reality, no system can be perfectly fair and each system has its advantages and disadvantages. The various parties will therefore emphasize those "fairness" arguments that align with their partisan interests. Of course, responsible citizens must avoid the genetic fallacy of thinking a position is false because it has been

---

15   Note, however, that the provincial NDP in British Columbia was strongly opposed to the initiatives to replace SMP with STV for elections in that province. Why? It is probably not coincidental that the NDP has formed several majority governments in that province thanks to the tendency of SMP to transform a minority of votes into a majority of seats.

16   The Bloc would actually have received more seats in 2015 under PR, but that is probably an exceptional case. Of course, it is also possible that the Bloc would reap a larger strategic advantage from a conversion to PR, even if PR provides them with fewer seats. PR will make majority governments rare; minority governments will be the rule. Minority government is the preferred environment for the Bloc because it provides greater opportunity for the Bloc to leverage concessions from the party in power.

advanced for self-interested motives. It is perfectly understandable that parties will emphasize the virtues of systems that benefit them and the vices of those that disadvantage them. The role of the citizen is to understand the impact of each system and to determine which, overall, is most conducive (or least harmful) to the health of the Canadian regime.

Key Terms

delegates

trustees

party member

mandate

floor-crossing

microcosm theory of representation

plurality

single-member plurality (SMP)

ridings

constituencies

first-past-the-post electoral system

electoral boundaries commissions

single transferable vote (STV)

community of interest

electoral quotient

general election

by-election

Chief Electoral Officer

returning officer

polls

enumerators

scrutineers

proportional representation (PR)

party list system

mixed member proportional (MMP)

Discussion Questions

1. Divide your class into groups representing each of the five parties with seats in the House of Commons. What would each group's objective be in negotiations concerning electoral reform? What compromises would each propose or accept, if any?

2. Moving away from the SMP system and toward some form of proportional representation would probably have the effect of creating a stronger multi-party system and thus make it less likely that any one party would gain a majority. Would this provide for better government?

Chapter Ten

Political Parties

10.1   Political Parties in the Canadian Regime

Political parties are publicly organized groups of people who are motivated by some common set of political ideas and whose goal is to have their particular members win public office so that those ideas can be put into practice.

It is obvious to even the most casual observer that Canadian political life is dominated by political parties. Every Canadian Parliament has been divided along party lines, and, except for a brief interlude during World War I, membership in every Canadian cabinet has been restricted to those who were members of the dominant political party at the time.[1] It is worth noting, however, that the dominant role of political parties is not something mandated by the law of the Constitution. CA 1867 and CA 1982 do not mention political parties. Nor could one claim that the role of political parties is a matter of constitutional convention: constitutional conventions are rules, and there is no rule requiring our MPs to be members of political parties. The truth of the matter is that the dominant role of our political parties is simply a matter of need. We have political parties because they are useful (as we shall see in 10.2) and because there is no law to prohibit them. Parties are useful to the leaders in Parliament or a legislature who need to muster continuing coalitions of legislators to support (or oppose) legislative programs. And they are useful to voters who appreciate how each party gathers policy positions into a coherent package based on a general vision of the nature of the country, the role of the state, and the meaning of ideas such as liberty and equality. To be sure, we often hear complaints to the effect that political parties constitute an impediment to reasonable democratic political life. The "party system" is accused of limiting our choices and stifling debate. It is blamed for focusing political deliberation on partisan advantage rather than the common good. Though Canadians often express frustration with the "party system," they almost never take advantage of their right to elect an "independent" candidate—a candidate with no party affiliation. It is well worth pondering why that is.

A lone MP in the House of Commons exercises little political power. He or she may be able to speak on behalf of constituents' interests without having to "toe the party line." On the other hand, the "independent" MP is unlikely to accomplish much within a political institution that runs on the principle of party discipline.

All things considered, the existence of political parties is a sign of a healthy democratic regime. Authoritarian and totalitarian forms of government usually move quickly to extinguish political opposition by means of outlawing opposition parties. They concentrate all power in the hands of the state by means of imposing a one-party state. In Frank Underhill's words,

> The acid test of freedom in a state is whether power and office can
> pass peaceably from one political party to another. "Her Majesty's

---

[1]   The "conscription crisis" of 1917 led to the formation of a "Union Government" that included all of the Conservative MPs and all of the Liberals who favoured conscription. Those Liberals who opposed conscription remained in opposition.

Opposition" is just as necessary to free government as "Her Majesty's Government."[2]

Liberal–democratic party politics is workable because the parties agree on at least one thing: different political parties have a right to exist, and should one party win an election, it has a legitimate right to rule until the next election. Parties are "parts" of the regime. Party politics is, therefore, non–revolutionary: it works because every party agrees on the fundamental principles of the regime.[3]

10.2 The Five Functions of Political Parties

In their efforts to win political power, parties perform a number of functions that are important to the health of the regime as a whole. The **five functions of political parties** are recruitment, fundraising, interest aggregation, policy development, and education.

First, parties recruit people into the party as members and, sometimes, as candidates. This recruitment function is obviously crucial, for modern democracies are constantly imperilled by apathy and lack of civic participation. The dangers of what Alexis de Tocqueville described as "individualism"—a way of life in which people tend to withdraw into their individual lives of work, family, and friends, and pay little attention to political affairs—are fairly obvious.[4] Democracy means the rule of the people, and it is endangered when the people lose their taste for politics. The parties supply us with our political leaders through national leadership conventions, our candidates by means of constituency elections, and the vast number of campaign workers needed to run all the aspects of a modern election.

Second, parties raise money for their organizations and election campaigns. This is still, by and large, a private activity. It is regulated by election finance laws. It is worth considering that if we did not have political parties to raise much of the money for elections, the costs would have to be borne by the taxpayer.

Third, parties identify, represent, and balance the diverse interests of Canadians. This process, often referred to as **interest aggregation**, is crucial to

---

2   Frank Underhill, *Canadian Political Parties*, Canadian Historical Association Booklet No. 8 (Ottawa: Canadian Historical Association, 1964), 3.

3   See Giovani Sartori, *Parties and Party Systems*, vol. 1 (Cambridge: Cambridge University Press, 1976).

4   *Democracy in America*, Vol. II, pp. 104ff.

the healthy functioning of a liberal democracy. It is rare that Canadian voters have a single common interest. In most cases, policy that is advantageous for one group ultimately comes at the expense of others. Fiscal transfers to have-not provinces do not go to the more prosperous provinces; companies in Winnipeg compete with companies in Montreal for lucrative government contracts. If Canada had no political parties, our MPs would be free to vote for whatever was in the best interests of their own constituents. But this would ultimately mean that the most demographically powerful regions—Ontario and Quebec—would make all the rules to their own advantage. Because the major national political parties seek votes in all constituencies—French and English, men and women, East and West, business and labour—they are forced to hammer out compromise positions that offer a relatively fair deal to all the major categories of voters. If we did not have political parties to perform this process of interest aggregation, our regime would likely be much less successful in its pursuit of fair treatment for all Canadians.

Fourth, in the process of attempting to aggregate interests and integrate them into a national whole, the parties formulate and influence public policy. Normally they design their policies at policy conventions, large gatherings of rank-and-file members who debate the current political issues and design or revise the party's main policies in light of these debates.

Finally, parties educate people about political life. Party membership provides an education in holding political office by means of providing elected offices within the party. Often a candidate has served as an elected member of a constituency organization before ever running for nomination. Parties meet to discuss policy and ideas and hold regular policy conventions. The educational function of parties thus extends beyond the party members to citizens at large, who benefit from media coverage and commercial advertising of party policy. It culminates in the way parties help to structure voter choice. The parties accomplish this by attempting to persuade voters to vote for them. One need only imagine an election without parties to see how essential their function has become.

10.3 Parties and Ideology

A political party is usually built on the basis of a loose set of fundamental political principles, commonly referred to as an **ideology**. Those principles are then used as the basis for generating ideas about the purposes of government, how it should be organized, and what public policies should be implemented.

Some might argue that this description is too "idealistic." They would instead emphasize that political parties are groups of people who are motivated primarily by the goal of winning public office, so they can obtain political power to serve their own interests. We would not disagree. Like most of us, those who enter directly into political life are rarely saints. And politics is inseparable from the desire for the benefits and honours that come with holding public office.

Here an important distinction should be made between kinds of partisanship. A partisan is a loyal follower of a cause. He or she is dependable, willing to defend the cause, and wants to see it succeed. **High partisanship** refers to a reasonable commitment to a set of political ideals that are related to the principles of the regime, as well as to the hope that these ideals prevail in a fair contest of ideas and argument. **Low partisanship** refers to the "retail," practical part of politics, to the actions and operations that must be performed to get people into government to achieve the higher ideals. Properly understood, low partisanship is necessary to high partisanship and is in service to it.[5] What most people find objectionable is low partisanship as the only form of partisanship—getting power by any means and for no worthy goal. The distinction between high and low partisanship is related to an older distinction between great and small political parties. Alexis de Tocqueville, in his magisterial study of democracy in America, noted that some parties are dedicated to grand, elevating principles linked to the general interests of the whole polity, while small parties, lacking a larger noble vision, advance the lower aims of small groups. "The means they employ," writes Tocqueville, "are miserable, as is the very goal they propose for themselves."[6]

Political parties in liberal democratic regimes are best understood as attempts to serve both the ideal and the practical. They must steer a moderate middle course between the extremes of powerless idealism on the one hand and the cynically unprincipled pursuit of power on the other. There is no point in pursuing ideals that are attractive to only a very few voters. Conversely, the public will soon sour on parties or politicians who are perceived to be without principles, often labelling them opportunistic and cynical. What we seem to want most are practical and pragmatic politicians who have political principles. The major Canadian political parties are **pragmatic** in this sense.

Most ideological questions turn on the issue of preservation and change. On most issues, some will favour change and some will prefer the status quo. One almost always finds both those who argue that conserving what we now have is the best course of action and those who argue that we can make progress and

---

5   Russell Muirhead, *The Promise of Party in a Polarized Age* (Cambridge, MA: Harvard University Press, 2014), chapter 8.

6   Alexis de Tocqueville, *Democracy in America*, trans. Harvey C. Mansfield and Delba Winthrop ([1835, 1840] Chicago: University of Chicago Press, 2000), I, 2.2, 167.

hence improve our present lot by following a different course. In other words, one almost always finds "conservatives" and "progressives" in any political arena.

This dichotomy between those who favour the present and those who favour change is best explained in terms of two factors. First, it seems to be a nearly universal human phenomenon that, within any group, some people are more inclined to have conservative dispositions than others. Some value caution and prudence; others are more daring and willing to take a chance. In other words, party politics seems to be rooted in the different dispositions of human beings. As Prime Minister Laurier said in a famous lecture, the inclinations to change and to conserve are "two attributes of our nature."[7] Second, there will always be those who have a vested interest in maintaining things as they are, as opposed to those whose interests would be best served by some new political arrangement. For example, it is hard to imagine professional athletes being in favour of a law that would limit their income to the salary of the highest paid police officers.

These days, the main ideological division between our parties is on socioeconomic matters. The dominant ideology at the time of Confederation (an ideology shared by both the Liberal and Conservative parties) might best be described as classical liberalism. Classical liberals emphasize the importance of individual liberty (freedom from governmental interference) and a free market economy. They also value equality, but they understand it to mean primarily equality of opportunity. In Canada, people or parties are labelled "conservative" when they are inclined to conserve the original principles of classical liberalism. In addition, conservatives usually raise practical objections to the ability of the state to solve society's various problems. They will often say that the state is as much a problem as a solution.

A "progressive," on the other hand, sees every person's fate to be bound up with that of the community, and the community, represented by the state, should protect people from the effects of contingencies such as illness, unemployment, and workplace danger that may threaten their ability to fulfill their own sense of purpose in life. In practice, progressives advocate greater income equality as a means to greater equality of opportunity. In the Canadian context, equality of condition is pursued mainly by the redistribution of wealth through the tax system and through state funding of social programs. Because the creation of greater equality of condition usually requires intervention by government, progressives are generally less concerned about "liberty" than are conservatives; or rather, they

---

7   Wilfrid Laurier, "Lecture on Political Liberalism (1877)," in *Essential Readings in Canadian Government and Politics*, ed. Peter H. Russell (Toronto: Emond Montgomery, 2010), 386.

will argue that the cause of advancing freedom *from* poverty or oppression justi-fies certain limitations on the freedom *to* pursue wealth or property. In general, they favour public regulation or even ownership of natural resources and key industries, and of economic institutions like banks.

10.4 Canada's Major Parties

Currently, four parties in Canada regularly elect members to the House of Commons. Two of these parties—the Conservatives and the Liberals—date back to the days of Confederation. These are the only two parties that have ever formed a national government. The NDP and the Bloc Québécois have historically also elected substantial numbers of members. Indeed, in the 2011 election, the NDP won twice as many seats as the Liberals and, for the first time, became the Official Opposition. Finally, the Green Party of Canada has received a substantial number of votes in recent elections; a Green candidate was elected for the first time in 2011.

1. The Conservative Party. The Conservative Party developed under the leader-ship of Canada's first prime minister, John A. Macdonald. Macdonald was able to build his party out of a coalition of "Liberal-Conservatives" from Upper Canada (pre-Confederation Ontario) and "Bleu" politicians from Lower Canada (pre-Confederation Quebec). Under Macdonald and his French-Canadian lieutenant George-Étienne Cartier, the Conservative Party dominated Canadian politics for the first 30 years after Confederation. The Conservatives put in place a "national policy" of protectionism against the United States, western expansion via the Canadian Pacific Railway, and strong central government. The party was not opposed to state intervention in the economy. Such intervention was seen as necessary for the development of Canada, and the party therefore traditionally favoured state enterprises. In the 1940s, the Conservatives absorbed the remnants of a Western agrarian protest movement called the Progressives and adopted the somewhat paradoxical name, the Progressive Conservative Party.

A remarkably similar story took place more recently. In the late 1980s, an Albertan named Preston Manning launched a new Western protest party called the Reform Party. Reform was both socially and fiscally conservative and therefore cut deeply into Progressive Conservative support in the West. Indeed, the emergence of Reform had much to do with the total collapse of the PCs in the 1993 election. Through most of the ensuing decade, the PCs and Reform fought a life-and-death struggle to be the right-of-centre alternative to the Liberal Party. This division of the political right made it easy for the Chrétien

Liberals to win solid majorities throughout this period. In 1998, Reform reconstituted itself as the Canadian Alliance Party in the hope that the PCs would join them. A few did but not enough to put an end to the war. Finally, in the run-up to the 2004 election, fear of a huge Liberal victory drove the two parties into a marriage of necessity. The result was the new Conservative Party of Canada (CPC). The former Canadian Alliance/Reform forces formed the more powerful faction within the new party, and their former leader, Stephen Harper, was easily elected leader. This new party stands for lower taxes and less government control, a more decentralized federation in which provincial jurisdictions are disentangled from federal government interference, global free trade, and a stronger free-market economy. It experiences some divisions on social issues, with those from the former Reform/Canadian Alliance wing tending to favour capital punishment and be against gun control and same-sex marriage while many of the former PCs incline to the opposite views. The Conservative Party supports a foreign policy that stresses the use of force as much as diplomatic activity in international affairs.

2. The Liberal Party. The second great party from the Confederation era was the Liberal Party, which emerged out of a coalition of Upper Canadian "Reformers" and the "Rouge" politicians of Quebec. During the first years of Confederation, the Liberal Party was united mainly by its opposition to the Macdonald Conservatives. It was not until Wilfrid Laurier became Canada's first French-Canadian prime minister in 1896 that the Liberals developed a coherent set of political ideas based on free trade and provincial rights. The Liberal Party has long been the national representative of the rights of French Canadians and therefore developed the tradition of alternating its leadership between anglophones and francophones. The view that Canada was a compact between two nations— English and French—is one that has had far greater influence within the Liberal Party than in the various incarnations of the Conservative Party.

In the 1960s the Liberal Government of Lester Pearson liberalized Canadian immigration policy, and Canada subsequently welcomed people from all over the world. The policies of official bilingualism and multiculturalism were instituted under Liberal governments. In recent years, the Liberal Party has come to stand for the maintenance of a strong national government and is generally suspicious of efforts to decentralize the Canadian federation. Like the Conservatives, the Liberals now favour global free trade (as they did 100 years ago), but they are more sympathetic to government intervention in the economy and are stronger advocates of the welfare state. On social issues, Liberals are generally in favour of measures such as gun control and same-sex marriage. In foreign affairs, they are more likely than the Conservatives to favour diplomacy over the use of force and to prize Canadian participation in UN peacekeeping missions.[8]

3. The New Democratic Party (NDP). The NDP is Canada's only important social democratic party. It originated in the regional protest politics of the Co-operative Commonwealth Federation (CCF), which began in reaction to the collapse of the prairie economy in the 1930s, for which capitalist interests, located mainly in central Canada, were held responsible. The reaction against free-market capitalism and liberalism was therefore long associated with the concern that Canada was a country run by central Canada to serve the interests of central Canada. The Liberals and the PCs were thought to represent the interests of the ruling elite or capitalist class, as opposed to the working class of industrial labour and farmers. The CCF was formed as a party to represent the interests of the working class.

In 1961, the NDP was formed by combining the largely Western CCF with the Canadian Labour Congress (CLC), Canada's most important labour organization, whose great strength was in Ontario. Until 2011, the NDP had had only modest success as a national political party. It did well provincially, having formed governments in six provinces, and it has been the Official Opposition in others. Traditionally, the party has drawn its strength from Ontario and Western Canada. But in 2011, it made spectacular gains in Quebec and gained substantial support in the Maritimes. For the first time, it became the Official Opposition party in Ottawa. Although the NDP has never formed the government in Ottawa, and in 2015 returned to more historical levels of voter support, it has had considerable influence on national policy. Over the years, many of its progressive ideas (medicare being the primary example) have been implemented by the Liberals, sometimes as the price for NDP support during a minority government.

4. The Bloc Québécois (the Bloc). The Bloc is an unusual political party in that it is dedicated to achieving independence for Quebec and hence to its own disappearance as a political party in Canadian politics. It came into existence after the failure of the Meech Lake Accord, when a handful of Quebec MPs quit the PC and Liberal caucuses and joined to form a new party. The 1993 election transformed the Bloc from a small group of disaffected MPs into a major political

---

8   Indeed, it is a point of pride for Liberals that Lester Pearson received the Nobel Peace Prize for his leadership in developing what is now called peacekeeping during the Suez Crisis of 1957. At the time, Pearson was the Minister of External Affairs in the Liberal government led by Louis St. Laurent.

party, which won 54 seats in Quebec. Because it had won more seats than any other opposition party, it ironically became "Her Majesty's Loyal Opposition."

Much to the surprise of many analysts, the Bloc has remained a substantial force in Ottawa. It is surprising because the Bloc is, in many respects, a typical regional party. Because the electoral system rewards regional party strength disproportionately, the party has been able to concentrate its efforts and appeal in one province. Yet regional protest parties usually fade in influence after a meteoric rise. The anger that drives them gradually subsides, and people begin to realize that, in a parliamentary regime, one cannot achieve much from the opposition side of the House. By 2003, the Bloc appeared to be on the brink of a major decline. It may well be that the party was saved only by the eruption of the sponsorship scandal, which in Quebec was of concern not simply because of the mismanagement involved but, more profoundly, because it was seen as a Liberal attempt to buy Quebec's loyalty through crude propaganda. Outrage over the sponsorship scandal propelled the Bloc to an unexpectedly handsome result in the 2004 election. In the 2011 election, however, the Bloc elected only four Members of Parliament. Defying predictions of its demise, the Bloc rebounded to 10 seats in 2015 though its leader, Gilles Duceppe, failed to win his riding.

5. The Green Party. The Green Party was formed in 1983 as a Canadian version of Green parties that had emerged in countries such as Germany and New Zealand. The party ideology is rooted in the "Charter of the Global Greens," which emphasizes six principles: ecological wisdom, social justice, participatory democracy, non-violence, sustainability, and respect for diversity. The Green Party is appealing to many voters—particularly younger voters—but it faces two massive challenges.

The first challenge for the Greens is their focus. Rightly or wrongly, the name of the party suggests that it is focused on a single issue, the environment. On the one hand, that implies to many voters that the Greens have nothing coherent to contribute in relation to the myriad non-environmental issues that a government must contend with. On the other hand, environmentalists such as David Suzuki have argued that a party focused on "Green" issues does the environmental movement a disservice by diverting the political efforts of environmentalists away from the parties that actually exercise power. For Suzuki, a better strategy for environmentalists would be to make existing parties "greener."

The second challenge for the Greens is to overcome the high threshold of electoral support required to elect candidates to the House of Commons. The party needs to appeal not just to Canadians across the country but to large numbers of voters in particular ridings. Whether one thinks of the Green Party as a single-issue party or as an ideological party, SMP will work against it systematically. The results of the 2008 election illustrate the point: with almost 7 per cent of the vote, the Greens did not win a single seat—did not even come close to winning one. In the 2011 election, however, they won only 4 per cent of the vote but elected a member from British Columbia, the province where they have the strongest regional base. One can therefore see that even with 15 per cent of the vote nationally, an ideologically based national party is unlikely to win many seats unless it has a strong regional base. The Green Party achieved a seat in the House in 2011 and in 2015 when the party decided to pour many of its scarce resources into leader Elizabeth May's Saanich-Gulf Islands riding to secure her victory. Most other Green candidates as a result were left to their own devices. So long as Canada uses SMP, it will probably prove difficult for the Green Party to establish itself as a major national party on par with the others.

10.5 The Canadian Party System

Political scientists often speak of **party systems**. What they mean by this is the number and types of parties that a regime is likely to have given the various factors that influence parties: the electoral system, party finance rules, federalism, political culture, and so on. For instance, because Canada has a democratic political culture, ours is a **multi-party system** rather than a **single-party system**. In many countries, only one political party is legally sanctioned. China, for example, allows no other political party than the Communist Party. The idea underlying such a system is that the public interest is best served by working out public policy within the party rather than by allowing diverse parties to develop competing alternatives. Liberal democratic regimes, however, are based on the principles of freedom of thought, freedom of association, and political participation. Because they protect a diversity of political opinion, liberal democracies are naturally home to a multiplicity of political parties. Canada's multi-party system allows for the development of different parties that represent different ideological positions and very different political interests and that put forward different political agendas. Ahead of the forty-second general election in 2015, 18 political parties were legally registered by Elections Canada, including the Christian Heritage Party, the Marijuana Party, the Libertarian Party, the Canada Action Party, and the Marxist-Leninist Party of Canada. Of course, the five parties just mentioned have very low profiles. Even though some of them consistently run candidates in a large number of ridings, they almost never elect anyone. So although we have a multi-party system, it is evidently more hospitable to some kinds of parties than to others.

Roughly speaking, we may classify political parties in four categories. First, we have **brokerage parties**: large, highly pragmatic parties that espouse middle-of-the-road ideologies and try to appeal to every region, every ethnic group, and every social class. The Liberals and the Conservatives are brokerage parties. Then there are **ideological parties** such as the Marxist-Leninists or the Christian Heritage Party. These parties espouse ideological views that are outside of the mainstream and are more concerned with promoting those views than with winning seats. In this context, it is important to note that the NDP has been on a long march from an ideological formation to a more pragmatic party, moderating its platform and adopting mainstream campaigning techniques as it has come closer to power. **Single-issue parties** resemble ideological parties in that they are more concerned with promoting a point of view than with electoral success, but in this case the point of view relates to a single issue rather than an ideology. The Marijuana Party would be an example of a single-issue party. Finally, there are **protest parties**. These are parties that emerge from time to time among people who believe that the dominant forces in political life systematically ignore them and who are angry enough about it to use their vote as a way of expressing a protest. In some countries, protest parties are national in scope but emerge in response to a particular issue such as immigration. In Canada, where regional divisions are often quite profound, protest parties have typically been regional in character. The Reform Party would be an example of a Western-based protest party. The Bloc and the Créditistes of the 1960s are examples of Quebec-based protest parties.

The Canadian regime is dominated by brokerage parties. There are two reasons for this. First, Canada's system of responsible government places a premium on being on the government side of the House of Commons. In a "separation-of-powers" regime, even small parties might have some influence in the legislative process. In our regime, legislation is controlled by the party in power. Those who are not in power will normally have significant influence only if they have a realistic hope of becoming the dominant party. The regime thus encourages a small number of large brokerage parties and discourages non-brokerage parties because the latter have no hope of forming a government. Of course, smaller parties might hope to exert influence in periods of minority government. Yet as we saw in Chapter Nine, our SMP electoral system systematically promotes majority governments by over-rewarding the large national brokerage parties. It is SMP, more than anything else, that shapes our party system. SMP systematically thwarts new national parties (for instance, the Green Party), single-issue parties, and small ideological parties. On the other hand, SMP does encourage regional protest parties when conditions for such parties are ripe because it rewards parties that concentrate their votes in a small number of ridings rather than dispersing them across the country.

In the early stages of Canadian history, the Liberals and the Conservatives were the only parties in Canada. One might refer to this period as the "two-party phase" in our multi-party system. In every election since World War I, at least one "third party" has tried to break their monopoly. The emergence of third parties led to what was commonly called a "two-and-a-half party" phase in our multi-party system. In the 1921 election, for example, a Western-based protest party called the Progressive Party actually won more seats than the Conservatives. But regional protest parties are by their very nature short-term phenomena. Because they are merely regional, they cannot hope to win a majority. Their supporters eventually realize that, in a regime based on responsible government, it is not terribly useful to be sitting constantly on the opposition side of the House of Commons. Support for the Progressives declined dramatically over the next few elections. By 1935, they were unable to elect a single member, and the remnants of the party merged with the Conservatives a few years later. The 1935 election marked the emergence of another "third party," the CCF. The CCF was to some extent a regional protest party, but it was also a party with a distinct ideology—democratic socialism. The NDP has been the leading third party during most of the last 50 years. However, because of the party's non-mainstream ideology, NDP candidates have until recently not been serious contenders for national power, and their lack of popularity has been compounded by our SMP electoral system, under which they have always received a smaller proportion of parliamentary seats than their proportion of the vote.

The general election of 1993 brought a significant change to Canada's party system. In that election, one of the traditional brokerage parties (the Liberals) won a solid majority (though not a majority of votes), but the other was handed a stunning defeat: the PCs came in fifth, winning a mere two seats. Two new regional parties had bolted ahead. In second place was the Bloc with 54 seats, followed closely by the Reform Party with 52. The PCs again finished fifth in both the 1997 and 2000 elections. At the time of the 1993 election, and in much of the ensuing decade, some observers predicted that the emergence of Reform and the Bloc spelled the end of the "two-and-a-half" party system that had characterized Canada for most of the twentieth century. But that judgement was rash. Even at the time, it was easy to see that at least some of the changes that took place in 1993 would be temporary. Because responsible government and SMP place such a premium on victory, it was almost inevitable that the PCs and the Reform Party would resolve their differences so as to create a national alternative to the Liberals. Given the nature of the Canadian regime, competition between two dominant national parties will probably remain a key feature of our party system.

Between 1993 and 2011, Liberal Party support steadily declined, and the party lost government in 2006. The Conservative Party of Canada under Stephen Harper won two minority governments and then a majority in 2011. Meanwhile, the NDP made a stunning foray into Quebec, winning 59 of 75 seats in 2011 and reducing the Bloc to a rump of 4 MPs. The Liberal Party, occupying the middle of the ideological continuum between the right-of-centre Conservatives and the left-of-centre NDP, has had difficulty defining itself and has also suffered from a succession of ineffective leaders. Its standing in Canadian politics seemed to be in long-term and perhaps terminal decline. It was a strategic goal of Stephen Harper to further polarize the Canadian party system by seeking to steer voters toward a clear choice between right and left, between the Conservatives and a left party. This strategy meant marginalizing the Liberals.

In the 2015 election, however, the Liberals, under young, photogenic, and optimistic Justin Trudeau, vaulted from third place in the Commons to majority government, the first time ever in Canada a third-place party won a federal election. Among other things, the 2015 election was an example of voter volatility: the NDP lost one-third of its 2011 popular vote and over half of its seats. The Conservatives lost a quarter of its voter support and government status. Meanwhile, the Liberals went from 19 per cent voter support in 2011 to over 39 per cent in 2015, and from 34 seats to 184. Conditions were perfect for a Liberal resurgence: a desire for "change" among voters, a visceral desire to remove Mr. Harper from the prime ministership, and a young leader who learned the craft of campaigning during a very long writ period and exceeded the low expectations set for him by a barrage of pre-writ Conservative advertising.[9] The Liberals in 2015 benefited, as they have over their history, from the SMP electoral system.[10]

It is tempting to conclude that federal politics has reverted to a more familiar 2½ party system: Liberals and Conservatives as the major parties with

---

9   Election writs are formal orders issued by the governor general on the advice of the prime minister to electoral officers to arrange elections for MPs. They mark the dissolution of Parliament and the official start of the election campaign period. Electoral laws set out a variety of things that can and cannot be done during this period. For example, party spending is regulated during the writ period but not before it.

10   Stephen Clarkson, *The Big Red Machine: How the Liberal Party Dominates Canadian Politics* (Vancouver: UBC Press, 2004), 271–73.

the NDP as the smaller player. However, a comparison between 2011 and 2015 reveals huge swings in both seat counts and popular vote. There is no reason to think such voter volatility is peculiar to the 2015 election. Further, the 2015 election is a vivid example of the importance of party leadership in Canadian politics. To a great extent, for example, the person of Justin Trudeau lifted the Liberals to majority government status. Leader-centred party politics are a more unpredictable politics. And of course, as discussed in Chapter Nine, our electoral system, if left unchanged, will continue to exaggerate the effect of vote swings.

10.6 The Organization of Political Parties

You will recall that a "national election" in Canada is really a collection of 338 separate simultaneous elections in the various electoral constituencies. Political parties are therefore organized at the constituency level. Each of Canada's major national parties has 338 local constituency organizations, which are set up for a number of purposes: attracting members into the party; raising money for the next election; choosing a candidate to run in the riding; and sending members to the provincial and national conventions to debate policy ideas, elect party officials, and help choose the party leader.

Each constituency has its own party association, with a constitution and an executive charged with responsibility for the association's ongoing business. Between elections, the association's full membership may meet merely once or twice a year. Constituency organizations become more active when they must select delegates to a national convention or when an election is approaching. One of the most important functions of a party's electoral district association is to select the party's candidate for an upcoming election. Increasingly, however, central party officers, including the leader, take an interest in candidate selection. Parties know that a candidate locally selected may have said or done things in the past that will embarrass the party if disclosed. Parties now undertake extensive vetting processes to prevent such candidates from winning nomination contests. In addition, as discussed in Chapter Nine, parties may be interested in ensuring that candidates as a group mirror the socio-cultural diversity of the country. This requires the leadership to encourage the selection of candidates representing various identity groups; in some cases, the leader will simply appoint a desired candidate. In extreme situations, the leader will refuse to sign the nomination papers of a locally selected but otherwise objectionable candidate.

Because Canada's parties are designed primarily for winning elections, they are organized in a way that gives the party leadership the power to set election strategy. The party leader usually plays the key role in providing the campaign platform, choosing the campaign strategy, and setting the party's course for the election campaign. Thus, the leader is the one who usually gets the credit for electoral success and pays the price for electoral defeat. A major defeat is most often followed by a reorganization of the party, which frequently includes a leadership convention. Often, leaders resign on their own initiative after electoral defeat, as did Mr. Harper on the night of the 2015 election.

How party leaders are chosen affects how much political power they wield over the party. At the beginning of the twentieth century, the parties still chose their leaders in a caucus meeting. Those members who were elected to Parliament would meet and choose who would lead them. This process of caucus leadership selection left individual MPs with some power over their leader, as he owed his position to them.

With the advent of the party leadership convention (in 1919, in the case of the Liberals), the power of party leaders has grown considerably. The leadership convention process is one in which the party sends a fixed number of delegates to a convention, and they in turn elect a leader. Many delegates will be representatives of their constituency associations. Others may be delegates representing various party associations. Still others will be MPs, senators, and elected members from provincial assemblies. All told, there may be 4,000 to 5,000 delegates at a convention. By a process of secret ballot, they vote on a leader from among a number of candidates. The usual procedure is for successive votes in which the field is reduced by dropping the candidate who has the fewest votes from the ballot until one candidate wins a majority.

The convention model greatly increases the power of the party leader over his or her caucus. Because the party leader no longer owes her or his position to the caucus but to the party organization as a whole, she or he can speak for the party over and against the caucus members who speak only for their individual constituencies. This system has been the dominant mode of leadership selection for most of this century. Recently, however, a new and allegedly more democratic process of selecting a leader has begun to be used: the all-member vote. This process resembles what the Americans call a "primary." Instead of a convention in which delegates represent the views of all the party's members, parties have elections in which each member gets to vote directly for a leadership candidate. As a part of a process of internal renewal after years of decline and ineffectiveness, the Liberal Party in 2012 created a category of "supporter" to encourage more people to associate with the party and vote for its leader without having to become formal dues-paying members. Ahead of the 2013 leadership convention, the party boasted about 300,000 members and supporters. Here the party opened its doors to people drawn not to the party so much as to a particular candidate for its leadership.

The all-member vote system thus marks a continuation of the trend toward making the leadership selection process more democratic. Whether this new process is more likely to produce better or more popular leaders remains to be seen, but there can be no doubt that it strengthens the hand of the leader relative to other officials in the party because leaders chosen in this mode owe their position to the party membership rather than the party's elite. Whether having increasingly powerful leaders makes parties more democratic is an open question.

Of the three levels of government—federal, provincial, and local—the only level at which party politics does not dominate is the local. Even there however, party politics has slowly crept in. In some cities, we now find slates of candidates running under the banner of a political party, and one often finds that there are close behind-the-scene links between civic politicians and provincial parties.

For the most part, however, Canada's parties are organized at both the provincial and federal levels. In some parties, the organizational links between the different levels are strong; in others, the federal and provincial parties are completely independent of each other. It is also important to note that it is not unusual for a party to be politically successful in a provincial election but not in a federal election even within the same province. Voters often distinguish between the provincial and federal wings of the same party and may at the same time like one and reject the other. In the 2000 federal election, for example, the PCs did not elect a single member in Ontario even though the Ontario PCs controlled the provincial legislature.

At each level, the party organization consists of two component parts: the parliamentary wing and the extra-parliamentary wing. The former consists of all those party members who have a seat in Parliament; the latter is made up of the party executive at the constituency, provincial, and national levels (see Figure 10.1).

Figure 10.1: Party Organization

Parliamentary Wing	Extra-Parliamentary Wing
Parliamentary Leader	Party President
Caucus	National Executive
	Constituency Associations

In Canadian political parties, the parliamentary wing wields power that far exceeds its size. This disproportion is to be expected, for the elected MPs necessarily view the party's policies and public positions in terms of what is conducive to being re-elected. Moreover, they must respond to the ongoing political events in the House of Commons. Therefore, the parliamentary wing of the party, and more specifically the leadership, is forced to formulate policies and take positions long before the next policy convention can decide party policy. Thus, while parties never cease discussing ways and means of making the parliamentary wing more responsive to the extra-parliamentary wing, such reforms will always be blunted by the reality of electoral politics. Canada's parties are electoral machines designed primarily for the purpose of winning elections. To the extent that the parliamentary wing of the party is best positioned to guide the party toward electoral success, it will continue to exercise a dominating role within the party.

10.7 Financing Political Parties

A substantial amount of money is necessary to run a successful national party. Major expenses are incurred for offices and staffing, for advertising, and for running leadership and electoral campaigns. The three main parties each spent about $20 million during the 2011 campaign. Where does this money come from? Where should it come from? Should there be limits on what donors can give and what parties and candidates can spend? The way in which we respond to these questions can have an important impact on what kinds of parties we have and what kinds of parties succeed.

In the early years of Canadian democracy, parties relied heavily on donations from wealthy individuals and large corporations. Of course, this approach made bribery and corruption a problem; in fact, two of our most successful prime ministers (John A. Macdonald and Mackenzie King) were defeated after soliciting large donations from business interests in exchange for government favours. Through much of the twentieth century, party leaders tried to keep their hands clean by shifting the responsibility for fundraising to "bag-men"—low-profile but well-connected individuals who could solicit large donations more discreetly.

Legislation passed in 1970 required parties to be registered with the Chief Electoral Officer, and their names for the first time accompanied the names of candidates on ballots. The age of the regulation of parties had begun. In 1974, laws were passed to encourage individual Canadians to donate to political parties, thus reducing the influence large corporate and union donors could wield. An individual donor would be able to claim a generous tax credit on his or her income tax return if he or she donated to a party. In 2004, another major change was implemented. Donations to parties from corporations and unions were sharply limited, and Parliament instituted a per vote public subsidy to help parties make up the shortfall. A party would get from the public treasury approximately $2.00 per year for every vote it garnered in the previous election. This policy added to party revenues and particularly assisted those parties that failed to generate donations from individual supporters. It meant a party would have money based on the votes it garnered, not necessarily on the seats it won. But it also encouraged parties to look to the state for funding rather than to their supporters. As prime minister, Stephen Harper eventually moved to terminate the subsidy, ban altogether donations from corporations and unions, increase the amount individuals could donate to parties and candidates, and increase the tax incentives for donors.

As of 2015, the regulatory framework for party finance looks like this:

1. *Contribution limits*. Only Canadian citizens and permanent residents can donate. In any one year, a person can give $1,500 to each party; $1,500 in total to constituency associations, nomination contests, and candidates of each registered party; and $1,500 in total for contestants in a party leadership contest. Candidates can commit higher amounts to their own campaigns.

2. *Spending limits*. Persons standing for nomination as candidate for a party are limited to about $15,000 in spending, or 20 per cent of the spending limit for a candidate in an election campaign. In 2015, a candidate could have spent anywhere from $170,000 to $270,000 on his or her election campaign. Candidate expense limits are tied to the number of electors per riding. The larger the number of electors, the higher the spending limit. They are also tied to the length of the campaign; the longer the campaign, the more candidates are allowed to spend. For example, the limit in Surrey Centre, BC, in 2015 was just over $200,000 while the limit in Charlottetown, PEI, was $170,000. Aside from candidates themselves, political parties are also able to spend money during the writ period. The maximum amount depends on the number of candidates they run in the election and on the length of the campaign. In 2015, parties running candidates in all 338 ridings were allowed to spend about $54,000,000. What counts as an expense is important to consider. New for 2015 was that neither spending on polls nor fundraising was considered an election expense. And of course, election expense limits cover only the campaign period. With fixed election dates, parties can spend on the "virtual" campaign long before the writs are issued.

3. *Reimbursements*. If a candidate wins at least 10 per cent of the vote in a riding and submits all his or her reports to Elections Canada, he or she can be reimbursed up to 60 per cent of his or her election expenses. (The reimbursements go to the electoral district association, not the candidate.) Parties are entitled to a reimbursement

of 50 per cent of their national expenses if they get at least 2 per cent of the national vote or 5 per cent of the vote in the ridings in which they ran candidates.

4. *Tax credits for political contributions.* Persons donating to a political party or candidate are eligible for a generous tax credit. For example, a donor is entitled to a 75 per cent tax credit for donations up to $400. When a person donates $400 to a party, the taxpayer is actually giving the party or candidate $300 and the donor is giving $100.

5. *Reporting requirements.* Parties and candidates must submit detailed reports of their donations and expenses. These are public documents. Parties and candidates are subject to fines and in extreme cases criminal charges for failures to report on time and other misrepresentations.

Because Canada is a federal regime, the provinces have the authority to regulate party politics according to their own priorities. Many of the provinces' rules are similar to the federal rules listed above. Several, however, provide annual public subsidies to parties based on those parties' vote counts in the previous election.

10.8 Party Government and Party Politics

Parliamentary government is party government, and Canadian politics is party politics. Though we may, from time to time, complain about this, it is probably both necessary and good that it is so, for the clear division of MPs into parties allows us to determine easily who has won a national election and consequently will form the next government. The governor general's obligation—to ensure that Canada has a workable government in Parliament—is thus easy to discharge. Political parties provide us both with clear outcomes to elections and the parliamentary leader who will become the prime minister. One need only imagine, for a moment, a scenario in which these results were all undetermined. The public would have no way of telling who the prime minister would be, and it is likely that, without party discipline, governments would come and go with problematic frequency. Party leadership and party discipline are what make for stable parliamentary government. One is left to conclude that the only thing worse than party politics would be parliamentary politics without parties.

This is not to say that party politics is simply good. Almost any observer of Canadian politics will soon notice troubling instances when party interests appear to take priority over national interests. Is the government of the day, which consists of the leadership of a particular political party, not always looking out for its future electoral interests at least as much as it is for the national interest?

A further question is the power of party leaders, both in and out of Parliament. Within Parliament, the party leader has the power to determine cabinet positions within the government. In the opposition party, the leader has the power to assign the "shadow cabinet" positions, the high profile positions of critics who follow the issues of particular government departments. An MP with such a position has a chance for frequent national media exposure as well as the opportunity to build up a specialized expertise in an area of public policy. It is not unusual for a finance critic to become a finance minister should the critic's party win the next election.

Have the party leaders become too powerful in Canadian politics? They certainly dominate both Parliament and the public view of political life, often leaving us with the impression that politics is a kind of struggle between three or four individuals (and their personal advisers). But it is important to remember that the political power of party leaders ultimately depends on public opinion. Can the leader lead the party to success, however that is conceived, in the next election? A leader's power, even a prime minister's, quickly begins to decline when those in the party begin to sense defeat. Although the liberal democratic regime is not a direct democracy, the political power of its parties and leaders ultimately rests on the votes, and therefore the opinions, of the people.

Key Terms

political parties	party systems
five functions of political parties	multi-party system
interest aggregation	single-party system
ideology	brokerage parties
high partisanship	ideological parties
low partisanship	single-issue parties
pragmatic	protest parties

Discussion Questions

1. What is the best way to choose the leader of a political party? Who should be involved in the selection?

2. For what reasons do people join political parties? What would motivate you to do so? What would prevent you from doing so?

CHAPTER ELEVEN

PUBLIC POLICY

11.1   The Canadian Regime and Public Policy

This book has described the major principles and institutions of the Canadian regime. Principles of equality and liberty have informed the creation and development of the institutions of federalism, parliamentary government, the Charter, and the electoral system. These institutions are not tangible things such as the Parliament Buildings in Ottawa. Rather, they are legitimate, continuing regularities of behaviour that are traceable to basic understandings of good government. These regularities or norms govern conduct by citizens and political office holders. They *constitute* the regime; accordingly, they form the Canadian Constitution.

Constitutional norms both limit and facilitate political action. One of the great conditions of political life is that we need government and want it to act in the interest of citizens' security and the peaceful settlement of disputes. But we are also wary of government. It has tremendous coercive capacity, and misuse of power by political actors and those who administer and enforce the law can bring misery and injustice. "Corruption" is the term applied to the condition in which political officials act not in the interest of the public but to advance their own private interests. Short of corruption, political officials can be incompetent or careless, and citizens individually and the political order as a whole can suffer because of their missteps. So we want governments to be able to act to advance the public good, but we want to ensure as much as possible that they are unable to act against the public good.

When we suggest that governments should be able to act, we refer to public policy. Public policy is what governments do—the decisions they make, the money they raise and spend, the laws they pass, the visits officials make, the pronouncements they utter, and even the things they refuse to say and do. Public policy is the output of government that is the stuff of debate, election campaigning, news reporting, and academic study. It is the regime in action. Public policy is what we get when politicians ask, "What shall we do?"

An analogy may clarify the relationship between public policy and the Canadian regime. Consider hockey, Canada's pastime. Hockey is played with a stick and a puck on ice. But not every use of these elements is hockey. A game of pick-up between two teams of four on a pond is not hockey. Hockey, properly speaking, is constituted by rules that define the surface on which the game is played, the number of players on the ice at any time, the equipment required, legal versus illegal contact, what constitutes offside passes, and so on. The rules of hockey distinguish it from shinny or indeed baseball and cricket.

So the rules of hockey are important. And note also that the rules of hockey can change. For many years, the NHL forbade a forward pass over two lines. This is no longer the case: a player can now pass over his or her blue line and the centre line, and that change in the rules has produced a change in the way the game is played. Fans need to know and understand the rules in order to appreciate the game, but it is ultimately the game that they care about, not the rules. They want to see how a team works together, how it adjusts to the other team, how it organizes its defence and offence, how it controls the puck, and ultimately how often it is able to score and win. The rules define and structure the game, but the game is the thing.

In politics, conceiving, implementing, and administering sound public policy is central to governing well. In order to understand the public policy process, one must bear in mind how the rules of the political game structure, enable, and limit what the players can do. This chapter will discuss the interaction of constitutional rules and the operation of the system so as to produce laws, budgets, and policies that animate public life and advance the common good.

11.2 Institutional Forces

Liberal democratic regimes empower governments to act and hold them account-able for their actions. They seek to balance the efficiency necessary for action with the necessary mechanisms designed to hold the government accountable. These mechanisms can, and often do, slow down government action. It is important to understand that we are often critical of governments for not acting quickly but, at the same time, demand that government powers be checked in various ways. We demand both things while sometimes forgetting that they are often compet-ing demands. Governments must seek to balance the demands for efficiency and accountability. The form of government used may lean more in one direction than the other. The more efficient form of government prizes the ability to act quickly and decisively. A form of government with greater checks on government power erects stronger obstacles to government action. This form of government does not make action impossible; it simply arranges the institutional forces to require a higher degree of consensus *before* action is possible.

Canada and the United States afford good examples of the principles of efficiency and accountability in action. The American Constitution, for example, distributes the power to legislate among the two houses of Congress (the House of Representatives and the Senate) and the president. Both houses, each elected by different constituencies of electors for different terms, must approve a bill in the same form. This is not easily accomplished. The president has the power to veto a bill that makes it through Congress. But Congress can override that veto by mustering a two-thirds vote in each house. American constitutional design makes it easier to kill a bill than pass it, especially because party discipline is not highly rigid. Historically, members of Congress voted their party lines about two-thirds of the time, though in recent years, party-line voting has increased.

In Canada, our SMP electoral system often (but not always) gives the win-ning party in a general election more seats than its popular vote would seem to dictate. The principles of responsible government assure the government of con-tinuation in office until the next election as long as it can maintain the support of a majority of members of the House of Commons on major elements of the gov-ernment's agenda or on explicit votes of confidence. In Canada, party discipline is very rigid. It is rare for an MP to vote against his or her party in Parliament. An MP is a rebel if he or she votes against the party six to eight times in a ses-sion. Bills are usually introduced by a member of the government, and if the government is committed to the passage of that bill, it can be passed despite the objections of the opposition, the media, and interest groups. The parliamentary system tilts in favour of efficiency in constitutional design, and, in the Canadian case, this is all the more true because the Canadian Senate was designed not to oppose government initiative but rather to be a chamber of review that, at most, delays legislation. The Senate has very occasionally killed government bills but, being appointed, lacks the democratic mandate to make a habit of it.

Is Canadian government so efficient, then, as to be potentially despotic as a result? The accusation is often made, particularly at election time when opposition candidates criticize the government party of the day. Several points are in order. First, Canadians are no strangers to minority government, and in such circumstances governments cannot afford to ignore the arguments and demands of MPs in other parties. Second, MPs do hew to the party line, but they may feel the pressure from constituents who disagree with a government's proposal on a policy matter. MPs know that they must face their constituents in the election campaign and so will be sure to represent their constituents' opinions to the government, if only in secret caucus meetings. Third, governments can act efficiently in Canada because they effectively control Parliament. But this also means they are quite justifiably held responsible for the legislation they pass. Prime ministers cannot blame others for laws they approved and arranged to have put through caucus and Parliament.

Fourth, a law rammed through Parliament may run afoul of other constitutional limits on government. The Charter of Rights and Freedoms protects a battery of rights against infringement by laws and other forms of official action. Aggrieved persons can challenge the constitutionality of laws in court. Likewise, a law passed by Parliament may concern a subject matter that is assigned to the provinces under the division of powers. Canada is implacably federal. One order of government cannot invade the jurisdiction of another. A province may wish to criminalize some noxious act in a province, but criminal law is a federal responsibility, not provincial. It has to choose another policy tool or request that the federal government amend the Criminal Code of Canada.

Finally, mention must be made of another major institutional player in public policy: the public service. Elected politicians come and go. They are not public policy experts. They know what they want to do while in government and feel they have the legitimacy to bring in the policies or programs that they promised to voters. But they are usually vague on the details of the policy they wish to implement. They may not know that the policy they champion was tried before and failed. They may not realize that the objectives they seek have been achieved by another government through alternative means.

The public service is that large phalanx of permanent government employees who ultimately report to ministers of the government of the day and who occupy their roles on the basis of non-partisan, merit-based competition.

The upper reaches of the public service assist the elected ministers in devising and implementing their policy priorities. Members of the public service are there to provide sound, impartial, evidence-based advice on what is the best way for government to proceed on a policy priority. Once a government has decided on a policy, the duty of the public service is to implement it and to evaluate its performance. This permanent executive assists the political executive in policy initiatives and in the execution of policies to which the government is committed.

Non-partisan though the public service may be, it is not without its own interests in the policy process. Bureaucracies are quite conservative by nature. They are committed to following established processes by which change is considered and implemented. And they naturally resist implementing changes whose effect is to compromise or otherwise diminish the ranks of the public service itself. The slow pace of change is a constant source of frustration for politicians. As a result, some parties in government have reorganized their operations to insulate ministers from senior civil servants who are adept at raising objections to a new government's policy agenda. In the Mulroney years of the 1980s, each minister was equipped with a chief of staff who would whisper into his or her ear the partisan priorities of the government so that a new member of the government would not be swayed by the expertise of a seasoned permanent public servant. In addition, the remarkable growth of the Prime Minister's Office since the 1970s can be attributed in part to the desire by prime ministers to have a source of policy expertise independent of that provided by the public service. This causes public servants no end of irritation.

11.3 Public Policy and Canadian Society

Governments are constrained by institutions. What other forces affect what they do?

First, there are interest groups. They come in two main varieties: **special interest groups** and **public interest groups**. The Canadian Wireless Telecommunications Association (CWTA), which represents companies involved in the wireless communications industry in this country, is an example of the first variety. It of course purports to advance the interest of millions of Canadians in affordable, reliable, and extensive wireless service, but it is also about advancing the objectives of the industry: blocking what it considers needless and costly regulation and supporting laws that discourage forms of competition harmful to its members' companies. The CWTA employs experts in policy analysis who monitor government policy and public opinion. Like many such groups, it often employs an ex-politician—in 2015 former premier of New Brunswick Bernard Lord—as its president and chief executive officer. Drawing on Mr. Lord's experience in government, the CWTA can effectively communicate with governments and the voters who elect them.

Public interest groups, by contrast, do not have hard economic interests to defend. Instead, they are committed to more abstract, general objectives. Consider, for example, the Canadian Civil Liberties Association (CCLA), whose work has been to promote and defend civil liberties. Not only does the CCLA conduct public education campaigns but its officers also regularly appear before parliamentary committees considering bills on such matters as anti-terrorism and criminal reform. And, like many public interest groups, the CCLA intervenes in court cases involving salient civil liberties issues. The CCLA depends on the donations of its membership and the pro bono work of lawyers who believe in its objectives.

Think tanks are akin to public interest groups in that they conduct and commission research and public policy proposals for consumption by media, government, scholars, and the general public. Think tanks provide some of the intellectual grist for the public policy mill. Each one generally claims to be independent, but it is also true that different think tanks tilt in one ideological direction or another. The Centre for Policy Alternatives publishes work reflecting a left, "progressive" view of economic policy, while the C.D. Howe Institute is a more market-friendly outfit.

The media are crucial players in the policy process. Their main contribution is in agenda setting. This refers to the manner in which an "issue" becomes a matter for public debate and public policy attention. Society is full of problems and difficulties, but only some rise to the level of a public policy issue. The media's stock-in-trade is the uncovering of issues that attract readers and viewers. Some of these take on a life of their own, generating extended public comment and reactions from politicians in office and those who aspire to political power. Some news stories embarrass governments whose policies are failing; others draw attention to problems no one has addressed. Still others tell the story of someone somehow ill-treated by a policy people favour. In any case, newspapers, radio, television, and social media put a matter before the attentive public, including those in government. The media do not tell us what to think, but they are effective at telling us what to think about.

Different media outlets also tell us how to think about issues. Regular readers of different news sources will notice that the same issue is reported differently in different outlets. The *Toronto Star*, for example, tilts to the progressive centre-left, while the *National Post* generally reflects a centre-right position on politics. Canadians should also be mindful of the distinction between public and private broadcasters. The CBC is a Crown corporation and is heavily dependent on public funding. This funding allows it to pursue activities or broadcast events that are in the public interest rather than just those that will attract a profitable audience. However, it also naturally has an interest in the continued public funding of its operations. It is hard not to think this interest does not colour its news broadcasting decisions. It is possible that its editorial officers are also favourable to public spending in general. In contrast, private broadcasters are less favourable to public monies supporting their market competition.

Finally, there are voters. Voters are the consumers of news and the objects of policy. Their lives are deeply influenced by governments. In the age of the sprawling administrative welfare state, where the economy is tightly regulated and citizens enjoy a range of entitlements to government programming and spending, people acquire a strong stake in programs that benefit them and have an interest in other state services not yet developed. But they are conflicted. Generally speaking, people want generous public programs: good, timely health care; access to cheap energy for their cars and houses; good schools for their children; and access to well-paying jobs near their homes. They also want low taxes so that more of their incomes remain with them. And other things being equal, they want governments not to go into debt. Interest payments on the debt mean less money for current government spending on programs people demand. They of course can have two of these three things—good services, low taxes, no public debt—but not all three. Politics is partly about reconciling the conflicting demands of voters.

A simple view of public policymaking holds that government perceives a problem, designs the perfect solution, implements it, and then the problem goes away. This simple view depends on an untenable notion that public policy is made by experts who know everything and have all the power to fashion the perfect solution. Neither assumption holds. The experts do not have all the power; and, in any case, experts disagree among themselves about the nature of the problem and the best solution. What we have instead are collections of agencies, groups, and individuals that cluster around certain policy issues, bringing different perspectives, degrees of expertise, and interests to bear. These **policy communities** include relevant government departments and agencies and interest groups. If the question, for example, is whether to explore for and develop oil resources in an untouched area of a province, the policy community that will emerge in response will include the federal departments of energy, natural resources, and environment; their provincial counterparts; energy industry associations; corporate proponents of natural resource development; environmental groups; Aboriginal groups whose lands may be affected by development; and other groups representing landowners. Elected politicians oversee the long and complex process of policy development and will take a particular position over the objections of at least some in the policy community. An election may be fought over the issue, and the outcome of the election may settle the matter. On other occasions, external events beyond anyone's control will shape the question. For example, if the world price of natural gas collapses due to oversupply, then the impetus for provincial natural gas development may evaporate.

Policy communities can be fertile environments for public policy change. One may think that public policies are in constant flux due to the ebb and flow of ideas, events, and the pressures asserted by groups and institutional actors. In fact, the array of forces and interests casts a rather conservative pall over the whole field. The reason is that once a public policy is in place it becomes hard to change. Myriad groups and individuals alter their activities and expectations to adjust to the new policy order, and habits once formed are hard to break. If it is a policy that provides citizens with entitlements to services, those citizens will be reluctant to give them up. Interest groups representing members benefiting from policies are in the same position. And government agencies with monies to disburse also resist changes depriving them of such tasks. In other words, as state and society interpenetrate, change is hard to achieve. When change occurs, it is more likely to happen at the margins rather than wholesale. Opposition politicians always campaign on change and reform. When they get into office, however, they realize how difficult it is to produce change.

11.4 Case Study: Health Care

Public health care insurance, or "medicare" as it is commonly known, is hallowed in Canada, one of the hallmarks of Canadian identity and citizenship. Its cachet is associated with a simple and attractive principle: medical attention is available to Canadians based on their need for care, not on their ability to pay. This principle accords with most Canadians' experience. You break an arm playing hockey or slipping on the ice, get to the hospital, and, upon presentation of your health-care insurance card, you are put in line in the fracture clinic. In a few hours, you are on the way home, not a penny out of pocket.

Behind this simple experience is a system that defies simple explanation. Under the constitutional division of powers, health is generally considered a provincial responsibility, though the federal order of government covers health care for military personnel, Aboriginal peoples, and some others. But for reasons to be explained shortly, the federal government is active in health care due to its spending power. A great deal of intergovernmental coordination is part of the health-care puzzle. Another layer of complexity is associated with the Charter of

Rights and Freedoms and the assertion of rights to achieve change in the delivery of health care in Canada.

An additional layer of complexity concerns the nature of health care itself. Each of us gets sick or otherwise has occasion to require medical attention. We all use the system and have opinions about it. We are increasingly informed about disease and its treatment by means of the Internet. Yet the fact remains that there is a yawning gap in knowledge between the medical experts and the rest of us. Thus, we all use the system but lack the precise expertise and knowledge to evaluate the kind of care we get or to judge the overall trade-offs associated with the operation of the system. What produces better health outcomes—pouring more money into acute care or concentrating on longer-term initiatives emphasizing prevention of disease? Experts themselves disagree. Citizens find it hard to judge the merits associated with the current system and those of alternative models in use in other countries.

Because doctors are in the business of making sick people healthy, and because they do this job quite well, they enjoy enormous trust and prestige. This means that they command not only high incomes but also substantial political influence. Medical professionals as a class are very articulate, politically well-connected, and more than able to defend their views and interests.

The system's complexity is matched by its cost. Health care may be free at point of treatment, but it is definitely expensive for the country as a whole, consuming an estimated $215 billion per year in 2014 or 11 per cent of GDP.[1] This works out to just over $6,000 for every Canadian each year. Seventy per cent of total health spending is public, so the bulk of the cost is covered by general tax revenues and in some cases health care insurance premiums. Public health spending consumes upwards of 40 per cent of provincial budgets, the single largest item of program spending. If left uncontrolled health-care spending can easily crowd out other government spending priorities.

A fundamental question is whether health care is a commodity like pizza or cars that can be purchased on open markets to everyone's net benefit. Markets are very good at responding to consumer choice and containing costs. But they depend on high levels of good information on the basis of which consumer choices can be made. Consumers can tell good coffee from rotgut and a good car from a lemon. But do they have the expertise to tell a good doctor from a bad one, a good insurance policy from a poor one? Can they intelligently evaluate a doctor's diagnosis or an advertisement for a medication for hypertension or arthritis? And because health

---

[1]   Canadian Institute for Health Information, *National Health Expenditure Trends, 1975 to 2014* (Ottawa: CIHI, 2014), 14.

care is "free" to patients at point of contact, is there an incentive to consume more of it? Experts disagree on the extent to which moral hazards accompany public health insurance, but many do worry that health costs are so high because people pay less attention to prevention and more to acute care because acute care is "free." If there is no out-of-pocket cost associated with getting treatment for a malady, is there an incentive for taking the steps to avoid poor health in the first place?

Markets ration demand through the price mechanism. How is demand rationed in health care? Health-care insurance in Canada is funded primarily from general revenues, so in what way is it actually insurance rather than just a publicly provided service? Public health insurance departs from standard insurance principles. In normal insurance plans, one pays for insurance based on the chance one will need the services insured against. House insurance is costlier for those houses with fireplaces because fireplaces increase the risk of the house burning down. In a free market for health care, one's access to insurance and the premiums one pays depend on a variety of factors including one's age and one's history of illness and disease—in other words, on the likelihood one will contract an expensive illness in future. Although illness is sometimes the result of one's own negligence—if you point a loaded gun at your feet and fire, your injury is your fault—in most cases illness occurs for reasons too difficult or expensive to plumb. What this means is that pure insurance models for health care impose high costs on the infirm and potentially infirm. And the incentive is for private providers of health insurance to insure the healthy, not the unhealthy, so as to improve the financial performance of the insurance provider. Private insurance may be efficient in the allocation of resources but it is not equitable. The poorer one is, the less likely one will have access to quality health care. Accordingly, health insurance in Canada provides all insured services to Canadians for a cost related to levels of taxation of their income, not the risk that they will use the system. It is thus more accurate to say Canadians are *ensured* against illness, not *insured* against it.

Canada's public insurance model is sometimes labelled socialistic. This is not quite true. Most doctors are private contractors who see the patients they wish and bill the provincial health insurance plan for the services they perform. Doctors' associations negotiate fee schedules with provincial authorities and help determine what is a "medically required service" to be covered by the insurance plan. Doctors and pharmacists also help governments determine what new drugs shall be part of a province's "formulary" of pharmaceuticals for those patients whose drug costs are publicly covered. Hospitals are usually private, not-for-profit corporations that receive budgets from provincial health authorities but are not government departments. Government priorities define annual spending allocations, but private actors are largely responsible for how those funds are spent on health care.

Furthermore, many health services are not covered by provincial insurance plans. Home care, the purchase of most drugs, ancillary medical services such as physiotherapy and dental care, and many aspects of seniors' care are not part of the medicare system. One must pay out of pocket for these or hold private insurance. So primary physician care and secondary services performed in hospitals and clinics are covered; much else is not.

Canadian federalism influences the delivery of health care. When the division of powers was set out in 1867, health care was a modest affair. Medicine could do little for people beyond obvious maladies. Provincial governments incurred no great costs. Now, provinces are responsible for the delivery of very expensive health programming, their single largest program and spending commitment. Yet they lack the tax revenues to do so sustainably. This is so for two reasons. First, the federal order of government is allotted most of the revenue-raising powers in the Constitution. Second, some provinces are poor, lacking the lucrative tax bases that yield substantial revenues to fund provincial services. In the 1960s, the federal government began to help finance provincial health care on the basis of 50/50 funding: every provincial dollar of health spending was matched by a federal dollar. This arrangement became unaffordable for the federal government as health spending rocketed and recession hit the country in the 1970s. In 1977, the federal government moved to a block grant to the provinces, fixing the level of federal contributions and dividing the federal contribution between cash transfers and "tax points"—pulling back on federal taxes so the provinces could take up that "room" to finance their own programs. It means that federal cash contributions today amount to about 20 per cent of provincial health spending.

When provinces, tight for money in the 1970s, tried to impose discipline on the system, doctors began extra-billing patients to boost their incomes. The federal government, particularly an assertive health minister, Monique Bégin, reacted by declaring that cash transfers from the federal level to the provinces would be reduced by the amount doctors extra-billed. This was the reason for the 1984 Canada Health Act, which set out five conditions provinces must meet in order to receive full funding from the federal government. Thus, the federal government used its spending power to impose national standards, supporting a national conception of what health care means in Canada. The provinces generally adhere to the act's five conditions but still grumble at the imposition of federal conditions on the delivery of services within provincial jurisdiction. However, as the federal government's cash contribution to the provinces declines relative to overall provincial spending, its clout in enforcing the five conditions weakens. Predictably, the provinces lobby for more money, arguing that it is needed if they are to meet the five conditions.

For a long time, pharmaceuticals were not a major part of health care. That has changed. Drugs now constitute over 15 per cent of total health spending. A patchwork of public programs covers 40 per cent of drug costs, but these programs are offered to limited sets of people, for example, to those over 65. As a result, there are people without private insurance and unable to pay for life-saving but prohibitively expensive drugs. In European countries, drugs are covered by public insurance schemes. Why not do the same in Canada? Political parties on the left routinely support a national pharmacare program. If government coordinated the purchase of drugs, some studies suggest that they could use their bargaining power to obtain costly drugs at much lower prices. It turns out that when a single purchaser represents a very large number of drug consumers, drug companies are willing to reduce their prices. Still, the costs of a public drug plan are considerable. But there is an important interaction effect between such a plan and the electoral cycle. One scholar explains:

> A more specific explanation of the cost barrier is that it does not fit the political timetable particularly well. A solid majority government confident of at least two terms in office might consider the implementation of a pharmacare program to be a reasonable political investment, as the up-front costs could be justified over time with reference to a slowdown in the rate of growth over a period of years. A minority government of any stripe fighting for survival, especially during inauspicious economic times, would see no conceivable payback for such a scheme.[2]

For health care and other public policies, important ideas run into a democratic wall: it is hard for politicians seeking re-election to sponsor policies whose benefits will only accrue *after* the elections they seek to win.

A major challenge in health care is to match spending and health-care outcomes. The system is such that it can absorb any amount of money spent on it. Not only are citizens' health needs potentially limitless—I can always imagine myself healthier than I am, and requiring health service more conveniently and quickly than I currently do, for example—but administrators, doctors, and other health-care workers can always argue that they are worth more than they are being

---

2   Katherine Fierlbeck, *Health Care in Canada: A Citizen's Guide to Policy and Politics* (Toronto: University of Toronto Press, 2011), 158.

paid. Indeed, most unconditional infusions of money into the health system are quickly absorbed by wages and salaries, and no other system change is produced.

In a system that is premised on patient care, should not the needs of patients dictate the shape and extent of the system? It is not that easy, as one observer explains:

> The health care system features, huge bureaucracies, large institutions, powerful professional associations, formidable unions, well-paid administrators, all nominally supervised and directed by a political party that, once in power, wishes to remain there. Each part of the system has its own ways of doing things and interests to protect. They are the producers and providers of a service (or product) called health care. Patients are consumers of that service.[3]

In other words, once in place, the health-care system creates a coterie of entrenched interests dependent on continued funding. These recipients quickly become privileged and resistant to change, particularly change that threatens their status and benefits. Once instituted, "producer entitlement is difficult to diminish, let alone eliminate. Producers or providers become, in economic parlance, 'rent-seekers' looking to appropriate unto themselves what they can of available resources."[4]

This rigidity in the system, its resistance to change, has created problems for expenditure control. For many years, provincial health-care spending exceeded the amount needed to account for population growth and inflation. Spending also exceeded rates of economic growth. The system simply could absorb as much money as a government was willing to put into it. And patients always say the system can work better. In most federal elections in recent memory (the 2015 election being a conspicuous exception), health was ranked by voters at or near the top of lists of important issues. No surprise: older people use health care frequently, and they vote in large numbers. We now spend more on health care than on education in Canada, from kindergarten to university.

As rigid as the system is, it attracts no end of discussion about reform. Though Canadians think highly of their system relative to that of the more complex and inegalitarian one south of the border, in fact on a number of criteria—for example, wait times before receiving treatments and overall health

---

3   Jeffrey Simpson, *Chronic Condition: Why Canada's Health-Care System Needs to Be Dragged into the 21st Century* (Toronto: Allen Lane, 2012), 168–69.

4   Simpson, *Chronic Condition*, 169–70.

outcomes when measured against the costs of the system—Canada's performance among the major industrial democracies is middling at best. Many European and Scandinavian systems produce better health outcomes at lower public cost and deliver health care in a more timely manner. Several European countries combine private, not-for-profit insurance with public insurance and cover the spectrum of health-care services more comprehensively. It is important to bear in mind that health is secured by more than access to acute care. Populations with regular exercise habits and better diets do have better health outcomes. On these points, North Americans have much to learn from other populations.

In the Charter era, citizens and groups have a new access point into the system to pursue change. If politicians cannot or will not act, people can try the courts. Two cases are pertinent. The first concerned a pregnant woman who, because of her deafness, was unable to understand instructions from her doctor. The BC health insurance plan did not cover sign language interpretation services for persons unable to understand their doctors when receiving medically required services. A unanimous Supreme Court panel found that the government's decision not to insure interpretation services was contrary to the equality rights provision of the Charter.[5]

A more controversial decision came down in 2005. Its complexities defy easy summary, but the issue was essentially whether long wait times—in this country associated with the rationing of health care by governments trying to contain costs—put patients in danger of physical or psychological harm. The right to security of the person in section 7 of the Charter has been interpreted by courts to mean the right to be free of state-imposed stress and injury unless the policy causing such stress is consistent with the principles of fundamental justice. A Quebec doctor, Jacques Chaoulli, proposed to solve the wait-time problem by offering private medical care to patients in a private hospital. He wanted to provide more timely care outside the public system for those willing to pay for it. But Quebec law prohibited the purchase of private health insurance, leaving Quebeckers to pay for timely health care out of pocket. This, of course, is prohibitively expensive for all but the very wealthy. Chaoulli's plan would work only if private health insurance could be purchased. So he challenged the ban on private health insurance as contrary to both the Canadian Charter and the Quebec Charter of Human Rights.

Chaoulli scored a surprise victory, shocking court watchers and defenders of medicare.[6] But the court was badly fractured, making the decision hard to

---

5   *Eldridge v. British Columbia (Attorney General)*, 1997 3 SCR 624.

6   *Chaoulli v. Québec (Attorney General)*, 2005 1 SCR 791.

understand and even obey. Given that the ban on private health insurance was held by the majority of justices to be linked to long wait times and patient harm, Quebec would thus have to allow private health insurance, on the theory (fiercely contested by defenders of medicare)[7] that access to private health care takes pressure off the public system and shortens wait lists. Quebec did allow limited access to private health insurance but also imposed other regulations making the practice of private health care in the province financially disadvantageous for doctors. So the *status quo ante* holds for now.

11.5 Case Study: Energy Policy

Although health-care policy is largely about the public provision of a tangible good or service to citizens, governments are active in many other fields where the product of their interventions is much less concrete. Regulating different kinds of industries or promoting international trade are examples of areas where governments expend a lot of effort but with less direct benefit to individuals. Energy policy potentially includes those kinds of efforts and many others as well. While our overall economy will benefit from supportive government policies that identify and promote international markets for products and services made or delivered by Canadians, and Canadians' overall well-being is improved by the protection of the environment and contributions to global environmental health, the impacts of these policies are still much more diffuse than the immediate result of treating an injury in a publicly funded hospital. In the fields of public policy that are like energy policy, the consequences of federalism are often even more pronounced. If we are talking about a variety of industries or pursuits, with different levels of activity across the provinces and trade-offs between regions and multiple headings of legislative jurisdiction, the complexity of policymaking and the interdependence of governments become quickly apparent. Health care is often thought of as a primary site of federal-provincial interaction and sometimes conflict. That may be true, but the provision of health-care services is still primarily a provincial matter with federal contributions and oversight. Because of the multiple ways in which both levels of government can potentially engage in energy policy, the policy process in this area is substantially more complex.

Energy producers are major generators of employment and wealth in the Canadian economy; the industry estimates that direct and supporting employment

---

7   Colleen Flood et al., eds., *Access to Care, Access to Justice: The Legal Debate over Private Health Care in Canada* (Toronto: University of Toronto Press, 2005).

to the oil and gas industry amounts to nearly three-quarters of a million Canadian workers. Moreover, we all rely to some degree on the products and prosperity that the industry generates. Drops in international prices for oil and gas can have a profound effect on the overall health of the Canadian economy and on the strength of the Canadian dollar in international markets; these drops can hit some regions of the country with particularly devastating effect. Governments are also major beneficiaries of the energy industry. Provinces collect "royalties" on the extraction of oil and gas that can make up a considerable share of government revenues, allowing the government to keep other taxes and charges lower for its residents. Apart from wealth, Canadians are also directly affected by the energy industry's contribution to climate change and to the more localized environmental effects of oil and gas extraction, which can include soil and air contamination or disruption of the natural environment at exploration and processing sites and along the transportation routes for the dangerous goods that those industries produce. Regulating those impacts in tandem with still wringing benefit from the industry will be a major challenge for Canadian governments for years to come. Canadian energy policy is affected by the dependence we have on natural resources for generating wealth and prosperity, and it is constrained by the negative impacts of carbon dependence and by our continuing and growing demand for energy to fuel industries, transportation needs, and consumer lifestyles.

Provinces are the primary governmental beneficiaries of the wealth generated by the energy industry in Canada. Provinces fought hard for the constitutional recognition of natural resource ownership in the patriation process and ultimately secured section 92A of CA 1982, which recognizes their right to own and to benefit financially from non-renewable natural resources such as oil and gas or forestry products. In turn, the provinces have a primary regulatory role for the industry, setting out standards for land and resource management, and for pollution reduction and containment and determining taxation levels. Provincial policies can encourage exploration and development of the natural resources that are the primary products of the energy industry. Provinces will offer tax credits to energy companies to offset the risks that these companies take in exploring for oil and gas reserves and the massive capital costs associated with extracting, refining, and transporting energy products. Stricter environmental controls, higher royalty rates, and lower tax credits for exploration can discourage investment in the industry. In provinces where oil and gas are central commodities, those are some of the most important trade-offs that the provincial government may have to consider. In the meantime, Canada is under increasing pressure to do its part to reduce global carbon emissions in order to help mitigate the impacts of climate change. Here, the federal government is often charged with taking the lead. It has primary responsibility for international relations and can commit the country to standards or practices that individual provinces may have too much self-interest to consider. If Canada is going to contribute to global efforts to address climate change, it will likely be at the lead of the federal government, but Ottawa has a limited set of tools to compel the provinces to help it reach those commitments.

The differential impact of the energy industry on different provinces is a major distinguishing characteristic of provincial economies. Since the discovery of major oil and gas deposits in Alberta and off the shores of Newfoundland and Labrador, those provinces have enjoyed relatively high prosperity and growth. Provincial government revenues in those provinces are highly dependent on oil and gas. Royalties from the energy economy allow the province of Alberta to be the only one in the country without a sales tax. Alberta has been a net contributor to the equalization program of the federal government for decades. Being a contributor does not mean that the province of Alberta actually shares its revenues with other provinces, but it doesn't get the same share of federal transfers that other provinces do. Alberta's prosperity as a consequence of its natural resource wealth has, at times, been so distorting that the province has had to be excluded from calculations of revenue averages so as not to make the federal government's obligations to other provinces through the equalization program excessively high. The fact that only a few provinces are the primary beneficiaries of wealth from oil and gas has also pitted provinces against one another. Provinces with economies and industries less reliant on carbon products are more likely to be supportive of national and international policies that seek to reduce carbon emissions and privilege other energy sources such as hydro dams or renewable energy.

When oil and gas prices are high, that tends to buoy Canada's currency, which in turn makes manufacturing industries that rely on exporting products less competitive. Those manufacturing industries are based largely in southern Ontario, which consequently bears some of the cost of the economic success of other regions in the country. When times are bad in the sector, Alberta and other energy producing provinces are asymmetrically impacted. Two-thirds of the employment generated by oil and gas activity in Canada takes place in Alberta. When oil prices are lower and investment is scaled back, Alberta bears a corresponding share of the national impact of that retrenchment. The decisions of provincial governments about how to deal with the boom and bust cycles of natural resource wealth are critical to the well-being of their residents. Most provinces consider oil and gas royalties a part of general tax revenue and use that money to pay for present-day services to their communities. Few take a "trust fund" approach to such revenue despite its non-renewable nature; in other words, most don't sock it away for a rainy day. Some northern European countries take this approach and have been able to build up substantial reserves of capital from oil and gas activity; they actually draw considerable wealth off the interest that such capital can generate. An alternative approach would be to distribute oil and gas revenues to the residents of the province as a dividend rather than to assume the revenues are an alternative form of taxation. This approach is taken in the United States by Alaska, where every resident gets an annual payment based on oil and gas activity in the state. The province of Alberta has flirted with both models, setting up a Heritage Trust Fund as a rainy day fund in the 1980s, but also distributing small dividends to every resident of the province now and then. The Canadian approach in most provinces is to rely on oil and gas revenue (if it exists) as a source of general revenue or to treat it as an occasional windfall to be spent on public goods or services.

Because energy products have to get to markets that need them, they inevitably need to cross provincial boundaries. Pipelines and transmission lines are disruptive to natural environments, and they pose risks for the communities and ecosystems that they traverse. Moving products beyond Canada's borders by sea also introduces risks for coastal communities and environments. Provincial governments that are not primary beneficiaries of the industry, but over whose territory or at whose ports those products arrive, are naturally reluctant to take these ecological risks and face strong calls from their constituents to resist such projects. When oil and gas or other energy traverses provincial borders, national regulators have the jurisdiction to approve the projects. Canada's National Energy Board oversees the regulatory and approval process for such applications. The board is made up of federal government appointees but works at arm's length from government. It is meant to consult widely and to make recommendations for approval based on evidence and best practices. But despite having nominal independence and expending considerable time and resources on hearings and opportunities for supporters and opponents to have their voices heard, inevitably the decisions of such boards are criticized as a fait accompli that will favour the industry. Opponents will make presentations to the National Energy Board, but they will also favour direct action in the form of protests and blockades designed to stop building or exploration from happening. The Liberal government of Justin Trudeau has promised that the environmental assessment process for such projects will be strengthened.

The federal government has also seen itself as responsible for trying to mitigate some of the regional inequities that are a consequence of differential wealth from energy activities. Mitigating the effects of inequality or trying to take advantage of an abundant supply of energy to help make domestic industries more competitive has often been at the heart of federal energy policymaking.

This has been very controversial in the past. In the 1980s, the Liberal government of Pierre Trudeau introduced the National Energy Program. The program was designed to increase Canadian ownership of the oil and gas industry and to set a "made in Canada" price for oil and gas commodities that would insulate the country from rising international prices and secure a reliable and cheap supply of energy for all of the country. National taxation of oil and gas producers on top of the royalties already paid to provincial governments was also part of the program, designed again to ensure that all of Canada was a beneficiary of resource wealth. The program was vehemently opposed by industry and by provinces such as Alberta, provinces that would bear the negative effects of a lower price for their commodities. To this day, mention of the National Energy Program (or any such policy) still rankles most Albertans, even those born long after its demise! The program is still considered responsible for some elements of Western alienation, and it led to the lobbying for greater provincial control that was recognized by the section 92A amendment to the Constitution. Most federal governments have backed away from such interventions, although the peril of climate change and efforts to retrofit the energy economy in Canada may require national initiatives again.

Because oil and gas can be a particularly lucrative industry when international demand is high and exploration costs are reasonable, the industry has considerable wealth. It is not afraid to use some of that wealth to protect its interests in government decision making. The industry has several associations to promote its interests to government and the public. The Canadian Association of Petroleum Producers (CAPP) is a leading advocacy group for the industry's interests. It has a presence in Ottawa as well as in Alberta, British Columbia, and Atlantic Canada. It lobbies governments to make decisions in the industry's interest, but CAPP also runs its own public relations campaigns to convince the general public that the industry is good for the economy and seeks to be environmentally responsible while it creates jobs and opportunities in the communities where the industry is active. It is not uncommon in parts of the country experiencing controversy over new projects or pipelines to see advertisements paid for by industry associations highlighting the good environmental record of oil and gas producers or the "ordinary Canadians" who have skilled jobs and good pay as a result of energy industry activity.

Oil and gas are not the only industries that make up the greater energy picture in Canada. Utilities, particularly those that generate electricity, are another important part of the energy equation. Unlike oil and gas explorers, many of the electrical generation and transmission companies in Canada are public or had their origins in public utility companies. Many of these companies were **Crown corporations**, operated on the general principles and structures of corporations at arm's length from government but owned and usually subsidized by governments. In return, the utilities had to provide services to communities and regions where privately owned corporations would be unlikely to invest. Public utilities also served as economic development engines. Their government owners set utility rates and prices and made the major capital investments necessary to expand their capacity and used that capacity to attract industrial clients with the lure of consistent and predictable (if not always cheap) electricity. Hydro-Quebec has been particularly adept at investing in the development of that capacity as a way to attract and maintain industrial investment in the province and to grow the internal economic capacity of the province. That its electricity is renewable and low in carbon emissions makes it even more competitive in a world increasingly concerned with those features.

Other methods of generating electricity include the burning of fossil fuels as well as nuclear energy. Coal and other fossil-fuelled electrical generation put provincial utilities in the sights of environmental activists. Transitioning to cleaner forms of energy for those utilities is one of the ways that provincial governments can try to live up to pledges to reduce the carbon emissions responsible for climate change. Nuclear energy, on the other hand, is virtually carbon free, but it is still potentially a problem for the environment. Nuclear power was not a topic of government activity anticipated by the writers of Canada's Constitution in 1867. There was, however, a good argument to be made that it fit under the presumed residual powers of the federal parliament. In a case on uranium mining in 1956, the Supreme Court essentially determined that the federal government would have primary jurisdiction for atomic energy. The building of nuclear power plants by provincial utilities in Ontario and New Brunswick was done in collaboration with the federal agency responsible for the development, design, and promotion of nuclear power. Those projects, most of which came on line during the oil crisis of the 1970s, have gone through expensive and time-consuming retrofits, again often with some dependence on further federal investment and oversight.

The Charter of Rights and Freedoms provides a less obvious platform for citizens to engage in influence over energy policy. That said, the judicial system is still a relevant institution for energy policy. The energy industry is disruptive to the natural environment and generally explores and develops resources in the less populated corners of the country. Though much of the land that oil and gas companies occupy for their activities belongs to the public, that ownership is not always uncontested. First Nations communities often have outstanding land claims to areas under oil and gas exploration or extraction. Given the history of displacement and resettlement to reserves experienced by many First Nations, they also find themselves in more remote areas of the country, in the communities nearest to major oil and gas projects. Consequently, those communities often feel the most direct effects of environmental contamination and disruption, especially when they are dependent on traditional hunting and fishing practices for economic gain or simply subsistence. Asserting the Aboriginal and treaty rights in the 1982 Constitution is one way those communities can fight back against the energy industry or seek adequate compensation and involvement in the development of resources so as to realize benefits for their communities.

Key Terms

special interest groups   policy communities
public interest groups   Crown corporations
think tanks

Discussion Questions

1. What would be some recent examples of the media's role in "agenda setting" on a matter of public policy? Do different types of media play that role in different ways?

2. One study suggests that, in 2014, over 50,000 Canadians travelled to private hospitals in the United States for medical care they would otherwise obtain in Canada. Observers cite long wait times in Canada as one reason for Canadians' decisions to pay directly for American medical attention that they would get for "free" in Canada. Should these "medical tourists" be allowed to obtain timely care in Canada at their own expense?

POLITICAL PARTICIPATION AND DEMOCRATIC CITIZENSHIP

The liberal democratic regime aims at the ideal of "government of the people, by the people, and for the people." Those who are elected to office and serve in the government are ordinary citizens like the rest of us. They are responsible to the people as a whole to do what is in the public interest. For the regime to have a reasonable chance of working well, there must therefore be a substantial amount of political participation on the part of its citizens. People must be willing to run for public office or take part in other aspects of electoral politics. Most important, all citizens require an education in politics that allows them to make reasonable judgements about who should hold public office and what constitutes good public policy. Democracy requires that citizens participate in politics and that this political participation is well informed. If we are to govern ourselves, we must be motivated and educated to do so.

With this fact in mind, we have tried to make clear the nature of the Canadian regime, the important purposes of its primary institutions, and the various forms of political participation in a liberal democracy. In the first instance, the most essential form of political participation is holding public office: legislating and governing. Those who seek election help to generate a new political agenda; those who win participate directly in the process of making law and public policy. Second is involvement in a political party: going to party meetings, fundraising, campaigning for the party's candidate, working on election day, and so on. Thousands of Canadians are involved in this fashion. A third and even more widespread form of participation is through interest groups. Almost all of us belong to various interest groups—unions, lobby groups, volunteer organizations, community leagues, and other associations—all of which participate, directly or indirectly, in the political process. As a result, they have an influence on public policy. Finally, there is the ongoing process of politics as it relates to the everyday lives of citizens and the ways in which we relate individually to government and our elected officials. We read newspapers, watch public affairs programs, attend political and civic meetings, discuss and debate political issues, write letters to editors and public officials, take part in public opinion polls, and ultimately vote in elections. The Internet and social media are making many forms of participation even easier. Whether they will lead to greater or more informed participation remains to be seen.

For the vast majority of Canadian citizens, participation in political life consists neither in running for office nor in working for a political party or interest group but simply in voting. To ask citizens to take a few minutes every few years to cast a ballot is not to ask very much. Incredibly, however, the number of people who neglect this simple democratic duty is now almost as large as the number of those who perform it. In the 2008 election, only 59 per cent of registered voters bothered to vote in the national election. (As many Canadians who are eligible to vote have not been registered to vote, the percentage of eligible voters who participated in the 2008 election was likely below 55 per cent.) Electoral participation increased slightly in 2011 and jumped up to 69 per cent in 2015, a rate not seen since the 1990s. It is encouraging to see that trend heading in the right direction, but electoral participation is still not at rates seen as recently as the 1980s, and we don't have any indication that it will stabilize or continue to grow.

Although Canada's poor voter participation rates are not so different from those of other liberal democracies, they are much lower than they used to be. Indeed, most democracies have experienced a steady decline in voter participation rates over the past four decades. Experts disagree to some extent about the cause of this decline. The most prominent explanation is Robert Putnam's thesis that declining voter turnout is a symptom of a deeper problem, a decline in social capital, which in turn is linked to a declining sense of trust by citizens in their governments and in their fellow citizens. Putnam argues that the democratic process is healthy only in places where there is a good deal of social capital, that is, a strong sense of connectedness and trust between citizens. Social capital is developed through participation in clubs, societies, organizations, and even sporting leagues, all of which teach people how to interact with each other to solve problems in accordance with agreed-upon rules and procedures. Putnam notes that there has been a dramatic decline in membership in clubs, societies, organizations, and leagues since the 1950s—probably, in large part, due to television. And his research suggests that the decline in voter participation rates is a direct result of this decline in social capital.[1]

In some democracies, it is simply not acceptable for a citizen to neglect to vote. In Australia, for instance, the law requires citizens to vote and imposes fines on those who do not. Some suggest that Canada should adopt this practice. Others disagree, arguing that the country is actually better off if people who are too apathetic to vote have no influence on the outcome of our elections. There are obviously problems with both positions. Clearly, the most desirable condition would be to have high participation rates from a well-informed public.

The question of how we create a well-informed public and hence intelligent public opinion necessarily brings us to the problem of political education. How should we educate people to be citizens in a liberal democracy? What kind of citizen does the liberal democratic regime require if it is to remain healthy? What sort of education is most likely to produce intelligent citizens who care about politics, understand the important political issues, can make prudent decisions in their electoral choices, and ultimately can be told the truth rather than merely be flattered?

One of the keystones in such an education is the right to free speech and the freedom of the press. The free exchange of ideas is essential in a liberal democracy. Only when we hear and listen to ideas being debated can we begin to make any sort of intelligent judgement on a particular issue. Only when citizens have the right to debate political issues in an atmosphere of toleration and respect, and use that right to do so, can the liberal democratic regime be sure that public opinion is reasonably well informed. Such debate must go beyond the issues of the day, although it must surely include those issues. It must include the ongoing controversies that surround the very principles of the liberal democratic regime itself: equality, liberty, rights, obligations, the rule of law, constitutionalism, federalism, and so on. Only when we are capable of debating the strengths and weaknesses of these principles, of understanding the competing interpretations of them, and of seeing how these principles are often at odds with one another, do we approach the education needed for the citizen of the liberal democratic regime. For only then can the citizen separate those issues that go to the question of the continued health of the regime from those that are merely transitory and ephemeral.

---

1   Robert D. Putnam, *Bowling Alone: The Collapse and Revival of American Community* (New York: Simon & Schuster, 2000).

Finally, political education in a liberal democracy must aim to encourage political participation. Citizens are far less likely to participate if they do not understand either the important political issues or the main institutions of politics. The reason for this is clear; without such an understanding, we tend to underestimate the value of participation. Often we hear people ask, "What difference does one vote in thousands make?" or "How can you fight the establishment?" An education in the history of Canadian politics reveals that the establishment can change very rapidly, that individuals can come out of nowhere and rise rapidly to prominence in politics, and that the political landscape is sometimes remade within months. In 1984, the Conservatives won the greatest electoral victory in Canadian history. Nine years later, their party was reduced to a mere two seats, and its future as a national party seemed questionable. The powerful Liberal machine that replaced them looked as though it might rule for decades. Yet the elections of 2004, 2006, 2008, and 2011 suggested that the Liberal Party was in steady, perhaps even terminal, decline.[2] The election of 2015 marked a remarkable turnaround, and the Liberals won a substantial majority. Citizens took a greater interest in the 2015 election, as evidenced by a 7 per cent increase in voter participation. The political landscape changed remarkably as a result.

Such changes are wrought by the actions of thousands of ordinary citizens, people who belong to political parties and interest groups, write letters, and generally act as though their actions have consequences. Political participation is thus encouraged by a strong sense that we have an obligation to take part in government, that our actions make a difference, and that we benefit both ourselves and our country when we do participate. An education in politics reveals that these beliefs are, by and large, well founded.

---

2   R. Kenneth Carty, *Big Tent Politics: The Liberal Party's Long Mastery of Canada's Public Life* (Vancouver: UBC Press, 2015).

THE CONSTITUTION ACTS 1867 AND 1982

Constitution Act, 1867

30 & 31 Victoria, c. 3. (U.K.)

(Consolidated with amendments)

An Act for the Union of Canada, Nova Scotia, and New Brunswick, and the Government thereof; and for Purposes connected therewith

[*29th March 1867.*]

Whereas the Provinces of Canada, Nova Scotia, and New Brunswick have expressed their Desire to be federally united into One Dominion under the Crown of the United Kingdom of Great Britain and Ireland, with a Constitution similar in Principle to that of the United Kingdom:

And whereas such a Union would conduce to the Welfare of the Provinces and promote the Interests of the British Empire:

And whereas on the Establishment of the Union by Authority of Parliament it is expedient, not only that the Constitution of the Legislative Authority in the Dominion be provided for, but also that the Nature of the Executive Government therein be declared: And whereas it is expedient that Provision be made for the eventual Admission into the Union of other Parts of British North America:

I Preliminary

Short title 1 This Act may be cited as the *Constitution Act, 1867.*

[Repealed] 2 Repealed.

II Union

Declaration of Union 3 It shall be lawful for the Queen, by and with the Advice of Her Majesty's Most Honourable Privy Council, to declare by Proclamation that, on and after a Day therein appointed, not being more than Six Months after the passing of this Act, the Provinces of Canada, Nova Scotia, and New Brunswick shall form and be One Dominion under the Name of Canada; and on and after that Day those Three Provinces shall form and be One Dominion under that Name accordingly.

Construction of subsequent Provisions of Act 4 Unless it is otherwise expressed or implied, the Name Canada shall be taken to mean Canada as constituted under this Act.

Four Provinces 5 Canada shall be divided into Four Provinces, named Ontario, Québec, Nova Scotia, and New Brunswick.

Provinces of Ontario and Québec 6 The Parts of the Province of Canada (as it exists at the passing of this Act) which formerly constituted respectively the Provinces of Upper Canada and Lower Canada shall be deemed to be severed, and shall form Two separate Provinces. The Part which formerly constituted the Province of Upper Canada shall constitute the Province of Ontario; and the Part which formerly constituted the Province of Lower Canada shall constitute the Province of Québec.

Provinces of Nova Scotia and New Brunswick 7 The Provinces of Nova Scotia and New Brunswick shall have the same Limits as at the passing of this Act.

Decennial Census 8 In the general Census of the Population of Canada which is hereby required to be taken in the Year One thousand eight hundred and seventy-one, and in every Tenth Year thereafter, the respective Populations of the Four Provinces shall be distinguished.

III Executive Power

9 The Executive Government and Authority of and over Canada is hereby declared to continue and be vested in the Queen.

Declaration of Executive Power in the Queen

10 The Provisions of this Act referring to the Governor General extend and apply to the Governor General for the Time being of Canada, or other the Chief Executive Officer or Administrator for the Time being carrying on the Government of Canada on behalf and in the Name of the Queen, by whatever Title he is designated.

Application of Provisions referring to Governor General

11 There shall be a Council to aid and advise in the Government of Canada, to be styled the Queen's Privy Council for Canada; and the Persons who are to be Members of that Council shall be from Time to Time chosen and summoned by the Governor General and sworn in as Privy Councillors, and Members thereof may be from Time to Time removed by the Governor General.

Constitution of Privy Council for Canada

12 All Powers, Authorities, and Functions which under any Act of the Parliament of Great Britain, or of the Parliament of the United Kingdom of Great Britain and Ireland, or of the Legislature of Upper Canada, Lower Canada, Canada, Nova Scotia, or New Brunswick, are at the Union vested in or exerciseable by the respective Governors or Lieutenant Governors of those Provinces, with the Advice, or with the Advice and Consent, of the respective Executive Councils thereof, or in conjunction with those Councils, or with any Number of Members thereof, or by those Governors or Lieutenant Governors individually, shall, as far as the same continue in existence and capable of being exercised after the Union in relation to the Government of Canada, be vested in and exerciseable by the Governor General, with the Advice or with the Advice and Consent of or in conjunction with the Queen's Privy Council for Canada, or any Members thereof, or by the Governor General individually, as the Case requires, subject nevertheless (except with respect to such as exist under Acts of the Parliament of Great Britain or of the Parliament of the United Kingdom of Great Britain and Ireland) to be abolished or altered by the Parliament of Canada.

All Powers under Acts to be exercised by Governor General with Advice of Privy Council, or alone

Application of Provisions referring to Governor General in Council

13 The Provisions of this Act referring to the Governor General in Council shall be construed as referring to the Governor General acting by and with the Advice of the Queen's Privy Council for Canada.

Power to Her Majesty to authorize Governor General to appoint Deputies

14 It shall be lawful for the Queen, if Her Majesty thinks fit, to authorize the Governor General from Time to Time to appoint any Person or any Persons jointly or severally to be his Deputy or Deputies within any Part or Parts of Canada, and in that Capacity to exercise during the Pleasure of the Governor General such of the Powers, Authorities, and Functions of the Governor General as the Governor General deems it necessary or expedient to assign to him or them, subject to any Limitations or Directions expressed or given by the Queen; but the Appointment of such a Deputy or Deputies shall not affect the Exercise by the Governor General himself of any Power, Authority, or Function.

Command of Armed Forces to continue to be vested in the Queen

15 The Command-in-Chief of the Land and Naval Militia, and of all Naval and Military Forces, of and in Canada, is hereby declared to continue and be vested in the Queen.

Seat of Government of Canada

16 Until the Queen otherwise directs, the Seat of Government of Canada shall be Ottawa.

IV Legislative Power

Constitution of Parliament of Canada

17 There shall be One Parliament for Canada, consisting of the Queen, an Upper House styled the Senate, and the House of Commons.

Privileges, etc., of Houses

18 The privileges, immunities, and powers to be held, enjoyed, and exercised by the Senate and by the House of Commons, and by the members thereof respectively, shall be such as are from time to time defined by Act of the Parliament of Canada, but so that any Act of the Parliament of Canada defining such privileges, immunities, and powers shall not confer any privileges, immunities, or powers exceeding those at the passing of such Act held, enjoyed, and exercised by the Commons House of Parliament of the United Kingdom of Great Britain and Ireland, and by the members thereof.

First Session of the Parliament of Canada

19 The Parliament of Canada shall be called together not later than Six Months after the Union.

[Repealed]

20 Repealed.

The Senate

21 The Senate shall, subject to the Provisions of this Act, consist of One   *Number of Senators*
Hundred and five Members, who shall be styled Senators.

22 In relation to the Constitution of the Senate Canada shall be deemed to   *Representation of Provinces*
consist of *Four* Divisions: *in Senate*

1. Ontario;
2. Québec;
3. The Maritime Provinces, Nova Scotia and New Brunswick, and
   Prince Edward Island;
4. The Western Provinces of Manitoba, British Columbia,
   Saskatchewan, and Alberta;

which Four Divisions shall (subject to the Provisions of this Act) be
equally represented in the Senate as follows: Ontario by twenty-four
senators; Québec by twenty-four senators; the Maritime Provinces
and Prince Edward Island by twenty-four senators, ten thereof representing Nova Scotia, ten thereof representing New Brunswick,
and four thereof representing Prince Edward Island; the Western
Provinces by twenty-four senators, six thereof representing Manitoba,
six thereof representing British Columbia, six thereof representing
Saskatchewan, and six thereof representing Alberta; Newfoundland
shall be entitled to be represented in the Senate by six members; the
Yukon Territory, the Northwest Territories and Nunavut shall be
entitled to be represented in the Senate by one member each.

In the Case of Québec each of the Twenty-four Senators represent-
ing that Province shall be appointed for One of the Twenty-four
Electoral Divisions of Lower Canada specified in Schedule A. to
Chapter One of the Consolidated Statutes of Canada.

23 The Qualifications of a Senator shall be as follows: *Qualifications of Senator*

(1) He shall be of the full age of Thirty Years:
(2) He shall be either a natural-born Subject of the Queen, or a Subject of
the Queen naturalized by an Act of the Parliament of Great Britain, or
of the Parliament of the United Kingdom of Great Britain and Ireland,
or of the Legislature of One of the Provinces of Upper Canada, Lower
Canada, Canada, Nova Scotia, or New Brunswick, before the Union, or of
the Parliament of Canada after the Union:

(3) He shall be legally or equitably seised as of Freehold for his own Use and Benefit of Lands or Tenements held in Free and Common Socage, or seised or possessed for his own Use and Benefit of Lands or Tenements held in Franc-alleu or in Roture, within the Province for which he is appointed, of the Value of Four thousand Dollars, over and above all Rents, Dues, Debts, Charges, Mortgages, and Incumbrances due or payable out of or charged on or affecting the same:

(4) His Real and Personal Property shall be together worth Four thousand Dollars over and above his Debts and Liabilities:

(5) He shall be resident in the Province for which he is appointed:

(6) In the Case of Québec he shall have his Real Property Qualification in the Electoral Division for which he is appointed, or shall be resident in that Division.

Summons of Senator 24 The Governor General shall from Time to Time, in the Queen's Name, by Instrument under the Great Seal of Canada, summon qualified Persons to the Senate; and, subject to the Provisions of this Act, every Person so summoned shall become and be a Member of the Senate and a Senator.

[Repealed] 25 Repealed.

Addition of Senators in certain cases 26 If at any Time on the Recommendation of the Governor General the Queen thinks fit to direct that Four or Eight Members be added to the Senate, the Governor General may by Summons to Four or Eight qualified Persons (as the Case may be), representing equally the Four Divisions of Canada, add to the Senate accordingly.

Reduction of Senate to normal Number 27 In case of such Addition being at any Time made, the Governor General shall not summon any Person to the Senate, except on a further like Direction by the Queen on the like Recommendation, to represent one of the Four Divisions until such Division is represented by Twenty-four Senators and no more.

Maximum Number of Senators 28 The Number of Senators shall not at any Time exceed One Hundred and thirteen.

Tenure of Place in Senate 29 (1) Subject to subsection (2), a Senator shall, subject to the provisions of this Act, hold his place in the Senate for life.

(2) A Senator who is summoned to the Senate after the coming into force of this subsection shall, subject to this Act, hold his place in the Senate until he attains the age of seventy-five years. *Retirement upon attaining age of seventy-five years*

30 A Senator may by Writing under his Hand addressed to the Governor General resign his Place in the Senate, and thereupon the same shall be vacant. *Resignation of Place in Senate*

31 The Place of a Senator shall become vacant in any of the following Cases: *Disqualification of Senators*

(1) If for Two consecutive Sessions of the Parliament he fails to give his Attendance in the Senate:

(2) If he takes an Oath or makes a Declaration or Acknowledgment of Allegiance, Obedience, or Adherence to a Foreign Power, or does an Act whereby he becomes a Subject or Citizen, or entitled to the Rights or Privileges of a Subject or Citizen, of a Foreign Power:

(3) If he is adjudged Bankrupt or Insolvent, or applies for the Benefit of any Law relating to Insolvent Debtors, or becomes a public Defaulter:

(4) If he is attainted of Treason or convicted of Felony or of any infamous Crime:

(5) If he ceases to be qualified in respect of Property or of Residence; provided, that a Senator shall not be deemed to have ceased to be qualified in respect of Residence by reason only of his residing at the Seat of the Government of Canada while holding an Office under that Government requiring his Presence there.

32 When a Vacancy happens in the Senate by Resignation, Death, or otherwise, the Governor General shall by Summons to a fit and qualified Person fill the Vacancy. *Summons on Vacancy in Senate*

33 If any Question arises respecting the Qualification of a Senator or a Vacancy in the Senate the same shall be heard and determined by the Senate. *Questions as to Qualifications and Vacancies in Senate*

34 The Governor General may from Time to Time, by Instrument under the Great Seal of Canada, appoint a Senator to be Speaker of the Senate, and may remove him and appoint another in his Stead. *Appointment of Speaker of Senate*

Quorum of Senate 35 Until the Parliament of Canada otherwise provides, the Presence of at least Fifteen Senators, including the Speaker, shall be necessary to constitute a Meeting of the Senate for the Exercise of its Powers.

Voting in Senate 36 Questions arising in the Senate shall be decided by a Majority of Voices, and the Speaker shall in all Cases have a Vote, and when the Voices are equal the Decision shall be deemed to be in the Negative.

The House Of Commons

Constitution of House of Commons in Canada 37 The House of Commons shall, subject to the Provisions of this Act, consist of two hundred and ninety-five members of whom ninety-nine shall be elected for Ontario, seventy-five for Québec, eleven for Nova Scotia, ten for New Brunswick, fourteen for Manitoba, thirty-two for British Columbia, four for Prince Edward Island, twenty-six for Alberta, fourteen for Saskatchewan, seven for Newfoundland, one for the Yukon Territory and two for the Northwest Territories.

Summoning of House of Commons 38 The Governor General shall from Time to Time, in the Queen's Name, by Instrument under the Great Seal of Canada, summon and call together the House of Commons.

Senators not to sit in House of Commons 39 A Senator shall not be capable of being elected or of sitting or voting as a Member of the House of Commons.

Electoral districts of the four Provinces 40 Until the Parliament of Canada otherwise provides, Ontario, Québec, Nova Scotia, and New Brunswick shall, for the Purposes of the Election of Members to serve in the House of Commons, be divided into Electoral Districts as follows:

1. Ontario

   Ontario shall be divided into the Counties, Ridings of Counties, Cities, Parts of Cities, and Towns enumerated in the First Schedule to this Act, each whereof shall be an Electoral District, each such District as numbered in that Schedule being entitled to return One Member.

2. Québec

   Québec shall be divided into Sixty-five Electoral Districts, composed of the Sixty-five Electoral Divisions into which Lower Canada is at the passing of this Act divided under Chapter Two of the Consolidated Statutes of Canada, Chapter Seventy-five of the Consolidated Statutes for Lower Canada, and the Act of the Province of Canada of the Twenty-third Year of the Queen, Chapter One, or any other Act amending the same in force at the Union, so that each such Electoral Division shall be for the Purposes of this Act an Electoral District entitled to return One Member.

3. Nova Scotia

Each of the Eighteen Counties of Nova Scotia shall be an Electoral District. The County of Halifax shall be entitled to return Two Members, and each of the other Counties One Member.

4. New Brunswick

Each of the Fourteen Counties into which New Brunswick is divided, including the City and County of St. John, shall be an Electoral District. The City of St. John shall also be a separate Electoral District. Each of those Fifteen Electoral Districts shall be entitled to return One Member.

41 Until the Parliament of Canada otherwise provides, all Laws in force in the several Provinces at the Union relative to the following Matters or any of them, namely,—the Qualifications and Disqualifications of Persons to be elected or to sit or vote as Members of the House of Assembly or Legislative Assembly in the several Provinces, the Voters at Elections of such Members, the Oaths to be taken by Voters, the Returning Officers, their Powers and Duties, the Proceedings at Elections, the Periods during which Elections may be continued, the Trial of controverted Elections, and Proceedings incident thereto, the vacating of Seats of Members, and the Execution of new Writs in case of Seats vacated otherwise than by Dissolution,—shall respectively apply to Elections of Members to serve in the House of Commons for the same several Provinces. *Continuance of existing Election Laws until Parliament of Canada otherwise provides*

Provided that, until the Parliament of Canada otherwise provides, at any Election for a Member of the House of Commons for the District of Algoma, in addition to Persons qualified by the Law of the Province of Canada to vote, every Male British Subject, aged Twenty-one Years or upwards, being a Householder, shall have a Vote.

42 Repealed. *[Repealed]*

43 Repealed. *[Repealed]*

As to Election of Speaker of 44 The House of Commons on its first assembling after a General Election
House of Commons   shall proceed with all practicable Speed to elect One of its Members to
be Speaker.

As to filling up Vacancy in 45 In case of a Vacancy happening in the Office of Speaker by Death,
Office of Speaker   Resignation, or otherwise, the House of Commons shall with all practicable Speed proceed to elect another of its Members to be Speaker.

Speaker to preside 46 The Speaker shall preside at all Meetings of the House of Commons.

Provision in case of Absence 47 Until the Parliament of Canada otherwise provides, in case of the
of Speaker   Absence for any Reason of the Speaker from the Chair of the House of
Commons for a Period of Forty-eight consecutive Hours, the House may
elect another of its Members to act as Speaker, and the Member so elected shall during the Continuance of such Absence of the Speaker have and
execute all the Powers, Privileges, and Duties of Speaker.

Quorum of House of 48 The Presence of at least Twenty Members of the House of Commons shall
Commons   be necessary to constitute a Meeting of the House for the Exercise of its
Powers, and for that Purpose the Speaker shall be reckoned as a Member.

Voting in House of 49 Questions arising in the House of Commons shall be decided by a
Commons   Majority of Voices other than that of the Speaker, and when the Voices
are equal, but not otherwise, the Speaker shall have a Vote.

Duration of House of 50 Every House of Commons shall continue for Five Years from the Day of
Commons   the Return of the Writs for choosing the House (subject to be sooner
dissolved by the Governor General), and no longer.

Readjustment of 51 (1) The number of members of the House of Commons and the repre-
representation in Commons   sentation of the provinces therein shall, on the completion of each
decennial census, be readjusted by such authority, in such manner,
and from such time as the Parliament of Canada provides from time
to time, subject and according to the following rules:

Rules   1. There shall be assigned to each of the provinces a number of members
equal to the number obtained by dividing the population of the
province by the electoral quotient and rounding up any fractional
remainder to one.

2. If the number of members assigned to a province by the application of rule 1 and section 51A is less than the total number assigned to that province on the date of the coming into force of the *Constitution Act, 1985 (Representation)*, there shall be added to the number of members so assigned such number of members as will result in the province having the same number of members as were assigned on that date.

3 After the application of rules 1 and 2 and section 51A, there shall, in respect of each province that meets the condition set out in rule 4, be added, if necessary, a number of members such that, on the completion of the readjustment, the number obtained by dividing the number of members assigned to that province by the total number of members assigned to all the provinces is as close as possible to, without being below, the number obtained by dividing the population of that province by the total population of all the provinces.

4 Rule 3 applies to a province if, on the completion of the preceding readjustment, the number obtained by dividing the number of members assigned to that province by the total number of members assigned to all the provinces was equal to or greater than the number obtained by dividing the population of that province by the total population of all the provinces, the population of each province being its population as at July 1 of the year of the decennial census that preceded that readjustment according to the estimates prepared for the purpose of that readjustment.

5 Unless the context indicates otherwise, in these rules, the population of a province is the estimate of its population as at July 1 of the year of the most recent decennial census.

6 In these rules, "electoral quotient" means.

(a) 111,166, in relation to the readjustment following the completion of the 2011 decennial census, and

(b) in relation to the readjustment following the completion of any subsequent decennial census, the number obtained by multiplying the electoral quotient that was applied in the preceding readjustment by the number that is the average of the numbers obtained by dividing the population of each province by the population of the province as at July 1 of the year of the preceding decennial census according to the estimates prepared for the purpose of the preceding readjustment, and rounding up any fractional remainder of that multiplication to one.

Population estimates (1.1) For the purpose of the rules in subsection (1), there is required to be prepared an estimate of the population of Canada and of each province as at July 1, 2001 and July 1, 2011—and, in each year following the 2011 decennial census in which a decennial census is taken, as at July 1 of that year—by such authority, in such manner, and from such time as the Parliament of Canada provides from time to time. (27)

Yukon Territory, Northwest (2) The Yukon Territory as bounded and described in the schedule to
Territories and Nunavut chapter Y-2 of the Revised Statutes of Canada, 1985, shall be entitled to one member, the Northwest Territories as bounded and described in section 2 of chapter N-27 of the Revised Statutes of Canada, 1985, as amended by section 77 of chapter 28 of the Statutes of Canada, 1993, shall be entitled to one member, and Nunavut as bounded and described in section 3 of chapter 28 of the Statutes of Canada, 1993, shall be entitled to one member. (28)

Constitution of House of 51A Notwithstanding anything in this Act a province shall always be entitled
Commons to a number of members in the House of Commons not less than the number of senators representing such province.

Increase of Number of 52 The Number of Members of the House of Commons may be from Time
House of Commons to Time increased by the Parliament of Canada, provided the proportionate Representation of the Provinces prescribed by this Act is not thereby disturbed.

Money Votes; Royal Assent

Appropriation and 53 Bills for appropriating any Part of the Public Revenue, or for imposing
Tax Bills any Tax or Impost, shall originate in the House of Commons.

54 It shall not be lawful for the House of Commons to adopt or pass any Vote, Resolution, Address, or Bill for the Appropriation of any Part of the Public Revenue, or of any Tax or Impost, to any Purpose that has

Recommendation of Money Votes

not been first recommended to that House by Message of the Governor General in the Session in which such Vote, Resolution, Address, or Bill is proposed.

55 Where a Bill passed by the Houses of the Parliament is presented to the Governor General for the Queen's Assent, he shall declare, according to his Discretion, but subject to the Provisions of this Act and to Her Majesty's Instructions, either that he assents thereto in the Queen's Name, or that he withholds the Queen's Assent, or that he reserves the Bill for the Signification of the Queen's Pleasure.

Royal Assent to Bills, etc.

56 Where the Governor General assents to a Bill in the Queen's Name, he shall by the first convenient Opportunity send an authentic Copy of the Act to One of Her Majesty's Principal Secretaries of State, and if the Queen in Council within Two Years after Receipt thereof by the Secretary of State thinks fit to disallow the Act, such Disallowance (with a Certificate of the Secretary of State of the Day on which the Act was received by him) being signified by the Governor General, by Speech or Message to each of the Houses of the Parliament or by Proclamation, shall annul the Act from and after the Day of such Signification.

Disallowance by Order in Council of Act assented to by Governor General

57 A Bill reserved for the Signification of the Queen's Pleasure shall not have any Force unless and until, within Two Years from the Day on which it was presented to the Governor General for the Queen's Assent, the Governor General signifies, by Speech or Message to each of the Houses of the Parliament or by Proclamation, that it has received the Assent of the Queen in Council.

Signification of Queen's Pleasure on Bill reserved

An Entry of every such Speech, Message, or Proclamation shall be made in the Journal of each House, and a Duplicate thereof duly attested shall be delivered to the proper Officer to be kept among the Records of Canada.

V Provincial Constitutions

Executive Power

Appointment of Lieutenant Governors of Provinces

58 For each Province there shall be an Officer, styled the Lieutenant Governor, appointed by the Governor General in Council by Instrument under the Great Seal of Canada.

Tenure of Office of Lieutenant Governor

59 A Lieutenant Governor shall hold Office during the Pleasure of the Governor General; but any Lieutenant Governor appointed after the Commencement of the First Session of the Parliament of Canada shall not be removeable within Five Years from his Appointment, except for Cause assigned, which shall be communicated to him in Writing within One Month after the Order for his Removal is made, and shall be communicated by Message to the Senate and to the House of Commons within One Week thereafter if the Parliament is then sitting, and if not then within One Week after the Commencement of the next Session of the Parliament.

Salaries of Lieutenant Governors

60 The Salaries of the Lieutenant Governors shall be fixed and provided by the Parliament of Canada.

Oaths, etc., of Lieutenant Governor

61 Every Lieutenant Governor shall, before assuming the Duties of his Office, make and subscribe before the Governor General or some Person authorized by him Oaths of Allegiance and Office similar to those taken by the Governor General.

Application of Provisions referring to Lieutenant Governor

62 The Provisions of this Act referring to the Lieutenant Governor extend and apply to the Lieutenant Governor for the Time being of each Province, or other the Chief Executive Officer or Administrator for the Time being carrying on the Government of the Province, by whatever Title he is designated.

Appointment of Executive Officers for Ontario and Québec

63 The Executive Council of Ontario and of Québec shall be composed of such Persons as the Lieutenant Governor from Time to Time thinks fit, and in the first instance of the following Officers, namely,—the Attorney General, the Secretary and Registrar of the Province, the Treasurer of the Province, the Commissioner of Crown Lands, and the Commissioner of Agriculture and Public Works, with in Québec the Speaker of the Legislative Council and the Solicitor General.

64 The Constitution of the Executive Authority in each of the Provinces of Nova Scotia and New Brunswick shall, subject to the Provisions of this Act, continue as it exists at the Union until altered under the Authority of this Act.

Executive Government of Nova Scotia and New Brunswick

65 All Powers, Authorities, and Functions which under any Act of the Parliament of Great Britain, or of the Parliament of the United Kingdom of Great Britain and Ireland, or of the Legislature of Upper Canada, Lower Canada, or Canada, were or are before or at the Union vested in or exerciseable by the respective Governors or Lieutenant Governors of those Provinces, with the Advice or with the Advice and Consent of the respective Executive Councils thereof, or in conjunction with those Councils, or with any Number of Members thereof, or by those Governors or Lieutenant Governors individually, shall, as far as the same are capable of being exercised after the Union in relation to the Government of Ontario and Québec respectively, be vested in and shall or may be exercised by the Lieutenant Governor of Ontario and Québec respectively, with the Advice or with the Advice and Consent of or in conjunction with the respective Executive Councils, or any Members thereof, or by the Lieutenant Governor individually, as the Case requires, subject nevertheless (except with respect to such as exist under Acts of the Parliament of Great Britain, or of the Parliament of the United Kingdom of Great Britain and Ireland,) to be abolished or altered by the respective Legislatures of Ontario and Québec.

Powers to be exercised by Lieutenant Governor of Ontario or Québec with Advice, or alone

66 The Provisions of this Act referring to the Lieutenant Governor in Council shall be construed as referring to the Lieutenant Governor of the Province acting by and with the Advice of the Executive Council thereof.

Application of Provisions referring to Lieutenant Governor in Council

67 The Governor General in Council may from Time to Time appoint an Administrator to execute the Office and Functions of Lieutenant Governor during his Absence, Illness, or other Inability.

Administration in Absence, etc., of Lieutenant Governor

68 Unless and until the Executive Government of any Province otherwise directs with respect to that Province, the Seats of Government of the Provinces shall be as follows, namely,—of Ontario, the City of Toronto; of Québec, the City of Québec; of Nova Scotia, the City of Halifax; and of New Brunswick, the City of Fredericton.

Seats of Provincial Governments

Legislative Power

1. Ontario

Legislature for Ontario 69 There shall be a Legislature for Ontario consisting of the Lieutenant Governor and of One House, styled the Legislative Assembly of Ontario.

Electoral districts 70 The Legislative Assembly of Ontario shall be composed of Eighty-two Members, to be elected to represent the Eighty-two Electoral Districts set forth in the First Schedule to this Act.

2. Québec

Legislature for Québec 71 There shall be a Legislature for Québec consisting of the Lieutenant Governor and of Two Houses, styled the Legislative Council of Québec and the Legislative Assembly of Québec.

Constitution of Legislative 72 The Legislative Council of Québec shall be composed of Twenty-four
Council Members, to be appointed by the Lieutenant Governor, in the Queen's Name, by Instrument under the Great Seal of Québec, one being appointed to represent each of the Twenty-four Electoral Divisions of Lower Canada in this Act referred to, and each holding Office for the Term of his Life, unless the Legislature of Québec otherwise provides under the Provisions of this Act.

Qualification of Legislative 73 The Qualifications of the Legislative Councillors of Québec shall be the
Councillors same as those of the Senators for Québec.

Resignation, 74 The Place of a Legislative Councillor of Québec shall become vacant in the
Disqualification, etc. Cases, *mutatis mutandis,* in which the Place of Senator becomes vacant.

Vacancies 75 When a Vacancy happens in the Legislative Council of Québec by Resignation, Death, or otherwise, the Lieutenant Governor, in the Queen's Name, by Instrument under the Great Seal of Québec, shall appoint a fit and qualified Person to fill the Vacancy.

Questions as to Vacancies, 76 If any Question arises respecting the Qualification of a Legislative Councillor
etc. of Québec, or a Vacancy in the Legislative Council of Québec, the same shall be heard and determined by the Legislative Council.

77 The Lieutenant Governor may from Time to Time, by Instrument under the Great Seal of Québec, appoint a Member of the Legislative Council of Québec to be Speaker thereof, and may remove him and appoint another in his Stead.

Speaker of Legislative Council

78 Until the Legislature of Québec otherwise provides, the Presence of at least Ten Members of the Legislative Council, including the Speaker, shall be necessary to constitute a Meeting for the Exercise of its Powers.

Quorum of Legislative Council

79 Questions arising in the Legislative Council of Québec shall be decided by a Majority of Voices, and the Speaker shall in all Cases have a Vote, and when the Voices are equal the Decision shall be deemed to be in the Negative.

Voting in Legislative Council

80 The Legislative Assembly of Québec shall be composed of Sixty-five Members, to be elected to represent the Sixty-five Electoral Divisions or Districts of Lower Canada in this Act referred to, subject to Alteration thereof by the Legislature of Québec: Provided that it shall not be lawful to present to the Lieutenant Governor of Québec for Assent any Bill for altering the Limits of any of the Electoral Divisions or Districts mentioned in the Second Schedule to this Act, unless the Second and Third Readings of such Bill have been passed in the Legislative Assembly with the Concurrence of the Majority of the Members representing all those Electoral Divisions or Districts, and the Assent shall not be given to such Bill unless an Address has been presented by the Legislative Assembly to the Lieutenant Governor stating that it has been so passed.

Constitution of Legislative Assembly of Québec

3. Ontario And Québec

81 Repealed.

[Repealed]

82 The Lieutenant Governor of Ontario and of Québec shall from Time to Time, in the Queen's Name, by Instrument under the Great Seal of the Province, summon and call together the Legislative Assembly of the Province.

Summoning of Legislative Assemblies

Restriction on election of 83 Until the Legislature of Ontario or of Québec otherwise provides, a Person
Holders of offices accepting or holding in Ontario or in Québec any Office, Commission, or
Employment, permanent or temporary, at the Nomination of the Lieutenant
Governor, to which an annual Salary, or any Fee, Allowance, Emolument, or
Profit of any Kind or Amount whatever from the Province is attached, shall
not be eligible as a Member of the Legislative Assembly of the respective
Province, nor shall he sit or vote as such; but nothing in this Section shall make
ineligible any Person being a Member of the Executive Council of the respective Province, or holding any of the following Offices, that is to say, the Offices
of Attorney General, Secretary and Registrar of the Province, Treasurer of the
Province, Commissioner of Crown Lands, and Commissioner of Agriculture
and Public Works, and in Québec Solicitor General, or shall disqualify him to
sit or vote in the House for which he is elected, provided he is elected while
holding such Office.

Continuance of existing 84 Until the legislatures of Ontario and Québec respectively otherwise pro-
Election Laws vide, all Laws which at the Union are in force in those Provinces respec-
tively, relative to the following Matters, or any of them, namely,—the
Qualifications and Disqualifications of Persons to be elected or to sit or
vote as Members of the Assembly of Canada, the Qualifications or
Disqualifications of Voters, the Oaths to be taken by Voters, the Returning
Officers, their Powers and Duties, the Proceedings at Elections, the
Periods during which such Elections may be continued, and the Trial of
controverted Elections and the Proceedings incident thereto, the vacating
of the Seats of Members and the issuing and execution of new Writs in
case of Seats vacated otherwise than by Dissolution,—shall respectively
apply to Elections of Members to serve in the respective Legislative
Assemblies of Ontario and Québec.

Provided that, until the Legislature of Ontario otherwise provides, at
any Election for a Member of the Legislative Assembly of Ontario for
the District of Algoma, in addition to Persons qualified by the Law of the
Province of Canada to vote, every Male British Subject, aged Twenty-one
Years or upwards, being a Householder, shall have a Vote.

Duration of Legislative 85 Every Legislative Assembly of Ontario and every Legislative Assembly of
Assemblies Québec shall continue for Four Years from the Day of the Return of the
Writs for choosing the same (subject nevertheless to either the Legislative
Assembly of Ontario or the Legislative Assembly of Québec being sooner
dissolved by the Lieutenant Governor of the Province), and no longer.

86 There shall be a Session of the Legislature of Ontario and of that of *Yearly Session of* Québec once at least in every Year, so that Twelve Months shall not *Legislature* intervene between the last Sitting of the Legislature in each Province in one Session and its first Sitting in the next Session.

87 The following Provisions of this Act respecting the House of Commons *Speaker, Quorum, etc.* of Canada shall extend and apply to the Legislative Assemblies of Ontario and Québec, that is to say,—the Provisions relating to the Election of a Speaker originally and on Vacancies, the Duties of the Speaker, the Absence of the Speaker, the Quorum, and the Mode of voting, as if those Provisions were here re-enacted and made applicable in Terms to each such Legislative Assembly.

4. Nova Scotia And New Brunswick

88 The Constitution of the Legislature of each of the Provinces of Nova *Constitutions of Legislatures* Scotia and New Brunswick shall, subject to the Provisions of this Act, *of Nova Scotia and New* continue as it exists at the Union until altered under the Authority of *Brunswick* this Act.

5. Ontario, Québec, And Nova Scotia

89 Repealed. *[Repealed]*

6. The Four Provinces

90 The following Provisions of this Act respecting the Parliament of Canada, *Application to Legislatures* namely,—the Provisions relating to Appropriation and Tax Bills, the *of Provisions respecting* Recommendation of Money Votes, the Assent to Bills, the Disallowance of *Money Votes, etc.* Acts, and the Signification of Pleasure on Bills reserved,—shall extend and apply to the Legislatures of the several Provinces as if those Provisions were here re-enacted and made applicable in Terms to the respective Provinces and the Legislatures thereof, with the Substitution of the Lieutenant Governor of the Province for the Governor General, of the Governor General for the Queen and for a Secretary of State, of One Year for Two Years, and of the Province for Canada.

VI Distribution of Legislative Powers

Powers of The Parliament

Legislative Authority of   91   It shall be lawful for the Queen, by and with the Advice and Consent of
Parliament of Canada   the Senate and House of Commons, to make Laws for the Peace, Order,
and good Government of Canada, in relation to all Matters not coming
within the Classes of Subjects by this Act assigned exclusively to the
Legislatures of the Provinces; and for greater Certainty, but not so as to
restrict the Generality of the foregoing Terms of this Section, it is hereby
declared that (notwithstanding anything in this Act) the exclusive
Legislative Authority of the Parliament of Canada extends to all Matters
coming within the Classes of Subjects next hereinafter enumerated; that
is to say,—

1. Repealed.

1A. The Public Debt and Property.

2. The Regulation of Trade and Commerce.

2A. Unemployment insurance.

3. The raising of Money by any Mode or System of Taxation.

4. The borrowing of Money on the Public Credit.

5. Postal Service.

6. The Census and Statistics.

7. Militia, Military and Naval Service, and Defence.

8. The fixing of and providing for the Salaries and Allowances of Civil
   and other Officers of the Government of Canada.

9. Beacons, Buoys, Lighthouses, and Sable Island.

10. Navigation and Shipping.

11. Quarantine and the Establishment and Maintenance of Marine
    Hospitals

12. Sea Coast and Inland Fisheries.

13. Ferries between a Province and any British or Foreign Country or
    between Two Provinces.

14. Currency and Coinage.

15. Banking, Incorporation of Banks, and the Issue of Paper Money.

16. Savings Banks.

17. Weights and Measures.

18. Bills of Exchange and Promissory Notes.

19. Interest.

20. Legal Tender.

21. Bankruptcy and Insolvency.

22. Patents of Invention and Discovery.

23. Copyrights.

24. Indians, and Lands reserved for the Indians.

25. Naturalization and Aliens.

26. Marriage and Divorce.

27. The Criminal Law, except the Constitution of Courts of Criminal Jurisdiction, but including the Procedure in Criminal Matters.

28. The Establishment, Maintenance, and Management of Penitentiaries.

29. Such Classes of Subjects as are expressly excepted in the Enumeration of the Classes of Subjects by this Act assigned exclusively to the Legislatures of the Provinces.

And any Matter coming within any of the Classes of Subjects enumerated in this Section shall not be deemed to come within the Class of Matters of a local or private Nature comprised in the Enumeration of the Classes of Subjects by this Act assigned exclusively to the Legislatures of the Provinces.

Exclusive Powers of Provincial Legislatures

92 In each Province the Legislature may exclusively make Laws in relation to Matters coming within the Classes of Subjects next hereinafter enumerated; that is to say,— *Subjects of exclusive Provincial Legislation*

1. Repealed.

2. Direct Taxation within the Province in order to the raising of a Revenue for Provincial Purposes.

3. The borrowing of Money on the sole Credit of the Province.

4. The Establishment and Tenure of Provincial Offices and the Appointment and Payment of Provincial Officers.

5. The Management and Sale of the Public Lands belonging to the Province and of the Timber and Wood thereon.

6. The Establishment, Maintenance, and Management of Public and Reformatory Prisons in and for the Province.

7. The Establishment, Maintenance, and Management of Hospitals, Asylums, Charities, and Eleemosynary Institutions in and for the Province, other than Marine Hospitals.

8. Municipal Institutions in the Province.

9. Shop, Saloon, Tavern, Auctioneer, and other Licences in order to the raising of a Revenue for Provincial, Local, or Municipal Purposes.

10. Local Works and Undertakings other than such as are of the following Classes:

    (a) Lines of Steam or other Ships, Railways, Canals, Telegraphs, and other Works and Undertakings connecting the Province with any other or others of the Provinces, or extending beyond the Limits of the Province:

    (b) Lines of Steam Ships between the Province and any British or Foreign Country:

    (c) Such Works as, although wholly situate within the Province, are before or after their Execution declared by the Parliament of Canada to be for the general Advantage of Canada or for the Advantage of Two or more of the Provinces.

11. The Incorporation of Companies with Provincial Objects.

12. The Solemnization of Marriage in the Province.

13. Property and Civil Rights in the Province.

14. The Administration of Justice in the Province, including the Constitution, Maintenance, and Organization of Provincial Courts, both of Civil and of Criminal Jurisdiction, and including Procedure in Civil Matters in those Courts.

15. The Imposition of Punishment by Fine, Penalty, or Imprisonment for enforcing any Law of the Province made in relation to any Matter coming within any of the Classes of Subjects enumerated in this Section.

16. Generally all Matters of a merely local or private Nature in the Province.

Non-Renewable Natural Resources, Forestry Resources and Electrical Energy

Laws respecting non-renewable natural resources, forestry resources and electrical energy

92A (1) In each province, the legislature may exclusively make laws in relation to

(a) exploration for non-renewable natural resources in the province;

(b) development, conservation and management of non-renewable natural resources and forestry resources in the province, including laws in relation to the rate of primary production therefrom; and

(c) development, conservation and management of sites and facilities in the province for the generation and production of electrical energy.

(2) In each province, the legislature may make laws in relation to the export from the province to another part of Canada of the primary production from non-renewable natural resources and forestry resources in the province and the production from facilities in the province for the generation of electrical energy, but such laws may not authorize or provide for discrimination in prices or in supplies exported to another part of Canada.

Export from provinces of resources

(3) Nothing in subsection (2) derogates from the authority of Parliament to enact laws in relation to the matters referred to in that subsection and, where such a law of Parliament and a law of a province conflict, the law of Parliament prevails to the extent of the conflict.

Authority of Parliament

(4) In each province, the legislature may make laws in relation to the raising of money by any mode or system of taxation in respect of

Taxation of resources

(a) non-renewable natural resources and forestry resources in the province and the primary production therefrom, and

(b) sites and facilities in the province for the generation of electrical energy and the production therefrom,

whether or not such production is exported in whole or in part from the province, but such laws may not authorize or provide for taxation that differentiates between production exported to another part of Canada and production not exported from the province.

(5) The expression "primary production" has the meaning assigned by the Sixth Schedule.

"Primary production"

(6) Nothing in subsections (1) to (5) derogates from any powers or rights that a legislature or government of a province had immediately before the coming into force of this section.

Existing powers or rights

Education

Legislation respecting Education

93 In and for each Province the Legislature may exclusively make Laws in relation to Education, subject and according to the following Provisions: —

(1) Nothing in any such Law shall prejudicially affect any Right or Privilege with respect to Denominational Schools which any Class of Persons have by Law in the Province at the Union:

(2) All the Powers, Privileges, and Duties at the Union by Law conferred and imposed in Upper Canada on the Separate Schools and School Trustees of the Queen's Roman Catholic Subjects shall be and the same are hereby extended to the Dissentient Schools of the Queen's Protestant and Roman Catholic Subjects in Québec:

(3) Where in any Province a System of Separate or Dissentient Schools exists by Law at the Union or is thereafter established by the Legislature of the Province, an Appeal shall lie to the Governor General in Council from any Act or Decision of any Provincial Authority affecting any Right or Privilege of the Protestant or Roman Catholic Minority of the Queen's Subjects in relation to Education:

(4) In case any such Provincial Law as from Time to Time seems to the Governor General in Council requisite for the due Execution of the Provisions of this Section is not made, or in case any Decision of the Governor General in Council on any Appeal under this Section is not duly executed by the proper Provincial Authority in that Behalf, then and in every such Case, and as far only as the Circumstances of each Case require, the Parliament of Canada may make remedial Laws for the due Execution of the Provisions of this Section and of any Decision of the Governor General in Council under this Section.

Québec 93A Paragraphs (1) to (4) of section 93 do not apply to Québec.

Uniformity of Laws in Ontario, Nova Scotia, and New Brunswick

Legislation for Uniformity of Laws in Three Provinces

94 Notwithstanding anything in this Act, the Parliament of Canada may make Provision for the Uniformity of all or any of the Laws relative to Property and Civil Rights in Ontario, Nova Scotia, and New Brunswick, and of the Procedure of all or any of the Courts in those Three Provinces, and from and after the passing of any Act in that Behalf the Power of the

Parliament of Canada to make Laws in relation to any Matter comprised in any such Act shall, notwithstanding anything in this Act, be unrestricted; but any Act of the Parliament of Canada making Provision for such Uniformity shall not have effect in any Province unless and until it is adopted and enacted as Law by the Legislature thereof.

Old Age Pensions

94A The Parliament of Canada may make laws in relation to old age pensions and supplementary benefits, including survivors' and disability benefits irrespective of age, but no such law shall affect the operation of any law present or future of a provincial legislature in relation to any such matter.

Legislation respecting old age pensions and supplementary benefits

Agriculture And Immigration

95 In each Province the Legislature may make Laws in relation to Agriculture in the Province, and to Immigration into the Province; and it is hereby declared that the Parliament of Canada may from Time to Time make Laws in relation to Agriculture in all or any of the Provinces, and to Immigration into all or any of the Provinces; and any Law of the Legislature of a Province relative to Agriculture or to Immigration shall have effect in and for the Province as long and as far only as it is not repugnant to any Act of the Parliament of Canada.

Concurrent Powers of Legislation respecting Agriculture, etc.

VII Judicature

96 The Governor General shall appoint the Judges of the Superior, District, and County Courts in each Province, except those of the Courts of Probate in Nova Scotia and New Brunswick.

Appointment of Judges

97 Until the Laws relative to Property and Civil Rights in Ontario, Nova Scotia, and New Brunswick, and the Procedure of the Courts in those Provinces, are made uniform, the Judges of the Courts of those Provinces appointed by the Governor General shall be selected from the respective Bars of those Provinces.

Selection of Judges in Ontario, etc.

98 The Judges of the Courts of Québec shall be selected from the Bar of that Province.

Selection of Judges in Québec

265

Tenure of office of Judges 99 (1) Subject to subsection two of this section, the Judges of the Superior Courts shall hold office during good behaviour, but shall be removable by the Governor General on Address of the Senate and House of Commons.

Termination at age 75 (2) A Judge of a Superior Court, whether appointed before or after the coming into force of this section, shall cease to hold office upon attaining the age of seventy-five years, or upon the coming into force of this section if at that time he has already attained that age.

Salaries, etc., of Judges 100 The Salaries, Allowances, and Pensions of the Judges of the Superior, District, and County Courts (except the Courts of Probate in Nova Scotia and New Brunswick), and of the Admiralty Courts in Cases where the Judges thereof are for the Time being paid by Salary, shall be fixed and provided by the Parliament of Canada.

General Court of Appeal, etc. 101 The Parliament of Canada may, notwithstanding anything in this Act, from Time to Time provide for the Constitution, Maintenance, and Organization of a General Court of Appeal for Canada, and for the Establishment of any additional Courts for the better Administration of the Laws of Canada.

VIII Revenues; Debts; Assets; Taxation

Creation of Consolidated Revenue Fund 102 All Duties and Revenues over which the respective Legislatures of Canada, Nova Scotia, and New Brunswick before and at the Union had and have Power of Appropriation, except such Portions thereof as are by this Act reserved to the respective Legislatures of the Provinces, or are raised by them in accordance with the special Powers conferred on them by this Act, shall form One Consolidated Revenue Fund, to be appropriated for the Public Service of Canada in the Manner and subject to the Charges in this Act provided.

Expenses of Collection, etc. 103 The Consolidated Revenue Fund of Canada shall be permanently charged with the Costs, Charges, and Expenses incident to the Collection, Management, and Receipt thereof, and the same shall form the First Charge thereon, subject to be reviewed and audited in such Manner as shall be ordered by the Governor General in Council until the Parliament otherwise provides.

104 The annual Interest of the Public Debts of the several Provinces of *Interest of Provincial* Canada, Nova Scotia, and New Brunswick at the Union shall form the *Public Debts* Second Charge on the Consolidated Revenue Fund of Canada.

105 Unless altered by the Parliament of Canada, the Salary of the Governor *Salary of Governor* General shall be Ten thousand Pounds Sterling Money of the United Kingdom *General* of Great Britain and Ireland, payable out of the Consolidated Revenue Fund of Canada, and the same shall form the Third Charge thereon.

106 Subject to the several Payments by this Act charged on the Consolidated *Appropriation from Time* Revenue Fund of Canada, the same shall be appropriated by the *to Time* Parliament of Canada for the Public Service.

107 All Stocks, Cash, Banker's Balances, and Securities for Money belonging *Transfer of Stocks, etc.* to each Province at the Time of the Union, except as in this Act mentioned, shall be the Property of Canada, and shall be taken in Reduction of the Amount of the respective Debts of the Provinces at the Union.

108 The Public Works and Property of each Province, enumerated in the *Transfer of Property in* Third Schedule to this Act, shall be the Property of Canada. *Schedule*

109 All Lands, Mines, Minerals, and Royalties belonging to the several *Property in Lands,* Provinces of Canada, Nova Scotia, and New Brunswick at the Union, *Mines, etc.* and all Sums then due or payable for such Lands, Mines, Minerals, or Royalties, shall belong to the several Provinces of Ontario, Québec, Nova Scotia, and New Brunswick in which the same are situate or arise, subject to any Trusts existing in respect thereof, and to any Interest other than that of the Province in the same.

110 All Assets connected with such Portions of the Public Debt of each *Assets connected with* Province as are assumed by that Province shall belong to that Province. *Provincial Debts*

111 Canada shall be liable for the Debts and Liabilities of each Province *Canada to be liable for* existing at the Union. *Provincial Debts*

112 Ontario and Québec conjointly shall be liable to Canada for the Amount *Debts of Ontario and* (if any) by which the Debt of the Province of Canada exceeds at the Union *Québec* Sixty-two million five hundred thousand Dollars, and shall be charged with Interest at the Rate of Five per Centum per Annum thereon.

Assets of Ontario and Québec 113 The Assets enumerated in the Fourth Schedule to this Act belonging at the Union to the Province of Canada shall be the Property of Ontario and Québec conjointly.

Debt of Nova Scotia 114 Nova Scotia shall be liable to Canada for the Amount (if any) by which its Public Debt exceeds at the Union Eight million Dollars, and shall be charged with Interest at the Rate of Five per Centum per Annum thereon.

Debt of New Brunswick 115 New Brunswick shall be liable to Canada for the Amount (if any) by which its Public Debt exceeds at the Union Seven million Dollars, and shall be charged with Interest at the Rate of Five per Centum per Annum thereon.

Payment of interest to Nova Scotia and New Brunswick 116 In case the Public Debts of Nova Scotia and New Brunswick do not at the Union amount to Eight million and Seven million Dollars respectively, they shall respectively receive by half-yearly Payments in advance from the Government of Canada Interest at Five per Centum per Annum on the Difference between the actual Amounts of their respective Debts and such stipulated Amounts.

Provincial Public Property 117 The several Provinces shall retain all their respective Public Property not otherwise disposed of in this Act, subject to the Right of Canada to assume any Lands or Public Property required for Fortifications or for the Defence of the Country.

[Repealed] 118 Repealed.

Further Grant to New Brunswick 119 New Brunswick shall receive by half-yearly Payments in advance from Canada for the Period of Ten Years from the Union an additional Allowance of Sixty-three thousand Dollars per Annum; but as long as the Public Debt of that Province remains under Seven million Dollars, a Deduction equal to the Interest at Five per Centum per Annum on such Deficiency shall be made from that Allowance of Sixty-three thousand Dollars.

Form of Payments 120 All Payments to be made under this Act, or in discharge of Liabilities created under any Act of the Provinces of Canada, Nova Scotia, and New Brunswick respectively, and assumed by Canada, shall, until the Parliament of Canada otherwise directs, be made in such Form and Manner as may from Time to Time be ordered by the Governor General in Council.

121 All Articles of the Growth, Produce, or Manufacture of any one of the   *Canadian Manufactures, etc.*
Provinces shall, from and after the Union, be admitted free into each
of the other Provinces.

122 The Customs and Excise Laws of each Province shall, subject to the   *Continuance of Customs*
Provisions of this Act, continue in force until altered by the Parliament   *and Excise Laws*
of Canada.

123 Where Customs Duties are, at the Union, leviable on any Goods,   *Exportation and*
Wares, or Merchandises in any Two Provinces, those Goods, Wares,   *Importation as between*
and Merchandises may, from and after the Union, be imported from   *Two Provinces*
one of those Provinces into the other of them on Proof of Payment of
the Customs Duty leviable thereon in the Province of Exportation, and
on Payment of such further Amount (if any) of Customs Duty as is leviable thereon in the Province of Importation.

124 Nothing in this Act shall affect the Right of New Brunswick to levy   *Lumber Dues in New*
the Lumber Dues provided in Chapter Fifteen of Title Three of the   *Brunswick*
Revised Statutes of New Brunswick, or in any Act amending that Act
before or after the Union, and not increasing the Amount of such Dues;
but the Lumber of any of the Provinces other than New Brunswick
shall not be subject to such Dues.

125 No Lands or Property belonging to Canada or any Province shall be   *Exemption of Public*
liable to Taxation.   *Lands, etc.*

126 Such Portions of the Duties and Revenues over which the respective   *Provincial Consolidated*
Legislatures of Canada, Nova Scotia, and New Brunswick had before the   *Revenue Fund*
Union Power of Appropriation as are by this Act reserved to the respective
Governments or Legislatures of the Provinces, and all Duties and
Revenues raised by them in accordance with the special Powers conferred
upon them by this Act, shall in each Province form One Consolidated
Revenue Fund to be appropriated for the Public Service of the Province.

IX Miscellaneous Provisions

General

127 Repealed.   *[Repealed]*

Oath of Allegiance, etc. 128 Every Member of the Senate or House of Commons of Canada shall before taking his Seat therein take and subscribe before the Governor General or some Person authorized by him, and every Member of a Legislative Council or Legislative Assembly of any Province shall before taking his Seat therein take and subscribe before the Lieutenant Governor of the Province or some Person authorized by him, the Oath of Allegiance contained in the Fifth Schedule to this Act; and every Member of the Senate of Canada and every Member of the Legislative Council of Québec shall also, before taking his Seat therein, take and subscribe before the Governor General, or some Person authorized by him, the Declaration of Qualification contained in the same Schedule.

Continuance of existing 129 Except as otherwise provided by this Act, all Laws in force in Canada, *Laws, Courts, Officers, etc.* Nova Scotia, or New Brunswick at the Union, and all Courts of Civil and Criminal Jurisdiction, and all legal Commissions, Powers, and Authorities, and all Officers, Judicial, Administrative, and Ministerial, existing therein at the Union, shall continue in Ontario, Québec, Nova Scotia, and New Brunswick respectively, as if the Union had not been made; subject nevertheless (except with respect to such as are enacted by or exist under Acts of the Parliament of Great Britain or of the Parliament of the United Kingdom of Great Britain and Ireland), to be repealed, abolished, or altered by the Parliament of Canada, or by the Legislature of the respective Province, according to the Authority of the Parliament or of that Legislature under this Act.

Transfer of Officers to 130 Until the Parliament of Canada otherwise provides, all Officers of the *Canada* several Provinces having Duties to discharge in relation to Matters other than those coming within the Classes of Subjects by this Act assigned exclusively to the Legislatures of the Provinces shall be Officers of Canada, and shall continue to discharge the Duties of their respective Offices under the same Liabilities, Responsibilities, and Penalties as if the Union had not been made.

Appointment of new Officers 131 Until the Parliament of Canada otherwise provides, the Governor General in Council may from Time to Time appoint such Officers as the Governor General in Council deems necessary or proper for the effectual Execution of this Act.

132 The Parliament and Government of Canada shall have all Powers nec- *Treaty Obligations*
essary or proper for performing the Obligations of Canada or of any
Province thereof, as Part of the British Empire, toward Foreign
Countries, arising under Treaties between the Empire and such Foreign
Countries.

133 Either the English or the French Language may be used by any Person *Use of English and French*
in the Debates of the Houses of the Parliament of Canada and of the *Languages*
Houses of the Legislature of Québec; and both those Languages shall
be used in the respective Records and Journals of those Houses; and
either of those Languages may be used by any Person or in any Pleading
or Process in or issuing from any Court of Canada established under
this Act, and in or from all or any of the Courts of Québec.
The Acts of the Parliament of Canada and of the Legislature of Québec
shall be printed and published in both those Languages.

Ontario and Québec

134 Until the Legislature of Ontario or of Québec otherwise provides, the *Appointment of Executive*
Lieutenant Governors of Ontario and Québec may each appoint under *Officers for Ontario and*
the Great Seal of the Province the following Officers, to hold Office *Québec*
during Pleasure, that is to say,—the Attorney General, the Secretary
and Registrar of the Province, the Treasurer of the Province, the
Commissioner of Crown Lands, and the Commissioner of Agriculture
and Public Works, and in the Case of Québec the Solicitor General,
and may, by Order of the Lieutenant Governor in Council, from Time
to Time prescribe the Duties of those Officers, and of the several
Departments over which they shall preside or to which they shall belong, and of the Officers and Clerks thereof, and may also appoint other
and additional Officers to hold Office during Pleasure, and may from
Time to Time prescribe the Duties of those Officers, and of the several
Departments over which they shall preside or to which they shall belong, and of the Officers and Clerks thereof.

135 Until the Legislature of Ontario or Québec otherwise provides, all *Powers, Duties, etc. of*
Rights, Powers, Duties, Functions, Responsibilities, or Authorities at *Executive Officers*
the passing of this Act vested in or imposed on the Attorney General,
Solicitor General, Secretary and Registrar of the Province of Canada,
Minister of Finance, Commissioner of Crown Lands, Commissioner of

Public Works, and Minister of Agriculture and Receiver General, by any Law, Statute, or Ordinance of Upper Canada, Lower Canada, or Canada, and not repugnant to this Act, shall be vested in or imposed on any Officer to be appointed by the Lieutenant Governor for the Discharge of the same or any of them; and the Commissioner of Agriculture and Public Works shall perform the Duties and Functions of the Office of Minister of Agriculture at the passing of this Act imposed by the Law of the Province of Canada, as well as those of the Commissioner of Public Works.

Great Seals 136 Until altered by the Lieutenant Governor in Council, the Great Seals of Ontario and Québec respectively shall be the same, or of the same Design, as those used in the Provinces of Upper Canada and Lower Canada respectively before their Union as the Province of Canada.

Construction of temporary Acts 137 The words "and from thence to the End of the then next ensuing Session of the Legislature," or Words to the same Effect, used in any temporary Act of the Province of Canada not expired before the Union, shall be construed to extend and apply to the next Session of the Parliament of Canada if the Subject Matter of the Act is within the Powers of the same as defined by this Act, or to the next Sessions of the Legislatures of Ontario and Québec respectively if the Subject Matter of the Act is within the Powers of the same as defined by this Act.

As to Errors in Names 138 From and after the Union the Use of the Words "Upper Canada" instead of "Ontario," or "Lower Canada" instead of "Québec," in any Deed, Writ, Process, Pleading, Document, Matter, or Thing shall not invalidate the same.

As to issue of Proclamations before Union, to commence after Union 139 Any Proclamation under the Great Seal of the Province of Canada issued before the Union to take effect at a Time which is subsequent to the Union, whether relating to that Province, or to Upper Canada, or to Lower Canada, and the several Matters and Things therein proclaimed, shall be and continue of like Force and Effect as if the Union had not been made.

140 Any Proclamation which is authorized by any Act of the Legislature of *As to issue of Proclamations* the Province of Canada to be issued under the Great Seal of the *after Union* Province of Canada, whether relating to that Province, or to Upper Canada, or to Lower Canada, and which is not issued before the Union, may be issued by the Lieutenant Governor of Ontario or of Québec, as its Subject Matter requires, under the Great Seal thereof; and from and after the Issue of such Proclamation the same and the several Matters and Things therein proclaimed shall be and continue of the like Force and Effect in Ontario or Québec as if the Union had not been made.

141 The Penitentiary of the Province of Canada shall, until the Parliament *Penitentiary* of Canada otherwise provides, be and continue the Penitentiary of Ontario and of Québec.

142 The Division and Adjustment of the Debts, Credits, Liabilities, *Arbitration respecting* Properties, and Assets of Upper Canada and Lower Canada shall be *Debts, etc.* referred to the Arbitrament of Three Arbitrators, One chosen by the Government of Ontario, One by the Government of Québec, and One by the Government of Canada; and the Selection of the Arbitrators shall not be made until the Parliament of Canada and the Legislatures of Ontario and Québec have met; and the Arbitrator chosen by the Government of Canada shall not be a Resident either in Ontario or in Québec.

143 The Governor General in Council may from Time to Time order that *Division of Records* such and so many of the Records, Books, and Documents of the Province of Canada as he thinks fit shall be appropriated and delivered either to Ontario or to Québec, and the same shall thenceforth be the Property of that Province; and any Copy thereof or Extract therefrom, duly certified by the Officer having charge of the Original thereof, shall be admitted as Evidence.

144 The Lieutenant Governor of Québec may from Time to Time, by *Constitution of Townships* Proclamation under the Great Seal of the Province, to take effect from *in Québec* a Day to be appointed therein, constitute Townships in those Parts of the Province of Québec in which Townships are not then already constituted, and fix the Metes and Bounds thereof.

X Intercolonial Railway

[Repealed] 145 Repealed.

XI Admission of Other Colonies

Power to admit 146 It shall be lawful for the Queen, by and with the Advice of Her Majesty's
Newfoundland, etc., Most Honourable Privy Council, on Addresses from the Houses of the
into the Union Parliament of Canada, and from the Houses of the respective Legislatures
of the Colonies or Provinces of Newfoundland, Prince Edward Island,
and British Columbia, to admit those Colonies or Provinces, or any of
them, into the Union, and on Address from the Houses of the Parliament
of Canada to admit Rupert's Land and the North-western Territory, or
either of them, into the Union, on such Terms and Conditions in each
Case as are in the Addresses expressed and as the Queen thinks fit to approve, subject to the Provisions of this Act; and the Provisions of any
Order in Council in that Behalf shall have effect as if they had been enacted by the Parliament of the United Kingdom of Great Britain and
Ireland.

As to Representation of 147 In case of the Admission of Newfoundland and Prince Edward Island,
Newfoundland and Prince or either of them, each shall be entitled to a Representation in the
Edward Island in Senate Senate of Canada of Four Members, and (notwithstanding anything in
this Act) in case of the Admission of Newfoundland the normal
Number of Senators shall be Seventy-six and their maximum Number
shall be Eighty-two; but Prince Edward Island when admitted shall be
deemed to be comprised in the third of the Three Divisions into which
Canada is, in relation to the Constitution of the Senate, divided by this
Act, and accordingly, after the Admission of Prince Edward Island,
whether Newfoundland is admitted or not, the Representation of Nova
Scotia and New Brunswick in the Senate shall, as Vacancies occur, be
reduced from Twelve to Ten Members respectively, and the
Representation of each of those Provinces shall not be increased at any
Time beyond Ten, except under the Provisions of this Act for the
Appointment of Three or Six additional Senators under the Direction
of the Queen.

Constitution Act, 1982

Schedule B
Constitution Act 1982

Part I
Canadian Charter of Rights and Freedoms

Whereas Canada is founded upon principles that recognize the supremacy of God and the rule of law:

Guarantee of Rights and Freedoms

1 The *Canadian Charter of Rights and Freedoms* guarantees the rights and freedoms set out in it subject only to such reasonable limits prescribed by law as can be demonstrably justified in a free and democratic society.

Rights and freedoms in Canada

Fundamental Freedoms

2 Everyone has the following fundamental freedoms:

  (*a*) freedom of conscience and religion;

  (*b*) freedom of thought, belief, opinion and expression, including freedom of the press and other media of communication;

  (*c*) freedom of peaceful assembly; and

  (*d*) freedom of association.

Fundamental freedoms

Democratic Rights

3 Every citizen of Canada has the right to vote in an election of members of the House of Commons or of a legislative assembly and to be qualified for membership therein.

Democratic rights of citizens

4 (1) No House of Commons and no legislative assembly shall continue for longer than five years from the date fixed for the return of the writs of a general election of its members.

Maximum duration of legislative bodies

(2) In time of real or apprehended war, invasion or insurrection, a House of Commons may be continued by Parliament and a legislative assembly may be continued by the legislature beyond five years if such

Continuation in special circumstances

continuation is not opposed by the votes of more than one-third of the members of the House of Commons or the legislative assembly, as the case may be.

Annual sitting of legislative bodies 5 There shall be a sitting of Parliament and of each legislature at least once every twelve months.

Mobility Rights

Mobility of citizens 6 (1) Every citizen of Canada has the right to enter, remain in and leave Canada.

Rights to move and gain livelihood (2) Every citizen of Canada and every person who has the status of a permanent resident of Canada has the right

(a) to move to and take up residence in any province; and

(b) to pursue the gaining of a livelihood in any province.

Limitation (3) The rights specified in subsection (2) are subject to

(a) any laws or practices of general application in force in a province other than those that discriminate among persons primarily on the basis of province of present or previous residence; and

(b) any laws providing for reasonable residency requirements as a qualification for the receipt of publicly provided social services.

Affirmative action programs (4) Subsections (2) and (3) do not preclude any law, program or activity that has as its object the amelioration in a province of conditions of individuals in that province who are socially or economically disadvantaged if the rate of employment in that province is below the rate of employment in Canada.

Legal Rights

Life, liberty and security of person 7 Everyone has the right to life, liberty and security of the person and the right not to be deprived thereof except in accordance with the principles of fundamental justice.

Search or seizure 8 Everyone has the right to be secure against unreasonable search or seizure.

9 Everyone has the right not to be arbitrarily detained or imprisoned.   *Detention or imprisonment*

10 Everyone has the right on arrest or detention   *Arrest or detention*

   (*a*) to be informed promptly of the reasons therefor;

   (*b*) to retain and instruct counsel without delay and to be informed of that right; and

   (*c*) to have the validity of the detention determined by way of *habeas corpus* and to be released if the detention is not lawful.

11 Any person charged with an offence has the right   *Proceedings in criminal and penal matters*

   (*a*) to be informed without unreasonable delay of the specific offence;

   (*b*) to be tried within a reasonable time;

   (*c*) not to be compelled to be a witness in proceedings against that person in respect of the offence;

   (*d*) to be presumed innocent until proven guilty according to law in a fair and public hearing by an independent and impartial tribunal;

   (*e*) not to be denied reasonable bail without just cause;

   (*f*) except in the case of an offence under military law tried before a military tribunal, to the benefit of trial by jury where the maximum punishment for the offence is imprisonment for five years or a more severe punishment;

   (*g*) not to be found guilty on account of any act or omission unless, at the time of the act or omission, it constituted an offence under Canadian or international law or was criminal according to the general principles of law recognized by the community of nations;

   (*h*) if finally acquitted of the offence, not to be tried for it again and, if finally found guilty and punished for the offence, not to be tried or punished for it again; and

   (*i*) if found guilty of the offence and if the punishment for the offence has been varied between the time of commission and the time of sentencing, to the benefit of the lesser punishment.

12 Everyone has the right not to be subjected to any cruel and unusual treatment or punishment.   *Treatment or punishment*

13 A witness who testifies in any proceedings has the right not to have any incriminating evidence so given used to incriminate that witness in any other proceedings, except in a prosecution for perjury or for the giving of contradictory evidence.   *Self-crimination*

Interpreter 14 A party or witness in any proceedings who does not understand or speak the language in which the proceedings are conducted or who is deaf has the right to the assistance of an interpreter.

Equality Rights

Equality before and under law and equal protection and benefit of law 15 (1) Every individual is equal before and under the law and has the right to the equal protection and equal benefit of the law without discrimination and, in particular, without discrimination based on race, national or ethnic origin, colour, religion, sex, age or mental or physical disability.

Affirmative action programs (2) Subsection (1) does not preclude any law, program or activity that has as its object the amelioration of conditions of disadvantaged individuals or groups including those that are disadvantaged because of race, national or ethnic origin, colour, religion, sex, age or mental or physical disability.

Official Languages of Canada

Official languages of Canada 16 (1) English and French are the official languages of Canada and have equality of status and equal rights and privileges as to their use in all institutions of the Parliament and government of Canada.

Official languages of New Brunswick (2) English and French are the official languages of New Brunswick and have equality of status and equal rights and privileges as to their use in all institutions of the legislature and government of New Brunswick.

Advancement of status and use (3) Nothing in this Charter limits the authority of Parliament or a legislature to advance the equality of status or use of English and French.

English and French linguistic communities in New Brunswick 16.1 (1) The English linguistic community and the French linguistic community in New Brunswick have equality of status and equal rights and privileges, including the right to distinct educational institutions and such distinct cultural institutions as are necessary for the preservation and promotion of those communities.

Role of the legislature and government of New Brunswick (2) The role of the legislature and government of New Brunswick to preserve and promote the status, rights and privileges referred to in subsection (1) is affirmed.

17 (1) Everyone has the right to use English or French in any debates and *Proceedings of Parliament* other proceedings of Parliament.

(2) Everyone has the right to use English or French in any debates and *Proceedings of New* other proceedings of the legislature of New Brunswick. *Brunswick legislature*

18 (1) The statutes, records and journals of Parliament shall be printed *Parliamentary statutes and* and published in English and French and both language versions *records* are equally authoritative.

(2) The statutes, records and journals of the legislature of New *New Brunswick statutes* Brunswick shall be printed and published in English and French *and records* and both language versions are equally authoritative.

19 (1) Either English or French may be used by any person in, or in any *Proceedings in courts* pleading in or process issuing from, any court established by Parliament. *established by Parliament*

(2) Either English or French may be used by any person in, or in any *Proceedings in New* pleading in or process issuing from, any court of New Brunswick. *Brunswick courts*

20 (1) Any member of the public in Canada has the right to communicate *Communications by public* with, and to receive available services from, any head or central of- *with federal institutions* fice of an institution of the Parliament or government of Canada in English or French, and has the same right with respect to any other office of any such institution where

(a) there is a significant demand for communications with and ser- vices from that office in such language; or

(b) due to the nature of the office, it is reasonable that communi- cations with and services from that office be available in both English and French.

(2) Any member of the public in New Brunswick has the right to communi- *Communications by public* cate with, and to receive available services from, any office of an institution *with New Brunswick* of the legislature or government of New Brunswick in English or French. *institutions*

21 Nothing in sections 16 to 20 abrogates or derogates from any right, *Continuation of existing* privilege or obligation with respect to the English and French lan- *constitutional provisions* guages, or either of them, that exists or is continued by virtue of any other provision of the Constitution of Canada.

Rights and privileges preserved 22 Nothing in sections 16 to 20 abrogates or derogates from any legal or customary right or privilege acquired or enjoyed either before or after the coming into force of this Charter with respect to any language that is not English or French.

Minority Language Educational Rights

Language of instruction 23 (1) Citizens of Canada

(*a*) whose first language learned and still understood is that of the English or French linguistic minority population of the province in which they reside, or

(*b*) who have received their primary school instruction in Canada in English or French and reside in a province where the language in which they received that instruction is the language of the English or French linguistic minority population of the province,

have the right to have their children receive primary and secondary school instruction in that language in that province.

Continuity of language instruction (2) Citizens of Canada of whom any child has received or is receiving primary or secondary school instruction in English or French in Canada, have the right to have all their children receive primary and secondary school instruction in the same language.

Application where numbers warrant (3) The right of citizens of Canada under subsections (1) and (2) to have their children receive primary and secondary school instruction in the language of the English or French linguistic minority population of a province

(*a*) applies wherever in the province the number of children of citizens who have such a right is sufficient to warrant the provision to them out of public funds of minority language instruction; and

(*b*) includes, where the number of those children so warrants, the right to have them receive that instruction in minority language educational facilities provided out of public funds

Enforcement

Enforcement of guaranteed rights and freedoms 24 (1) Anyone whose rights or freedoms, as guaranteed by this Charter, have been infringed or denied may apply to a court of competent jurisdiction to obtain such remedy as the court considers appropriate and just in the circumstances.

(2) Where, in proceedings under subsection (1), a court concludes that evidence was obtained in a manner that infringed or denied any rights or freedoms guaranteed by this Charter, the evidence shall be excluded if it is established that, having regard to all the circumstances, the admission of it in the proceedings would bring the administration of justice into disrepute.

Exclusion of evidence bringing administration of justice into disrepute

General

25 The guarantee in this Charter of certain rights and freedoms shall not be construed so as to abrogate or derogate from any aboriginal, treaty or other rights or freedoms that pertain to the aboriginal peoples of Canada including

Aboriginal rights and freedoms not affected by Charter

(a) any rights or freedoms that have been recognized by the Royal Proclamation of October 7, 1763; and

(b) any rights or freedoms that now exist by way of land claims agreements or may be so acquired.

26 The guarantee in this Charter of certain rights and freedoms shall not be construed as denying the existence of any other rights or freedoms that exist in Canada.

Other rights and freedoms not affected by Charter

27 This Charter shall be interpreted in a manner consistent with the preservation and enhancement of the multicultural heritage of Canadians.

Multicultural heritage

28 Notwithstanding anything in this Charter, the rights and freedoms referred to in it are guaranteed equally to male and female persons.

Rights guaranteed equally to both sexes

29 Nothing in this Charter abrogates or derogates from any rights or privileges guaranteed by or under the Constitution of Canada in respect of denominational, separate or dissentient schools.

Rights respecting certain schools preserved

30 A reference in this Charter to a Province or to the legislative assembly or legislature of a province shall be deemed to include a reference to the Yukon Territory and the Northwest Territories, or to the appropriate legislative authority thereof, as the case may be.

Application to territories and territorial authorities

Legislative powers not extended 31 Nothing in this Charter extends the legislative powers of any body or authority.

Application of Charter

Application of Charter 32 (1) This Charter applies

(a) to the Parliament and government of Canada in respect of all matters within the authority of Parliament including all matters relating to the Yukon Territory and Northwest Territories; and

(b) to the legislature and government of each province in respect of all matters within the authority of the legislature of each province.

Exception (2) Notwithstanding subsection (1), section 15 shall not have effect until three years after this section comes into force.

Exception where express declaration 33 (1) Parliament or the legislature of a province may expressly declare in an Act of Parliament or of the legislature, as the case may be, that the Act or a provision thereof shall operate notwithstanding a provision included in section 2 or sections 7 to 15 of this Charter.

Operation of exception (2) An Act or a provision of an Act in respect of which a declaration made under this section is in effect shall have such operation as it would have but for the provision of this Charter referred to in the declaration.

Five year limitation (3) A declaration made under subsection (1) shall cease to have effect five years after it comes into force or on such earlier date as may be specified in the declaration.

Re-enactment (4) Parliament or the legislature of a province may re-enact a declaration made under subsection (1).

Five year limitation (5) Subsection (3) applies in respect of a re-enactment made under subsection (4).

Citation

Citation 34 This Part may be cited as the *Canadian Charter of Rights and Freedoms*.

Part II

Rights Of The Aboriginal Peoples Of Canada

35 (1) The existing aboriginal and treaty rights of the aboriginal peoples of Canada are hereby recognized and affirmed.

Recognition of existing aboriginal and treaty rights

(2) In this Act, "aboriginal peoples of Canada" includes the Indian, Inuit and Métis peoples of Canada.

Definition of "aboriginal peoples of Canada"

(3) For greater certainty, in subsection (1) "treaty rights" includes rights that now exist by way of land claims agreements or may be so acquired.

Land claims agreements

(4) Notwithstanding any other provision of this Act, the aboriginal and treaty rights referred to in subsection (1) are guaranteed equally to male and female persons.

Aboriginal and treaty rights are guaranteed equally to both sexes

35.1 The government of Canada and the provincial governments are committed to the principle that, before any amendment is made to Class 24 of section 91 of the "*Constitution Act, 1867*", to section 25 of this Act or to this Part,

Commitment to participation in constitutional conference

(a) a constitutional conference that includes in its agenda an item relating to the proposed amendment, composed of the Prime Minister of Canada and the first ministers of the provinces, will be convened by the Prime Minister of Canada; and

(b) the Prime Minister of Canada will invite representatives of the aboriginal peoples of Canada to participate in the discussions on that item.

Part III

Equalization And Regional Disparities

36 (1) Without altering the legislative authority of Parliament or of the provincial legislatures, or the rights of any of them with respect to the exercise of their legislative authority, Parliament and the legislatures, together with the government of Canada and the provincial governments, are committed to

Commitment to promote equal opportunities

(a) promoting equal opportunities for the well-being of Canadians;

(b) furthering economic development to reduce disparity in opportunities; and (*c*) providing essential public services of reasonable quality to all Canadians.

Commitment respecting
public services

(2) Parliament and the government of Canada are committed to the principle of making equalization payments to ensure that provincial governments have sufficient revenues to provide reasonably comparable levels of public services at reasonably comparable levels of taxation.

Part IV
Constitutional Conference

[Repealed]   37 Repealed.

Part IV.I
Constitutional Conferences

[Repealed]   37.1 Repealed.

Part V
Procedure For Amending Constitution Of Canada

General procedure for
amending Constitution of
Canada

38 (1) An amendment to the Constitution of Canada may be made by proclamation issued by the Governor General under the Great Seal of Canada where so authorized by

(*a*) resolutions of the Senate and House of Commons; and

(*b*) resolutions of the legislative assemblies of at least two-thirds of the provinces that have, in the aggregate, according to the then latest general census, at least fifty per cent of the population of all the provinces.

Majority of members

(2) An amendment made under subsection (1) that derogates from the legislative powers, the proprietary rights or any other rights or privileges of the legislature or government of a province shall require a resolution supported by a majority of the members of each of the Senate, the House of Commons and the legislative assemblies required under subsection (1).

(3) An amendment referred to in subsection (2) shall not have effect in a province the legislative assembly of which has expressed its dissent thereto by resolution supported by a majority of its members prior to the issue of the proclamation to which the amendment relates unless that legislative assembly, subsequently, by resolution supported by a majority of its members, revokes its dissent and authorizes the amendment.

Expression of dissent

(4) A resolution of dissent made for the purposes of subsection (3) may be revoked at any time before or after the issue of the proclamation to which it relates.

Revocation of dissent

39 (1) A proclamation shall not be issued under subsection 38(1) before the expiration of one year from the adoption of the resolution initiating the amendment procedure thereunder, unless the legislative assembly of each province has previously adopted a resolution of assent or dissent.

Restriction on proclamation

(2) A proclamation shall not be issued under subsection 38(1) after the expiration of three years from the adoption of the resolution initiating the amendment procedure thereunder.

Idem

40 Where an amendment is made under subsection 38(1) that transfers provincial legislative powers relating to education or other cultural matters from provincial legislatures to Parliament, Canada shall provide reasonable compensation to any province to which the amendment does not apply.

Compensation

41 An amendment to the Constitution of Canada in relation to the following matters may be made by proclamation issued by the Governor General under the Great Seal of Canada only where authorized by resolutions of the Senate and House of Commons and of the legislative assembly of each province:

Amendment by unanimous consent

(a) the office of the Queen, the Governor General and the Lieutenant Governor of a province;

(b) the right of a province to a number of members in the House of Commons not less than the number of Senators by which the province is entitled to be represented at the time this Part comes into force;

(*c*) subject to section 43, the use of the English or the French language;

(*d*) the composition of the Supreme Court of Canada; and

(*e*) an amendment to this Part.

Amendment by general procedure 42 (1) An amendment to the Constitution of Canada in relation to the following matters may be made only in accordance with subsection 38(1):

(*a*) the principle of proportionate representation of the provinces in the House of Commons prescribed by the Constitution of Canada;

(*b*) the powers of the Senate and the method of selecting Senators;

(*c*) the number of members by which a province is entitled to be represented in the Senate and the residence qualifications of Senators;

(*d*) subject to paragraph 41(*d*), the Supreme Court of Canada;

(*e*) the extension of existing provinces into the territories; and

(*f*) notwithstanding any other law or practice, the establishment of new provinces.

Exception (2) Subsections 38(2) to (4) do not apply in respect of amendments in relation to matters referred to in subsection (1).

Amendment of provisions relating to some but not all provinces 43 An amendment to the Constitution of Canada in relation to any provision that applies to one or more, but not all, provinces, including

(*a*) any alteration to boundaries between provinces, and

(*b*) any amendment to any provision that relates to the use of the English or the French language within a province,

may be made by proclamation issued by the Governor General under the Great Seal of Canada only where so authorized by resolutions of the Senate and House of Commons and of the legislative assembly of each province to which the amendment applies.

Amendments by Parliament 44 Subject to sections 41 and 42, Parliament may exclusively make laws amending the Constitution of Canada in relation to the executive government of Canada or the Senate and House of Commons.

Amendments by provincial legislatures 45 Subject to section 41, the legislature of each province may exclusively make laws amending the constitution of the province.

46 (1) The procedures for amendment under sections 38, 41, 42 and 43 may   *Initiation of amendment*
be initiated either by the Senate or the House of Commons or by the   *procedures*
legislative assembly of a province.

(2) A resolution of assent made for the purposes of this Part may be re-   *Revocation of authorization*
voked at any time before the issue of a proclamation authorized by it.

47 (1) An amendment to the Constitution of Canada made by proclamation   *Amendments without Senate*
under section 38, 41, 42 or 43 may be made without a resolution of   *resolution*
the Senate authorizing the issue of the proclamation if, within one
hundred and eighty days after the adoption by the House of
Commons of a resolution authorizing its issue, the Senate has not
adopted such a resolution and if, at any time after the expiration
of that period, the House of Commons again adopts the resolution.

(2) Any period when Parliament is prorogued or dissolved shall not be   *Computation of period*
counted in computing the one hundred and eighty day period re-
ferred to in subsection (1).

48 The Queen's Privy Council for Canada shall advise the Governor   *Advice to issue proclamation*
General to issue a proclamation under this Part forthwith on the
adoption of the resolutions required for an amendment made by
proclamation under this Part.

49 A constitutional conference composed of the Prime Minister of Canada   *Constitutional conference*
and the first ministers of the provinces shall be convened by the Prime
Minister of Canada within fifteen years after this Part comes into force
to review the provisions of this Part.

Part VI
Amendment To The Constitution Act, 1867

50 (1) (The amendment is set out in the Consolidation of the *Constitution
Act*, 1867, as Section 92A thereof.)

51 (2) (The amendment is set out in the Consolidation of the *Constitution
Act*, 1867, as the sixth schedule thereof.)

Part VII
General

Primacy of Constitution of Canada

52. (1) The Constitution of Canada is the supreme law of Canada, and any law that is inconsistent with the provisions of the Constitution is, to the extent of the inconsistency, of no force or effect.

Constitution of Canada

(2) The Constitution of Canada includes

(*a*) the *Canada Act 1982*, including this Act;

(*b*) the Acts and orders referred to in the schedule; and

(*c*) any amendment to any Act or order referred to in paragraph (*a*) or (*b*).

Amendments to Constitution of Canada

(3) Amendments to the Constitution of Canada shall be made only in accordance with the authority contained in the Constitution of Canada.

Repeals and new names

53. (1) The enactments referred to in Column I of the schedule are hereby repealed or amended to the extent indicated in Column II thereof and, unless repealed, shall continue as law in Canada under the names set out in Column III thereof.

Consequential amendments

(2) Every enactment, except the *Canada Act 1982*, that refers to an enactment referred to in the schedule by the name in Column I thereof is hereby amended by substituting for that name the corresponding name in Column III thereof, and any British North America Act not referred to in the schedule may be cited as the *Constitution Act* followed by the year and number, if any, of its enactment.

Repeal and consequential amendments

54 Part IV is repealed on the day that is one year after this Part comes into force and this section may be repealed and this Act renumbered, consequentially upon the repeal of Part IV and this section, by proclamation issued by the Governor General under the Great Seal of Canada.

[Repealed] 54.1

55 A French version of the portions of the Constitution of Canada referred to in the schedule shall be prepared by the Minister of Justice of Canada as expeditiously as possible and, when any portion thereof sufficient to warrant action being taken has been so prepared, it shall be put forward for enactment by proclamation issued by the Governor General under the Great Seal of Canada pursuant to the procedure then applicable to an amendment of the same provisions of the Constitution of Canada. *French version of Constitution of Canada*

56 Where any portion of the Constitution of Canada has been or is enacted in English and French or where a French version of any portion of the Constitution is enacted pursuant to section 55, the English and French versions of that portion of the Constitution are equally authoritative. *English and French versions of certain constitutional texts*

57 The English and French versions of this Act are equally authoritative. *English and French versions of this Act*

58 Subject to section 59, this Act shall come into force on a day to be fixed by proclamation issued by the Queen or the Governor General under the Great Seal of Canada. *Commencement*

59 (1) Paragraph 23(1)(a) shall come into force in respect of Québec on a day to be fixed by proclamation issued by the Queen or the Governor General under the Great Seal of Canada. *Commencement of paragraph 23(1)(a) in respect of Québec*

(2) A proclamation under subsection (1) shall be issued only where authorized by the legislative assembly or government of Québec. *Authorization of Québec*

(3) This section may be repealed on the day paragraph 23(1)(a) comes into force in respect of Québec and this Act amended and renumbered, consequentially upon the repeal of this section, by proclamation issued by the Queen or the Governor General under the Great Seal of Canada. *Repeal of this section*

60 This Act may be cited as the *Constitution Act, 1982*, and the Constitution Acts 1867 to 1975 (No. 2) and this Act may be cited together as the *Constitution Acts, 1867 to 1982*. *Short title and citations*

61 A reference to the "*Constitution Acts, 1867 to 1982*" shall be deemed to include a reference to the "*Constitution Amendment Proclamation, 1983*". *References*

Index

Reform Act (1832), 19
Reform Party, 117, 142, 200, 205–6
refugee claims, 98
regime, 3, 50
    Aristotle's typology, 4
    Canada *vs.* US, xii–xiii
regional disparities, 69, 73
regional parties, 185, 203
rent seekers, 227
Report on the Affairs of British North America, 39
report state (bills), 132
representation, 169–72
    Canadian model, 171
    microcosm theory of, 172–73
    by population, 75, 138
    trustee theory of, 170–72
representative democracy, 6–7, 169
republican regimes, 7
reservation, 63, 93
residential schools, 87
residual power, 15, 62
resolutions, adoption of, 132
responsible government, xii, xiv, 7, 37–57, 110, 124, 171, 217
    accountability, 55–56
    collective responsibility, 111–12
    compared to separation of powers, 54–57
    conventions of, 40–43
    democratic legitimacy in, 170
    efficiency, 55
    federalism and, 74
    fixed election dates and, 51, 178
    forming a government, 43–47
    Governor General as guardian of, 107–8
    institutional implications, 50–54
    liberty and, 56
    ministerial responsibility, 119–21
    premium on victory, 205–6
returning officer, 179–80
ridings, 127, 176
right not to be subjected to cruel or unusual punishments, 88, 90
right to enjoyment of property, 87
right to non-discriminatory treatment under the law, 88
right to retain legal counsel upon arrest, 87
right to security of person, 91, 175, 228

right to vote, 87–88, 169
rights and freedoms. *See also* Charter of Rights and Freedoms; human rights
    Aboriginal people, 87–88, 151
    Charter of Rights and Freedoms, 10
    charter or bill of rights, 15, 87
    "inalienable" rights, 8–9
    Japanese Canadians, 86
    natural rights, 8–9
Rothstein, Marshall, 163
"Rouge" politicians of Quebec, 201
royal assent, 17–18, 105, 132
Royal Canadian Mounted Police (RCMP), 148
Royal Proclamation (1763), 71
rule of law, 10, 154
Rupert's Land, 25, 70
Russell, Peter, 90, 151, 156
Russia, 14

S

sales taxes, 67
same-sex marriage, 93, 98, 201
Saskatchewan, 25, 70
    use of notwithstanding clause, 93
Schreyer, Ed, 106
scrutineers, 181
second reading (bills), 132
Section 1 (Canadian Charter of Rights and Freedoms), 94–96
section 92 courts, 158
section 96 courts, 158
section 101 courts, 158
section 52 remedy (of CA 1982), 83
Selinger, Greg, 118
Senate (Canada), 4, 124, 132, 138–40, 173
    appointment to, 115, 139
    Charlottetown Accord, 32
    constitutional conventions, 18
    designed not to oppose government, 218
    Governor General reserve power to make appointments, 109
    non-partisan senators, 143
    powers of, 139
    questionable expense claims, 130
    reform (*See* Senate reform)
    regional equality, 75, 138
    sober second thought, 138